Academic Biliteracies

BILINGUAL EDUCATION & BILINGUALISM

Series Editors: Nancy H. Hornberger, *University of Pennsylvania, USA* and Wayne E. Wright, *Purdue University, USA*

Bilingual Education and Bilingualism is an international, multidisciplinary series publishing research on the philosophy, politics, policy, provision and practice of language planning, Indigenous and minority language education, multilingualism, multiculturalism, biliteracy, bilingualism and bilingual education. The series aims to mirror current debates and discussions. New proposals for single-authored, multiple-authored, or edited books in the series are warmly welcomed, in any of the following categories or others authors may propose: overview or introductory texts; course readers or general reference texts; focus books on particular multilingual education program types; school-based case studies; national case studies; collected cases with a clear programmatic or conceptual theme; and professional education manuals.

Full details of all the books in this series and of all our other publications can be found on http://www.multilingual-matters.com, or by writing to Multilingual Matters, St Nicholas House, 31–34 High Street, Bristol BS1 2AW, UK.

BILINGUAL EDUCATION & BILINGUALISM: 107

Academic Biliteracies

Multilingual Repertoires in Higher Education

Edited by
**David M. Palfreyman and
Christa van der Walt**

MULTILINGUAL MATTERS
Bristol • Blue Ridge Summit

Library of Congress Cataloging in Publication Data
A catalog record for this book is available from the Library of Congress.
Names: Palfreyman, David, 1954- editor. | Van der Walt, C. (Christa) editor.
Title: Academic Biliteracies: Multilingual Repertoires in Higher Education/
    edited by David M. Palfreyman and Christa van der Walt.
Description: Bristol: Multilingual Matters, [2017] |
Series: Bilingual Education and Bilingualism: 107 |
Includes bibliographical references and index.
Identifiers: LCCN 2016046328 | ISBN 9781783097418 (hbk : alk. paper) |
ISBN 9781783097401 (pbk : alk. paper) | ISBN 9781783097425 (Pdf) |
    ISBN 9781783097432 (Epub) | ISBN 9781783097449 (Kindle)
Subjects: LCSH: Language and languages—Study and teaching (Higher)—China—
    Hong Kong. | Language and education—China—Hong Kong. | Multiculturalism—
    China—Hong Kong. | Education, Bilingualism—China—Hong Kong.
Classification: LCC P57.C6 A324 2017 | DDC 404/.20711—dc23 LC record available at
    https://lccn.loc.gov/2016046328

British Library Cataloguing in Publication Data
A catalogue entry for this book is available from the British Library.

ISBN-13: 978-1-78309-741-8 (hbk)
ISBN-13: 978-1-78309-740-1 (pbk)

Multilingual Matters
UK: St Nicholas House, 31–34 High Street, Bristol BS1 2AW, UK.
USA: NBN, Blue Ridge Summit, PA, USA.

Website: www.multilingual-matters.com
Twitter: Multi_Ling_Mat
Facebook: https://www.facebook.com/multilingualmatters
Blog: www.channelviewpublications.wordpress.com

The policy of Multilingual Matters/Channel View Publications is to use papers that are natural, renewable and recyclable products, made from wood grown in sustainable forests. In the manufacturing process of our books, and to further support our policy, preference is given to printers that have FSC and PEFC Chain of Custody certification. The FSC and/or PEFC logos will appear on those books where full certification has been granted to the printer concerned.

Typeset by Nova Techset Private Limited, Bengaluru and Chennai, India.
Printed and bound in the UK by the CPI Books Group Ltd.
Printed and bound in the US by Edwards Brothers Malloy, Inc.

Contents

List of Contributors

Bassey E. Antia, Professor, University of the Western Cape, South Africa.

Beverly Baker, Assistant Professor, University of Ottawa, Canada.

Tracey Costley, Lecturer, University of Essex, United Kingdom.

Charlyn Dyers, Professor, University of the Western Cape, South Africa.

Alberto Esquinca, Associate Professor, Biliteracy/Bilingual Education, University of Texas at El Paso, United States.

Guillaume Gentil, Associate Professor, Carleton University, Canada.

Gwenn Hiller, Director of the Center for Intercultural Learning, European University Viadrina, Germany.

Rhian Hodges, Lecturer, Coleg Cymraeg Cenedlaethol, Prifysgol Bangor University, United Kingdom.

Ellen Hurst, Senior Lecturer, University of Cape Town, South Africa.

Gwawr Ifan, Lecturer, Coleg Cymraeg Cenedlaethol, Prifysgol Bangor University, United Kingdom.

Julia E. Kiernan, Assistant Professor, Kettering University, Canada.

Mbulungeni Madiba, Associate Professor, University of Cape Town, South Africa.

Zina Manu, Manager (Education Delivery), Te Wānanga o Aotearoa, New Zealand.

Catherine M. Mazak, Professor, University of Puerto Rico (Mayagüez).

Erika Mein, Associate Professor, Literacy/Biliteracy Education, University of Texas at El Paso, United States.

Angélica Monárrez, Graduate Assistant, Teaching, Learning and Culture, University of Texas at El Paso, United States.

Shannon Morreira, Lecturer, University of Cape Town, South Africa.

David M. Palfreyman, Associate Professor, Zayed University, United Arab Emirates.

Lauren Pérez Mangonéz, Research Assistant, University of Puerto Rico (Mayagüez).

Wilson Poha, Education Advisor (Adult), Te Wānanga o Aotearoa, New Zealand.

A.J. Rivera, Lecturer, Indiana University-Purdue University Fort Wayne, United States.

Christa van der Walt, Professor, Stellenbosch University, South Africa.

Elsa Q. Villa, Research Assistant Professor, University of Texas at El Paso, United States.

Danping Wang, Lecturer, University of Auckland, New Zealand.

Acknowledgements

The editors of this book would like to express their thanks and appreciation to the book contributors for their valuable insights and efforts which form the core of the book; to series editor, Nancy Hornberger, and all the staff with Multilingual Matters who have helped to bring the book to fruition; and to our spouses and families, without whose support we could not have brought the book together.

1 Introduction: Biliteracies in Higher Education

David M. Palfreyman and
Christa van der Walt

Literacy is a key element of higher education: learning and teaching in universities and colleges is supported and evidenced via a range of texts and genres from reference works to lecture handouts, essays, portfolios and research articles. As higher education becomes more widely available and more internationalized, it is increasingly common for this literacy to involve more than one language in some way. This book deals with biliteracy in academic contexts: that is (adapting a definition from Hornberger (1990)) *the use in a higher education context of two or more languages in or around written text for the purpose of broadening or deepening knowledge.* Our aim in this book is to bring together studies of academic biliteracy in diverse parts of the world and to consider how it may be an integral element of learning at the tertiary level. The chapters in this book range from cases of informal student use of different written languages, to pedagogical, institutional and disciplinary strategies leveraging multilingual resources to develop literacy.

Globalised Higher Education, Multilingual Campuses and Implications for Teaching and Learning

Much has been written in the past 20 years on the way in which globalising forces influence higher education both positively and negatively. Terms such as *student mobility* and *internationalisation* are used to describe challenges and opportunities at organisational, political and financial levels, with sporadic attention to the internationalisation of the curriculum and the desirability of educating for international citizenship (Palfreyman & McBride, 2010). In truth, academics and students have always moved across national borders; for example, from the 13th and 14th centuries, student mobility became a key feature of universities in Europe (Perraton, 2014). Of course the situation today is very different because of the large numbers of students and academics who travel to follow or present courses at higher education institutions elsewhere. Moreover (contrary to some perceptions), there is currently no undisputed academic language with a status matching that of Latin in the Middle Ages, because academic material is available in a wide variety of languages. Students and academics are schooled in many languages; and although English can be seen as similar to Latin in its status as *the* language of the academy, students and scholars can now also read and write about their disciplines in other languages.

Another striking difference from Medieval Europe can be found in the modern global student population, which is no longer so limited to an elite corps of wealthy and high-status men. At national level, governments and funding agencies actively encourage an increase in domestic student numbers in an attempt to broaden participation in higher education. Far from being limited to upper class males, higher education is now seen as a prerequisite for social mobility (among students and their parents) and for national, economic progress (among government agencies). In a UNESCO (2015) *Education for All* position paper, education is presented

> as a key lever for development, is understood as a way of achieving social well-being, sustainable development and good governance. (pp. 1–2)

and post-basic and tertiary education are identified as priority areas. It is therefore clear that higher or tertiary education is expanding both in terms of international networks and in terms of increased access by minoritized communities nationally, all in the service of growth and development.

These increases in international student movement and in access to higher education at national level have led to increasing diversity of the student and staff body; and this is nowhere more evident than in the language profile of higher education institutions. Both types of change imply the spreading use of high-status, standardized codes (languages or language varieties) as well as minoritized, non-standard ones. As students become increasingly mobile and English is increasingly seen as a necessary condition for internationalisation (Van der Walt, 2013), it is easy to fall into a deficit perspective, focusing attention mainly on access measures that test English language proficiency, or on extensive academic support and development in English. Against this background,

> language policies designed to support and promote indigenous languages can be perceived as problematic and even deleterious. (Balfour, 2007: 36)

This chapter and indeed this book argue from a different perspective: one that accepts the languages that students bring to their higher education studies as resources for learning, irrespective of the status or spread of such languages. The movement by policy-makers, students and academics *towards*

English has, paradoxically, resulted in increased multilingualism on campuses, as increasing numbers of students from different language backgrounds use the lingua franca to access and develop knowledge and competencies in a variety of languages. As Hornberger and Link (2012) point out for pre-tertiary education,

> [w]hether or not there is an officially or unofficially sanctioned medium of instruction, the rich and varied communicative repertoires educators, learners, and their families bring to school mean that what is inevitably occurring is biliteracy. (p. 243)

From the perspective of 'language as resource' (Ruiz, 1984), educational institutions are encouraged to use students' language backgrounds to strengthen academic performance and concept literacy (Madiba, 2014), thus linking up with their language practices in non-academic contexts (and often in their future work contexts), where practices like code switching, multilingual note-making and translation are widespread. As García (2009a) points out,

> if multilingualism in most of the world today is characterized by its widespread nature, along with the fuzziness of language boundaries and fluidity and multiplicity in language practices and language identities, then multilingual education must develop ways of supporting not only multiple languages and literacies, but also interrelated functional complementarity of language practices. (p. 157)

Developing such support is the main focus of this volume, by presenting case studies in higher education where the multilingual nature of student writing is evidence of a need for support for multiple languages and literacies. We will now consider how literacy is embedded in higher education contexts.

Literacy as Social Practice

That literacy is socially significant is is very clear, but its significance is viewed in different ways. Theorists such as Ong and Goody saw a 'Great Divide' of thought and culture separating 'literate' societies from 'oral' ones (Street, 1988). In some ways, a similar division is often seen between academic and non-academic life – although a view is often taken that any person who comes to study at university should already be 'literate' in a particular sense of having mastered in secondary education certain literacy skills (reading 'deeply', perhaps 'critically' and writing 'clearly and correctly') which are associated with academic ways of thinking. Language and cognition are linked in Vygotskyan-influenced concepts of languaging (Swain, 1985) and meaning-making (van Leeuwen, 2005), which suggest that engaging in processes of writing and reading can clarify and crystallize understandings. For this reason, 'writing to learn' has been proposed even in scientific disciplines which have traditionally had less focus on language (Reynolds *et al.*, 2012).

On the other hand, the New Literacy Studies highlighted how 'reading' and 'writing' can refer to very different activities and skills, depending on the different social contexts in which they are used; thus

> literacy is best understood as a set of social practices; these are observable in [literacy] events which are mediated by written texts. (Barton & Hamilton, 2000: 9)

From this point of view, literacy becomes plural: each kind of social context has different 'literacies' associated with it. A specific *text* such as the one you are now reading is a product of a series of *literacy events* (authors, editors and publishers writing, discussing, critiquing and rewriting), which is largely structured by the social *practice* of academic publishing: conventions and expectations according to which knowledge is produced and distributed. It is also (we hope) the starting point for a further range of literacy events, as people read, reflect, annotate, cite, apply and/or adapt the ideas, words and organizing principles which they extract from this text, in their roles as researcher, teacher, student and so on.

The 'academic literacies' approach proposed by Lea and Street (1998) emphasizes the range and dynamic nature of literacies in higher education and the identity work involved in its development. We (writers and readers of this book) all participate in some way in an academic community; socialization into this community is an ongoing process which involves the individual as well as the community, thinking as well as language. For Duff (2010), academic discourse in general and academic literacy in particular is

> a social, cognitive, and rhetorical process and an accomplishment, a form of enculturation, social practice, positioning, representation, and stance-taking. [...] Academic discourse is therefore a site of internal and interpersonal struggle for many people, especially for newcomers or novices. [...] Affective issues and tensions [...] may be especially acute in intercultural contexts – in which local and global (or remote) language codes, cultures, and ideologies of literacy may differ; furthermore, the expectations of students producing academic language and those assessing it (instructors, journal editors, or reviewers) may be at odds. (p. 170)

Academic authors, editors, teachers and students engage with this process of enculturation, and through it with bodies of disciplinary knowledge/discourse (Kuteeva & Airey, 2014). The role of professors has typically been an active one, as they strive to make their mark by contributing to ongoing conversations through conference debates, journal articles and books; the role of the student has traditionally been a more receptive one. Yet the advent of online 'new media' or 'social media' such as blogs or social networking services has brought about a 'changing balance of agency' (Cope & Kalantzis, 2007: 76) in literacy practices among youth: readers increasingly become *reader–writers*, highlighting, commenting, remixing and reworking text and other content in ways that reflect their local context as well as the (often global) online communities in which they participate (Thorne & Ivkovic, 2015). The entry of a generation of students with this more agentic conception of literacy into an academic community which works in a parallel way but with a (traditionally) distinct body of knowledge, offers interesting possibilities for education.

In engaging with academic literacy practices, students and teachers make use of the linguistic resources at their disposal: their *repertoire* of forms, meanings and communicative acts, based upon various linguistic codes (varieties, registers, modes and often languages). A focus on a person's communicative repertoire (rather than on a particular language or genre) is key to the model of biliteracy proposed by Hornberger and Skilton-Sylvester (2000). Their 'continua of biliteracy' highlight firstly that biliteracy involves not simply two (or more) language codes, but various dimensions of communication; and secondly that for each dimension, there is a range of communicative resources, rather than one or more fixed or mutually exclusive options.

What Hornberger and Link (2012) term the *media* of biliteracy include

> the language varieties and scripts through which multilingual literacies are expressed and the sequence or configurations in which they are acquired and used.

Cases of biliteracy discussed in this book involve – in addition to the ever-present English – Afrikaans, Arabic, Chinese, French, German, isiXhosa and other African languages, Korean, Māori, Polish, Spanish and Welsh. Some of these languages are written (depending on the context) with more than one script; in some cases, different varieties of the language come into play (in or around writing); and these various codes can be acquired and used sequentially or concurrently. Each of these variables is a continuum: each literacy event will involve a different mix of skills in the two languages, and may at different times move towards one end or the other of a continuum.

Another set of continua is concerned with *contexts* and purposes of language use. In higher education, these include locating information in library resources, deepening understanding of texts or displaying knowledge in essays. Some chapters in this book consider macro contextual factors (for example Baker *et al.*'s chapter) and how these connect with more micro contexts, such as the specific interactions considered in Esquinca *et al.*'s chapter. The focus in some cases is very much on written language (Costley's, Kiernan's and Wang's chapters); but as Street (1988) argues,

> literacy practices are always embedded in oral uses, and the variations between cultures are generally variations in the mix of oral/literate channels. (p. 5)

For example, while Esquinca *et al.*'s chapter looks at multimodal (including oral) interaction around a multimodal written product, Hurst *et al.*'s chapter draws on interactive written discussion (a hybrid genre) around mini-texts on an online forum.

Hornberger's *development* continua concern individuals' 'paths of acquisition and [...] degrees of expertise' (Hornberger, 2001: 356): the varying ways in which people's biliteracy shifts (not always in a consistent direction) between their first language (L1) and second language (L2), between receptive and productive use, and between oral and written use. Chapters by Costley and by Ifan and Hodges show some biliterate individuals who feel they have greater academic literacy in their L2 than in their L1; while Antia and Dyers show learners discussing their deepening understanding of course concepts presented in different languages, as a bridge to productive application of these concepts.

The *content* of biliterate language use is particularly salient in higher education, as tertiary programmes typically aim to convey and develop students' understanding of concepts – indeed, the main concern of several contributors to the present volume is with how well students learn and understand content, rather than how well they use a language or languages. In terms of Hornberger and Skilton-Sylvester's (2000) model, this content may be rooted in majority and/or minority concerns, in literary and/or vernacular discourses and be more or less contextualized or personalized in terms of the specific writer and/or reader. Particular subject content may be linked to and/or decoupled from particular languages, as with the courses in Māori traditional arts or Islamic Studies discussed in Baker *et al.*'s chapter. Note that academic literacy, in the sense used in this book, focuses on development of knowledge and skills, and does not necessarily involve scholarly written texts of the kind represented by this book or by the publications of Chinese scholars discussed in Wang's chapter; for example, written personal narratives may be analysed and discussed to deepen students' understanding of issues underlying them (chapters by Hurst *et al.*, Kiernan).

Although each continuum of biliteracy represents a range of possibilities, each also has a power dimension which skews those possibilities: social or historical circumstances may well limit a person in a particular situation (or prompt them to orient themselves) to one or the other end/part of a continuum (Hornberger & Skilton-Sylvester, 2000). Typically, the broader context will construct power and/or prestige around one linguistic code (usually a variety of English, in the contexts described in this book). Hornberger and Skilton-Sylvester point out how the different continua tend to align in this respect: for example, university contexts in general assign greater value to literate contexts and to less immediately contextualized content. However, the chapters in this book show how more local discourses can assign prestige to a different code, sometimes in terms of a local identity (Welsh in Ifan & Hodges' chapter), sometimes in terms of an influential, non-English academic or professional discourse community (Chinese in Wang's chapter).

It is important to note that many of the issues captured in the continua of biliteracy are relevant also to 'monolingual' higher education contexts. Monolingual speakers of English, for example, engage with new media of literacy as they are socialized into an academic community (Lillis, 2003; Duff, 2010). Students are expected to develop from receptive reading skills to synthesis, critique and (by doctoral level) production of knowledge. As noted earlier, higher education generally has also seen changes in the content of literacy, with widening minority participation and an emphasis on contextualizing knowledge with respect to the worlds students come from on the one hand and, on the other hand, to the professional communities they aspire to join in the future (Laurillard, 2013; Kennedy et al., 2015). These changes all indicate the way higher education literacy has become hybridized as it spreads to new areas of these continua; the studies in this book show how different languages are involved in these processes.

In terms of pedagogy, Hornberger and associates have suggested that

> [t]he more their learning contexts and contexts of use allow learners and users to draw from across the whole of each and every continuum, the greater are the chances for their full biliterate development and expression: there tends to be an implicit privileging of one end over the other and there is a need to contest that traditional power weighting. (Hornberger & Skilton-Sylvester, 2000: 99)

As well as finding justification in the contestation of power, this idea of drawing on the range of available possibilities resonates with the contextualization of learning mentioned above, and with the value of diversity in learning ecologies (Lai et al., 2015). It also fits with dynamic models of multilingual competence (Herdina & Jessner, 2002) which see multilingualism not as the coexistence of parallel linguistic systems, but as unified: an 'overall system of a mind or a community that uses more than one language' (Cook & Singleton, 2014: 147). Notions of translanguaging – mixing different (aspects of) languages to communicative effect (see below) – seem also to sit well with this discourse of connecting diverse areas of literacy.

It should be noted that multilingual writing is by no means a modern nor necessarily a transgressive phenomenon in academia. Piller (2015) gives the example of a 1909 article by the German linguist Hugo Schuchardt:

> a 'German' article [which] extensively quotes from work published in French, Italian, Portuguese and Spanish. These quotes are simply part of the running text and no translation is provided. (p. 6)

Schuchardt was part of a transnational academic community with particular practices which assumed and valued receptive proficiency in several European languages. Times have changed and a more monolingual perspective currently prevails in academic publishing, showing the contingent nature of academic literacy. In recent years, although the use of multiple languages/ varieties has achieved some acceptance when it preserves social context boundaries (for example using one language to discuss a text written in another language), there is more resistance to such fluidity *within* functions/ texts – especially where this runs counter to the power differentials described by Hornberger and Skilton-Sylvester (2000), as when vernacular discourse is used as a communicative resource in a written essay.

Understanding and Using Multilingual Repertoires in Academic Contexts

The introduction of English medium instruction in many higher education institutions worldwide means that multilingual students can draw on more than one language in academic contexts. Although there might be a simplistic assumption that lecturers and students will be using English only, there is a variety of studies, some reported in this volume, that demonstrate the use of more than one language in higher education classes (for example Canagarajah, 2011; Madiba, 2014). In such contexts a student is able to use a language other than English to complete academic work. Multilinguals can draw on different strategies and practices in their repertoire and these can be activated for learning, depending on the degree to which such languages are available for reading or writing or discussion. When lecturers are multilingual too, and share one or more of their students' other languages, this can help them actively support or structure the use of whatever languages they have at their disposal.

Language proficiency, or lack thereof, has often been raised as an argument against the use of other languages in the English medium classroom. Students may well have developed some level of academic literacy in their other language; furthermore, it can be argued that

> [i]n the case of African languages, and possibly other minoritised languages, the idea of languages having to 'develop' first before they are

useful for teaching and learning is, at best, a diversionary tactic, since any kind of discussion, even when much code-switching takes place, can facilitate learning. (Van der Walt, 2015: 106)

In these multilingual contexts it is difficult and, one might argue, unnecessary to determine which language, the 'second', 'third' or 'fourth' one, could best be used for teaching and learning. Jessner (2008) points out that

> [d]ue to the dynamics of multilingualism, that is, the changes which usually take place in the course of time with regard to language proficiency and consequently language dominance in a multilingual repertoire, the use of the terms 'L1', 'L2' and 'L3' becomes [...] problematic. (p. 18)

Canagarajah (2013) emphasizes that communication in most contexts (academic and non-academic) involves *translingual* practice, in the sense of using whatever linguistic or other means are available and judged appropriate in order to express and explore meaning. Against this background, the term '*translanguaging*' becomes useful to describe a range of strategies and practices of 'blending' language that are present and used in a multilingual classroom.

Much has been written in the past ten years on translanguaging, from its origins as a term developed in Welsh education (Lewis *et al.*, 2012) to descriptions of contexts where translanguaging takes place, as will be discussed below. In this discussion the use of words like *strategies* and *practices* suggests that translanguaging is both a communicative action by individuals in a variety of situations and, by extension, a pedagogy, when a lecturer creates the opportunity for translanguaging to occur. The discussion below is meant to contribute to ongoing debates about a clearer description of what translanguaging could be, but does not aim to make a definitive pronouncement.

Beyond tracing the term to its roots in Welsh–English bilingual education, Lewis *et al.* (2012) note that it has moved from being viewed

> as a disadvantage to an advantage, from causing mental confusion to the benefits of dual language capability, from solitudes to synergies. (p. 643)

They link translanguaging explicitly to biliteracy (what they call 'dual literacy'). Drawing on a discussion paper released by Estyn, the Inspectorate for Education and Training in Wales, translanguaging was originally seen as using one language to strengthen another (especially speaking or writing in one language to show understanding of content heard or read in another), and is described as a learner-centred classroom strategy. Creese and Blackledge (2010) use the term more broadly to refer to a multilingual pedagogy, a principled set of 'bilingual instructional strategies' (p. 103). García (2009b: 45) uses the term in the plural to refer to multilingual communication not only in the classroom but more generally:

> For us, translanguagings are *multiple discursive practices* in which bilin-guals engage in order to *make sense of their bilingual worlds*. (Italics in the original.)

Most recently, Gorter and Cenoz (2015) describe a translingual perspective on linguistic landscapes which enables the 'co-occurrence of different lin-guistic forms, signs and modalities' (p. 54).

Although translanguaging draws on a range of abstract linguistic sys-tems, it does not presuppose a functional distinction (or 'movement') between these systems. García (2009b) states that unlike the concept of 'code switching' (which assumes languages as separate entities), translan-guaging treats linguistic systems as resources in a fluid communicative rep-ertoire. Along similar lines, Canagarajah (2011) suggested the alternative term 'code meshing':

> Whereas code switching treats language alternation as involving bilin-gual competence and switches between two different [communicative] systems, codemeshing treats the languages as part of a single integrated system. (p. 403)

Because of this integrated quality, translanguaging strategies can help 'to mediate cognitive, social and affective processes in literacy and learning' (Palmer et al., 2014: 759). An example of how this could happen is provided in Madiba's (2014) study of Tshivenda–English bilinguals, which describes how conceptual knowledge is strengthened when students discuss concepts in a mix of Tshivenda and English, with reference to an English textbook. He concludes that

> translanguaging is used as a productive strategy to support discussion and deeper understanding of the two concepts. (p. 99)

The languages used are not as important as the result of translanguaging: deeper and more efficient learning. This is why Ifan and Hodges's chapter in the present volume recommends that 'biliterate students need to be encouraged to be confident when interpreting resources in both languages, rather than the tendency of merely translating work from one language into another'.

Lewis et al. (2012) argue that translanguaging

> may not be valuable in a classroom when children are in the early stages of learning and developing their second language. (p. 644)

This belief is shared by Baker (2011) who argues (following Cummins, 1979) for a certain threshold level of language proficiency for students to derive cognitive benefits from using more than one language. This would certainly be a key factor in a situation of academic biliteracy: any reading, writing or communication can only happen on the basis of a particular threshold level of comprehension. However, this threshold level needs clarification with reference to context. Canagarajah (2011) shows with pedagogical examples how scaffolding and reader engagement can help students to engage with and construct meaning around even a text (Arabic calligraphy) whose script and structure they do not 'understand' in a linguistic sense. From the perspective of Hornberger's (2007) continua of biliteracy, students should be encouraged to draw on whatever they know of a particular language. She states that

> what is needed is attention to oral, multilingual interaction at the micro level of context and to learners' first language, oral, and receptive language skills development (that is, to the traditionally less powerful ends of the continua). (Hornberger, 2007: 186)

In the case of minoritized languages and languages that have not featured in academic domains, calling on students to use such languages in the classroom may be difficult, as Michael-Luna and Canagarajah (2007) found when higher education students who used a non-standard variety in online discussions were unwilling to use it in class. This is also evident in Costley's chapter in the present volume, with students who find the idea of writing essays in Cantonese out of the question.

From a continuum or translanguaging perspective, languages are seen as communicative resources to be integrated in practice (Canagarajah, 2013); similarly, the boundaries between literacy and oracy may be blurred, with writing in a dominant academic language supported by discussion and outlining in minoritized vernaculars. The fluid use of more than one language in writing is clearly seen in the chapter by Kiernan, where students insert phrases and words from other languages into their English assignments. However, an uncomfortable imbalance between two languages can also be experienced, as is succinctly put by one of the participants in the Ifan and Hodges' chapter: 'I'm more comfortable speaking Welsh, but I'm more confident writing in English'. This situation is typical at South African universities too, where minority languages are used freely outside the classroom, but seldom inside the classroom as academic languages and almost never in a written format. The results of the study presented in Antia and Dyers' chapter show that students need examples of academic language use in a minoritized language (in PowerPoint presentations) to support the meaning-making process: lecturers need to demonstrate translanguaging practices if they expect them from the students.

García and Li (2013) emphasize a connection between translanguaging and two key features espoused by the academic discourse community. The first is *creativity*, which García and Li define as

> the ability to choose between obeying and breaking the rules and norms of behavior, including the use of language. (p. 67)

There is little doubt that the fluid use of more than one language in the classroom results in translations, code switching, interpreting among students and between students and lecturer. In this process much creativity results, as noted by students in Ifan and Hodges' chapter as well as in Hurst *et al.*'s. The unavailability of terms in one language may result in direct translations (as described in Wang's chapter in the case of Chinese and English). Creativity is linked to a second characteristic valued by the academy which García and Li (2013) associate with translanguaging: *criticality*, or

> the ability to use available evidence to inform considered views of cultural, social, political and linguistic phenomena, to question and problematize received wisdom and to express views adequately through reasoned responses to situations. (p. 67)

Chapters by Kiernan and by Antia and Dyers highlight how rhetorical choices made in translanguaging can foster critical reflection as well as creativity, as students 'step back' and consider the different aspects of the academic and personal linguistic repertoires available to them.

The space created by lecturers for translanguaging practices will shape the learning process. The situation described by Mazak's chapter seems effective, with the lecturer not only creating space for such practices, but also modelling them. Ifan and Hodges similarly make the point that 'offering examples of scholarly writing in both languages' is a prerequisite for students to do the same. It would not make much sense to expect students to use translanguaging strategies for which they have no example.

These descriptions of translanguaging and translingual practices suggest a rich classroom context in which multilinguals use the linguistic resources at their disposal to engage with each other and with texts to create meaning and deepen learning. In this context a variety of strategies are used, including (but not limited to) code switching, translation, co-languaging and interpreting, without any attempt to limit communication or the production of text to one language. Lewis *et al.* (2012) point out that 'the effectiveness of translanguaging strategies [have] yet to be researched, evaluated, and critiqued' (p. 650). In response, this book presents several cases of translanguaging pedagogies in the context of academic biliteracy, and showcases divergent views of translanguaging in an attempt to build on current conceptions. Creese and Blackledge (2010) note that how to harness and build on this [moving between languages] will depend on the sociopolitical and historical environment in which such practice is embedded and the local ecologies of schools and classrooms. (p. 107)

The next section provides a foretaste of how this book attempts to illuminate these contextual aspects of academic biliteracy.

Outline of the Book

The chapters are ordered according to two broad themes. The first includes accounts of different multilingual contexts where biliteracy practices emerge in response to the demands of academic reading and writing. The second theme focuses on more deliberate attempts to teach biliteracy or to teach in a way that supports biliteracy.

Tracey Costley's chapter explores the ways in which students make use of their linguistic resources during their studies at an English medium university in Hong Kong. The chapter draws on data collected from audio-recorded interviews with multilingual and multi-literate undergraduate students to provide insight into how the medium of instruction experienced by these students shapes their academic language and literacy practices in their university studies. Some of the complex ways in which the medium of instruction shapes and determines the practices of these students at university are highlighted in the context of the language choices they make in their day-to-day lives.

Alberto Esquinca, Erika Mein, Elsa Q. Villa and Angélica Monárrez present the US/Mexico borderlands as the context for a study of how languaging resources are used and developed to author and talk about a multimodal text (ePortfolio). Countering deficit notions of bilingualism, they present an ethnographic account of academic biliteracy practices drawing on multiple sources of data. They use discourse analysis to highlight the variety of semiotic resources participants used to design and talk about their ePortfolio, with translanguaging and gesture used productively to present, critique and make sense of students' textual designs. The authors provide a theoretical perspective based on social semiotics, translanguaging and the continua of biliteracy. The value of drawing on multiple points along the continua of biliteracy is discussed and implications for policymakers are provided.

Catherine Mazak, A.J. Rivera and Lauren E. Perez Mangonez examine the texts and talk-around-text of Spanish–English bilingual students in an upper-level university psychology classroom as they negotiate written assignments using translanguaging. They collected data as part of an ethnographic case study over the course of one academic semester in a classroom where the professor taught bilingually. The analysis presents the complex bilingual talk and writing used as students come to understand the subject matter to complete their written tasks. Results show that students deftly leverage what they have learned from the English textbooks as they complete written assignments and exams using a combination of Spanish and English.

Ellen Hurst, Mbulungeni Madiba and Shannon Morreira begin their chapter by arguing that higher education in South Africa still carries the legacy of the colonial era, not least in the dominance of English as the medium of instruction. In this chapter, they take a decolonial perspective to argue that the use of African languages in academic spaces can contest dominant discourses and Eurocentrism in the academy. They present two sets of research data drawn from an undergraduate extended degree programme in the Humanities. The first data are a set of language histories written by the students in their first week at university. These histories uncover the multilingual backgrounds and identities of the class, and challenge preconceived notions of homogenous groups of monolingual speakers of linguistically marginalised African languages. The histories allow lecturers to surface and value their students' linguistic resources. The second set of data analysed is from the use of multilingual glossaries in class. Students were required to translate key concepts, as identified by lecturers, to their African languages and to then share their translations with the class through an online forum. This utilisation of students' language resources to scaffold concept literacy can be beneficial at both linguistic and conceptual levels. The approaches described in this chapter opened up spaces for translingual practice in the classrooms, changed the dynamics of what (linguistic) resources were valued, and gave a voice to students who are too often silenced by the academy. The authors argue that these pedagogical literacy activities are fundamentally decolonial.

Julia E. Kiernan explores the problematic nature of assigning monolingual narrative projects in North American writing classrooms populated by multilingual students, and offers an alternative: the Translation Narrative. Specific to this chapter are the ways that translation narratives allow students to explore language negotiation within their own writing practices. Consequently, this study considers how students develop academic writing proficiency in English by drawing on academic texts in their home languages. In this way, student choice and ideologies of choice are presented as central to translingual writing processes. Analysis of student translanguaging communicates textual evidence of the benefits of language negotiation and illustrates how the encouragement of language negotiation can develop critical thinking among multilingual students.

Bassey Antia and Charlyn Dyers argue that increasingly multilingual and multicultural lecture halls in South Africa and elsewhere require greater recognition of the challenges posed to teaching and learning by the linguistic diversity and literacy heterogeneity of students. This chapter reports on a study at the University of the Western Cape, South Africa, in which Hornberger's continua of biliteracy model both provided the design principles for a set of multilingual learning resources made available to students on a course, and served as framework for discussing students' responses to these resources. Effects associated with these resources include enhanced understanding of threshold concepts, destabilization of traditional relations of power, empathy with co-learners or appreciation of co-learner vulnerabilities, and impetus for wanting to be academically biliterate. A literacy practices framework is used to draw out further implications of the model for the development of multilingual lecture resources in South African higher education.

Gwawr Ifan and Rhian Hodges write from the perspective of a bilingual, Welsh National College. The objectives of this chapter are to discuss a pioneering interdisciplinary module *Cymdeithaseg Cerddoriaeth yng Nghymru* (Sociology of Music in Wales). This module is funded by the Coleg Cymraeg Cenedlaethol (Welsh-medium National College), and is offered to Welsh-speaking students of the School of Music and School of Social Sciences, Bangor University. This interdisciplinary module combines key themes from Sociology and Music and draws upon cultural, musical and social factors often unique to the Welsh language and Wales. This chapter discusses, in particular, the challenges faced by Welsh-medium academics in creating a pioneering module through the medium of Welsh based on mainly English-language sources; and highlights students' efforts to write in Welsh.

Moving to lecturers' biliteracy, Danping Wang investigated bilingual teachers' experiences of developing Chinese/English academic biliteracy in foreign language education research in China. Qualitative data were collected from three native Chinese language teachers who had research degrees from English-speaking countries. The findings presented analyze their everyday language choice and use in research activities, and identify three levels of factors which influence their choice of languages. Their bilingual academic writings were also analyzed to demonstrate their perceptions of academic conventions in Chinese and English. The chapter ends by suggesting possible methods to enhance bilingual research literacy for foreign language teachers.

The chapter by Beverly Baker, David M. Palfreyman, Gwenn Hiller, Wilson Poha and Zina Manu highlights policies around biliteracy, presenting bilingual and multilingual policies and practices in four higher education institutions:

- *a multilingual university in a border area in Europe*: European University Viadrina in Germany;
- *a bilingual university in a minority language context*: Te Wānanga o Aotearoa in New Zealand;
- *a bilingual university in a highly globalized emerging state*: Zayed University in the United Arab Emirates;
- *a bilingual university in a bilingual country context* : The University of Ottawa in Canada.

Using Baldauf's (2006) categories to distinguish different levels of policy formation and implementation, they move from the historical, macro level to the meso level where policies and language plans are developed at institutional level; this is further connected to a micro view of literacy and translanguaging practices among students, teachers, and other stakeholders in the classroom and in other university spaces.

In his afterword, Gentil draws together the take-home messages from this volume as well as parting thoughts on the direction that future research could take. Most importantly, he notes that theorization needs to progress in tandem with empirical and pedagogical studies to help avoid 'sloganization' of terms and concepts in language education (Breidbach et al., 2014). This afterword suggests next steps to consolidate research by developing a grounded theory of translanguaging in general and biliteracy in particular.

References

Baker, C. (2011) *Foundations of Bilingual Education and Bilingualism* (5th edn). Bristol: Multilingual Matters.

Baldauf, R.B. Jr. (2006) Rearticulating the Case for Micro Language Planning in a Language Ecology Context. *Current Issues in Language Planning* 7, 147–170. http://dx.doi.org/10.2167/cilp092.0

Balfour, R. (2007) University language policies, internationalism, multilingualism, and language development in South Africa and the UK. *Cambridge Journal of Education* 37, 35–49.

Barton, D. and Hamilton, M. (2000) Literacy practices. In D. Barton, M. Hamilton and R. Ivanic (eds) *Situated Literacies: Reading and Writing in Context*. London: Psychology Press.

Breidbach, S., Küster, L. and Schmenk, B. (2014) Sloganizations in language education discourse. Humboldt-Universität zu Berlin, Germany. See https://www.angl.hu-berlin.de/news/conferences/Archive/2014/sloganizations-in-language-education-discourse (accessed 16 December 2016).

Canagarajah, S. (2011) Codemeshing in academic writing: Identifying teachable strategies of translanguaging. *The Modern Language Journal* 95 (3), 401–417.

Canagarajah, S. (2013) *Translingual Practice: Global Englishes and Cosmopolitan Relations*. Abingdon: Routledge.

Cook, V. and Singleton, D. (2014) *Key Topics in Second Language Acquisition*. Bristol: Multilingual Matters.

Cope, B. and Kalantzis, M. (2007) New media, new learning. *International Journal of Learning* 14 (1), 75–79.

Creese, A. and Blackledge, A. (2010) Translanguaging in the bilingual classroom: A pedagogy for learning and teaching? *Modern Language Journal* 94 (1), 103–115.

Cummins, J. (1979) Linguistic interdependence and the educational development of bilingual children. *Review of Educational Research* 49, 222–251.

Duff, P. (2010) Language socialization into academic discourse communities. *Annual Review of Applied Linguistics* 30, 169–192.

García, O. (2009a) Education, multilingualism and translanguaging in the 21st century. In T. Skutnabb-Kangas (ed.) *Social Justice Through Multilingual Education* (pp. 140–158). Bristol: Multilingual Matters.

García, O. (2009b) *Bilingual Education in the 21st Century*. Malden, MA: Blackwell.

García, O. and Li, W. (2013) *Translanguaging: Language, Bilingualism and Education*. New York, NY: Palgrave.

Gorter, D. and Cenoz, J. (2015) Translanguaging and linguistic landscapes. *Linguistic Landscape: An International Journal* 1 (1–2), 54–74.

Herdina, P. and Jessner, U. (2002) *A Dynamic Model of Multilingualism: Perspectives of Change in Psycholinguistics.* Clevedon: Multilingual Matters.

Hornberger, N. (2007) Multilingual language policies and the continua of biliteracy: An ecological approach. In O. García and C. Baker (eds) *Bilingual Education: An Introductory Reader* (pp. 177–194). Clevedon: Multilingual Matters.

Hornberger, N.H. (1990) Creating successful learning contexts for bilingual literacy. *Teachers College Record* 92, 212–229.

Hornberger, N.H. (2001) Multilingual literacies, literacy practices, and the continua of biliteracy. In M. Martin-Jones and K.E. Jones (eds) *Multilingual Literacies: Reading and Writing Different Worlds* (pp. 353–368). Amsterdam: John Benjamins.

Hornberger, N.H. and Link, H. (2012) Translanguaging and transnational literacies in multilingual classrooms: A biliteracy lens. *International Journal of Bilingual Education and Bilingualism* 15 (3), 261–278.

Hornberger, N.H. and Skilton-Sylvester, E. (2000) Revisiting the continua of biliteracy: International and critical perspectives. *Language and Education* 14 (2), 96–122.

Jessner, U. (2008) Teaching third languages: Findings, trends and challenges. *Language Teaching* 41 (1), 15–56.

Kennedy, M., Billett, S., Gherardi, S. and Grealish, L. (eds) (2015) *Practice-Based Learning in Higher Education: Jostling Cultures.* New York: Springer.

Kuteeva, M. and Airey, J. (2014) Disciplinary differences in the use of English in higher education: Reflections on recent language policy developments. *Higher Education* 67 (5), 533–549.

Lai, C., Zhu, W. and Gong, G. (2015) Understanding the quality of out-of-class English learning. *TESO Quarterly* 49 (2), 278–308.

Laurillard, D. (2013) *Rethinking University Teaching: A Conversational Framework for the Effective Use of Learning Technologies.* London: Routledge.

Lea, M.R. and Street, B.V. (1998) Student writing in higher education: An academic literacies approach. *Studies in Higher Education* 23 (2), 157–172.

Lewis, G., Jones, B. and Baker, C. (2012) Translanguaging: Origins and development from school to street and beyond. *Educational Research and Evaluation* 18, 641–654.

Lillis, T. (2003) Student Writing as 'Academic Literacies': Drawing on Bakhtin to Move from Critique to Design. *Language and Education* 17 (3), 192–207.

Madiba, M. (2014) Promoting concept literacy through multilingual glossaries: A translanguaging approach. In: L. Hibbert and C. Van der Walt (eds) *Multilingual Universities in South Africa* (pp. 68–87). Bristol: Multilingual Matters.

Michael-Luna, S. and Canagarajah, A.S. (2007) Multilingual academic literacies: Pedagogical foundations for code meshing in primary and higher education. *Journal of Applied Linguistics* 4, 55–77.

Palfreyman, D.M. and McBride, D.L. (eds) (2010) *Learning and Teaching Across Cultures in Higher Education.* London: Palgrave.

Palmer, D.K., Martinez, R.A., Mateus, S.G. and Henderson, K. (2014) Reframing the debate on language separation: Toward a vision for translanguaging pedagogies in the dual language classroom. *The Modern Language Journal* 98 (3), 757–772.

Perraton, H. (2014) *A History of Foreign Students in Britain.* London: Palgrave.

Piller, I. (2015) Monolingual ways of seeing multilingualism. *Journal of Multicultural Discourses* 11 (1), 25–33.

Reynolds, J.A., Thaiss, C., Katkin, W. and Thompson, R.J. (2012) Writing-to-Learn in Undergraduate Science Education: A Community-Based, Conceptually Driven Approach. *Cell Biology Education* 11 (1), 17–25.

Ruiz, R. (1984) Orientations in language planning. *NABE Journal* 8 (2), 15–34.

Street, B. (1988) A critical look at Walter Ong and the 'Great Divide'. *Literacy Research Center* 4 (1), 1–5.

Swain, M. (1985) Communicative competence: Some roles of comprehensible input and comprehensible output in its development. *Input in Second Language Acquisition* 15, 165–179.

Thorne, S.L. and Ivkovic, D. (2015) Multilingual Eurovision meets plurilingual YouTube. In D.A. Koike and C.S. Blyth (eds) *Dialogue in Multilingual and Multimodal Communities* (pp. 167–192). Amsterdam, Netherlands: John Benjamins.

UNESCO (2015) *UNESCO Position Paper on Education Post-2015*. See http://unesdoc.unesco.org/images/0022/002273/227336E.pdf (accessed 16 December 2016).

Van der Walt, C. (2013) *Multilingual Higher Education*. Bristol: Multilingual Matters.

Van der Walt, C. (2015) Reconsidering the role of language-in-education-policies in multilingual higher education contexts. In A. Knapp and K. Aguado (eds) *Fremdsprachen in Studium und Lehre: Chancen und Herausforderungen für den Wissenserwerb* (pp. 97–121). Frankfurt: Peter Lang.

van Leeuwen, T. (2005) *Introducing Social Semiotics*. New York: Routledge.

2 'No Way, I Could Never Write My Essays in Cantonese. I Only Know How to Do It in English': Understanding Undergraduate Students' Languages and Literacies at a Hong Kong University

Tracey Costley

Introduction

This chapter explores the ways in which a small sample of undergraduate students at a university in Hong Kong make sense of and use their language resources, with a particular focus on literacy. In order to do this, the chapter looks at the different ways in which the students describe their linguistic resources and identities, and how they make use of this range of resources in their day-to-day lives as well as in the course of their academic studies. A key goal here is to understand more about how these students do different things in different domains with the languages at their disposal. The chapter begins with an overview of schooling and the Medium of Instruction in the context of Hong Kong before moving on to a discussion of how bilingualism has been understood at the policy level in the territory. The chapter moves on to present students' accounts of how they make use of their different languages in the course of their studies. The discussion focuses on the types of literacy practices and activities they engage in and the choices they make in the process of navigating their multilingual worlds (Lea & Street, 1998; Safford & Costley, 2006, 2008). The chapter concludes with some potential implications for pedagogy as well some reflections on current and future policy in relation to medium of instruction.

The Hong Kong Context

The 2013 National Survey on Use of Language in the Hong Kong Special Administrative Region (HKSAR) carried out by the Census and Statistics Department (CSD, 2013) found that, of those aged between 6 and 65 (approximately 5.6 million people), 90.3% indicated Cantonese as their mother tongue language. This is in keeping with Li's statement that

> over 95% of the [Hong Kong] population is ethnic Chinese, with the majority – about nine out of 10 – having Cantonese as their usual (home) language. [...] Cantonese is a vibrant regional vernacular whose vitality is sustained by its use in everyday communication and the electronic media, in miscellaneous artistic forms from movies and opera to Canto-pop and stand-up comedy. (Li, 2012: 79)

Whilst the dominant language of Hong Kong is Cantonese, Mandarin[1] and English also play key roles in day-to-day life. The 2013 CSD survey found that 3.2% of those surveyed indicated Mandarin as their mother tongue, with 1.4% selecting English as their mother tongue. For Mandarin, 24.1% of the respondents indicated that their level of proficiency in the language was *very good* to *good* and 39.8% reported their level as *average*. The corresponding figures for English were 23.7% and 36.9% respectively. The relative similarity of these figures is interesting but as Li (2012) describes,

> English is regarded by Hong Kongers as an important form of linguistic capital, which is precious for sustaining the economic vitality of this former colony (Morrison & Liu, 2000). Putonghua (Mandarin) is no less important, given its status as the national language of China (Li, 2006). Both languages are generally looked upon by local parents as indispensable assets as their children struggle to climb up the social ladder. (pp. 67–68)

Hong Kong is also home to a sizeable South Asian community as well as high numbers of Indonesian, Filipino, Thai and Japanese residents. The 2011 population census stated that there were 451,183 ethnic minority residents in Hong Kong, making up 6.4% of the total population (CSD, 2011). A high number of these people may be in Hong Kong somewhat temporarily as migrant workers; but for many others, Hong Kong is where they, their parents and grandparents before them were born. It is where they consider home and they see themselves as Hong Kongers. This also means that on a day-to-day basis, there are many other languages in use in Hong Kong. While moving around the territory, it is not uncommon to hear people interacting in Tagalog, Indonesian or Hindi for example as well as in English, Mandarin and other languages.

Much has been written about the complex interplay of languages and language policy in Hong Kong and how these have been directly influenced by its status as a territory under British colonial rule and more recently as part of China (Evans, 2000; O'Halloran, 2000; Johnson, 1997; Lin, 2012; Perez-Milans, 2014; Poon, 2000; Tollefson & Tsui, 2004). In general, as Morrison and Lui (2000) state,

> the language policy in Hong Kong was, and is, a deliberate action on the part of the ruling class (formerly the British Administration and latterly the Chinese government respectively) to perpetuate its power in Hong Kong. (p. 474)

Schooling in Hong Kong

The Hong Kong Education Bureau (EDB) has responsibility for developing and implementing education policies across the HKSAR. The following quote taken from the EDB's website not only clearly frames the current policy intentions in relation to the linguistic profiles of Hong Kong students, but also has clear implications for the ways in which languages and literacies are positioned in current Hong Kong society:

> Hong Kong is an international city. To increase our competitiveness in the international arena and to enhance our role in fostering exchange and stronger ties with Mainland China, we need to nurture talents who are proficient in both Chinese and English [...] The language education policy of the Government of the HKSAR aims to enable our students to become biliterate and trilingual. We expect that our secondary school graduates will be proficient in writing Chinese and English and able to communicate confidently in Cantonese, English and Putonghua. (EDB, 2015a)

What is important in regard to these policy goals is the way that they have influenced ideas of what bilingualism means and the role that these languages play in relation to the medium of instruction (MOI) in government state-funded education in Hong Kong education from primary through to tertiary levels.

At present, government-funded education in Hong Kong is organised along relatively specific linguistic lines. Within the local context Hong Kong students who attend government-funded schools (not international schools) are likely to have experienced the following model of education. Students are likely to have had their primary schooling conducted predominantly in

Cantonese. This would be the dominant language of instruction, with reading and writing taking place through Cantonese using the traditional Chinese[2] script. English is also taught at primary schools and many students will be exposed to English in the wider Hong Kong society, through their parents, domestic helpers (CSD, 2013), tutorial classes and popular media (see Evans, 2000; Li, 2012; Lin, 2012; Morrison & Lui, 2000; Poon, 2000 for further discussion). Mandarin has also begun to occupy a larger role in the curriculum; it is a·core subject at primary and secondary school and also has increasing currency as a language required in workplaces. Both English and Mandarin benefit from a significant amount of government funding to provide schools with a wide range of resources such as native speaker teachers, books and extended library facilities (EDB, 2015b). Although English and Mandarin play a significant role in the primary curriculum, mother-tongue instruction has a long history at the primary level with the aim of facilitating learning, and as such Cantonese is still likely to be the main language of operation in the primary context.

Secondary schooling is a more complex arrangement. Until 2010, schools were separated into Chinese[3] Medium Instruction (CMI) or English Medium Instruction (EMI) schools. This pattern of organisation had, in some form, been in place since the late 1970s and was a source of much discussion, debate and at times vehement disagreement and protest (Evans, 2000; Johnson, 1997; Lin, 2012; Poon, 2000). The CMI or EMI designations were made based on the English levels of the school's students as well as the linguistic profiles of the teaching staff. Schools had to demonstrate that both students and staff had a high enough standard of English in order to be an EMI school. This, over many years, has become part of the commodification of English and has made EMI schools highly desirable for parents, so much so that their views have shaped and determined both school and government policy decisions (see Evans, 2000; Horner & Lu, 2012; Johnson, 1997; Li, 2012; Lin, 2012 for detailed discussion).

A 'fine-tuning' policy introduced in 2010 has blurred these distinctions (Poon, 2000). The policy has done away with the traditional CMI/EMI distinction and has made it possible for schools to create their own school MOI policy. Although there is choice, there is still a need to demonstrate that students and teachers have sufficient 'ability' to ensure that teaching and learning can take place through English. Schools can, based on the expertise of the teachers and the levels of the students, choose to teach some subjects through English and others through Chinese. This means that all the classes for that subject should be delivered, conducted and assessed through the specified language. The intention of this policy change is to give schools the flexibility to make the best use of their resources in order to achieve the trilingual/biliterate policy intentions. This means that within the course of a school day, students and teachers are required to make use of the different languages across different subjects. However, the focus is still very much on making sure that the languages are kept separate and that code-mixing is not the default. As the EDB (2009: 4) states:

> should schools claim to adopt English as the MOI for any non-language subject, the medium for delivering the subject content in the lesson, the basic textbooks, assignments for learning reinforcement and assessment/evaluation for learning should primarily be in English.

At the tertiary level there are eight government-funded universities in the territory. Seven of these are English MOI institutions, with The Chinese University of Hong Kong (CUHK) the only official Chinese–English bilingual institution. For the approximately 20% of the student population who go on to study at one of the eight government-funded universities, English is the main currency used to gain a place to study. This means that places at these institutions, CUHK included, are largely determined by a student's success in English at secondary school.

Although the seven universities are officially EMI in terms of the language used for instruction and assessment, the campuses are not monolingual English environments. In the institution where I was based, for example, a visitor walking round the campus would hear local students and staff predominantly speaking in Cantonese, and different languages being used by the international students. Signs, posters and other student-oriented materials were often in Cantonese (and English) and amenities such as student canteens, shops and the library were Cantonese dominant in that transactions were generally conducted in Cantonese with limited English used/available. English, Mandarin and other languages were often used, but the dominant mode of communication was Cantonese. The use of different languages was not, in my experience limited to outside of the classroom; however, there was a certain degree of institutional pressure on staff to ensure the use of English in teaching and assessment. For example, every semester, students are asked to complete a standardised feedback form for each class. One question they are asked concerns what percentage of their classes was conducted through English. The results of these surveys are centralised and go directly to the senior management. The surveys were apparently introduced to allay concerns that Cantonese was being used too much in classrooms. My linguistic background meant that the MOI for my teaching was limited to English, but my students regularly switched between languages throughout the classes and these switches tended to be between Cantonese and English. Some of my Cantonese-speaking colleagues said that they insisted on English only in the classroom and that they would not use Cantonese in classes. Students also commented that they had never heard some of their Hong Kong professors speak in Cantonese. On the other hand, there are of course many colleagues who do use Cantonese as well as English in lectures and tutorials (see Yang & Lau, 2003).

Bilingualism and the avoidance of code-mixing

The MOI has been a key theme in the history of Hong Kong's education policy debates. Most of these debates have focused not necessarily on the different pedagogical approaches of EMI or CMI, or necessarily the pedagogical value of the use of mother tongue in instruction, but more in terms of which MOI is more effective at ensuring a bilingual or, in the current context, trilingual population. Discussions have mostly focused on the effectiveness of instruction in terms of creating and developing skilled language users, and the focus has been on students' 'mastery' of the individual languages and an equal proficiency in both. There has been a concern for ensuring the minimal use of code-mixing and an attempt to prevent this from being the default means for teaching and classroom interaction (see Evans, 2000 for a full discussion). The consequence of such views, as O'Halloran (2000) suggests,

> has been to place Chinese and English in complementary distribution as media of instruction in separate school systems when they are not placed so in the community at large. (p. 152)

Mixed codes and code-switching have consistently concerned Hong Kong policy makers and public opinion (see Evans, 2000; Glenwright & Wang, 2013; Johnson, 1997; Luk & Lin, 2015; O'Halloran, 2000). For some, the use of code-mixing has been understood as a healthy and expected way of learning languages and has been considered to be a natural part of functioning as a bilingual speaker (Evans, 2000). In the main, though, policy and popular opinion seem to have been dominated by approaches to bilingualism that see the learning of languages as separate processes, and any kind of mixing of the languages as a threat to the mastery of one or the other. The Hong Kong government has consistently 'blamed "mixed-code teaching" as the main factor contributing to failing standards' (Luk & Lin, 2015: 17). Although much research has attested to the value of mixed-code teaching and uses of L1 in classrooms (see Luk & Lin's, 2015 work on the teaching of science, for example), and has found that many teachers draw on a variety of codes in classrooms even within a '"one language only" policy' (Glenwright & Wang, 2013: 87), there is still a sense of 'taboo' surrounding code-mixing vis-à-vis effective language learning. Swain *et al.* (2011) are among many scholars and practitioners advocating for a change in public attitudes through developing teaching materials and classroom strategies for teachers that celebrate multilingual teachers and classrooms. The title of their handbook (*How to Have a Guilt-Free Life Using Cantonese in the English Class*) effectively reflects the lived reality of many teachers and the wider perception of mixed-code teaching.

The dominant approach to bilingualism (and present-day trilingualism) in Hong Kong policy has thus been what García (2009) would refer to as 'monoglossic' (p. 7). García uses this term to refer to approaches to bilingualism based on the belief that languages exist as discrete entities, to be mastered in equal ways and with equal but distinct skills and abilities. Monoglossic approaches to bilingualism would, for García, be grounded in the belief that the development of 'balanced bilinguals' i.e. learners with equal language abilities in both/all languages, is the dominant goal and purpose of pedagogy. For García (as well as many others writing on the complex ways in which bilingualism and multilingualism develop),

> bilingual education is not simply about *one language plus a second language equals two languages*. The vision of bilingual education as a sum of equals reduces bilingual education to the use of two or more separate languages, usually in different classroom spaces, time frames, contexts, or as spoken by different teachers. (García, 2009: 7, original emphasis)

García and others interested in bilingual pedagogy take a very different starting point, challenging the idea that it is productive to understand bilingualism as having a balanced knowledge of and fluency in two languages and arguing instead for a more nuanced view, based on the idea that

> a bilingual is a person that 'languages' differently and that has diverse and unequal experiences with each of the two languages. (García, 2009: 44–45)

In this sense then, we can see that for García and others, bilingualism does not manifest as a mastery of two separate codes, but it is more a case of languages co-existing, overlapping, and meshing (Canagarajah, 2006). This perspective has obvious implications for how notions of code-switching and code-mixing are understood in the social context of Hong Kong and poses a fundamental challenge to the idea of 'balance' in bilingualism, and in many ways to concepts of bilingualism itself.

Canagarajah's (2013) work is important in terms of the contribution it has made to our understanding of bilingualism. For him, the term 'bilingualism', although well-established and underlying many years of pedagogy and practice, is not necessarily the most useful way for us to conceptualise and understand how people both learn and deploy the languages in their repertoires. He feels it is necessary to move beyond the dichotomy implied in traditional approaches to bilingualism; and to do to this he adopts the idea of 'translingual practice', which foregrounds activity and communication rather than linguistic systems. This

> enables a consideration of communicative competence as not restricted to predefined meanings of individual languages, but the ability to merge different language resources in situated interactions for new meaning construction. (Canagarajah, 2013: 1–2)

Here then, is an understanding of language and language use very different to that which has characterised language policy in Hong Kong (as well as many other contexts). Instead, what is being argued for by many is a different starting point based on

> the concept of translanguaging[, which] makes obvious that there are no clear-cut boundaries between the languages of bilinguals. What we have is a languaging continuum that is accessed. (García, 2009: 47)

This leads to a number of interesting questions about the ways in which young people in Hong Kong perceive their bi/multilingualism and how this shapes what they do. As Lu and Horner (2013) suggest, the everyday contexts of language use are navigated by

> involving choices made in particular situations and in light of particular purposes. Rather than asking whether writers should code-switch or code-mesh, a translingual approach asks us to consider how, when, where, and why specific language strategies might be deployed. (p. 27)

Participants and Data Collection

The data presented in the following sections of this chapter come from semi-structured interviews conducted with 13 undergraduate students over a period of six months in 2014. The students were all aged between 17 and 21 and included nine female and four male students. Some of the students came for interview in small groups or pairs, and others came alone. The interviews took place either in my office or in another agreed upon location at the university and resulted in close to six hours of recorded data. The interviews sought to gain insight into how the students understand and make use of their linguistic resources during their studies at an English medium university in Hong Kong. Through the interviews I hoped to generate narrative accounts of how they mobilize their different linguistic resources in their academic work, in order to gain a more emic perspective on the day-to-day language worlds of these students. All of the interviews were conducted in English and based on the same set of questions, provided below in Table 2.1.

It is important to note here that these interviews took place in a context where codeswitching has been constructed in a very particular way in policy rhetoric and public discourses. There are many accounts in the research literature in which codeswitching is considered to be a negative classroom practice (see Li & Martin, 2009 for example) rather than a positive resource for learning. As was shown in the opening discussion, codeswitching has been actively discouraged in Hong Kong classrooms (Ferguson, 2003; Lin, 1996). As Li and Martin (2009) suggest,

Table 2.1 Guiding questions for interviews

Ideas about your languages:
- What languages do you use on a daily basis?
- What do you use them for/to do?
- Do you translate from one language to another?
- Can you do all the same things in all of the languages you have?
- Do you prefer to use one language over another?
- Would you describe yourself as multilingual?
- Would you describe yourself as multiliterate?

When you are doing academic work what languages do you use:
- To read in
- To discuss ideas in
- To think in
- To write in

How are languages used in schools and universities in Hong Kong?

How are languages used outside of schools and universities in Hong Kong?

> whereas codeswitching in community contexts is regarded as acceptable bilingual talk, in many classroom contexts codeswitching is deemed inappropriate or unacceptable, and as a deficit or dysfunctional mode of interaction. (p. 117)

Such a backdrop is likely to shape the ways in which people not only recall and talk about their languages and literacy practices, but also the ways in which they identify with them; and this needs to be taken into account with regard to the interview data presented here. The point here is that in the interviews the students were presenting aspects of their lifeworlds that might have looked and sounded different if they had done the interviews with different people, in different contexts. This is not to suggest that their responses are somehow invalid, but rather it is a caution that these responses are socially situated and should be interpreted as reflecting these young peoples' particular ideological positionings.

Students' Language Backgrounds

All of the students were born in Hong Kong and consider themselves to be Hong Kongers although not all are ethnically Chinese. All of their education took place in state-funded primary and secondary schools in Hong Kong except for one student who spent a portion of her primary schooling in the Philippines but completed her secondary school exams in Hong Kong. All of the students are multilingual and the languages they described themselves as using on a day-to-day basis were Cantonese, English, Mandarin, Tagalog,

Hindi and Urdu. Many of the students also described other languages of which they had some working knowledge from school or through personal study, such as Japanese, Korean, French and German. From the interviews it was clear that these young people are members of complex and overlapping language worlds through which they move throughout the course of a day. In talking about the languages used at home for example, one student whose father is from Hong Kong and whose mother is from Malaysia said that at home she speaks both Cantonese and English as she has to help translate between her father and her mother: she described her language use in these contexts as being 'the bridge between them [the parents]'. Another student talked about how she moved to the Philippines when she was young and then back to Hong Kong a few years later. As a result she said her family all speak Cantonese, English and Tagalog. She spoke about her home as being one in which many languages were used, in very clear ways. She spoke of using English predominantly with her mother, Cantonese with both her father and mother, and Tagalog with her siblings. She said that it was not something she had really thought about much before the interview, but that she felt that for herself and her siblings using Tagalog together was their way of maintaining a Philippine culture and identity.

The question of which language students considered to be their mother tongue produced a variety of interesting answers. While most cited Cantonese, this was not the case for all students. For two students of South Asian heritage the answers were more complex. One felt that Hindi was his mother tongue in terms of his home and family language, but Cantonese was the language he used for all other aspects of his life. The other felt that she identified mostly with Urdu as this was the language of her home and family, but Cantonese was her primary language outside the home. One interviewee said that his mum spoke Mandarin and as such he felt that he had to consider that literally as his 'mother's tongue'. He felt, however, that Cantonese was the language he used most often, including with his mum, and that this was the language and identity he connected the most with. He said he did not identify with Mainland China and actively resisted using Mandarin where possible. This student's identity work in opposition to Mandarin is important in terms of understanding the current local context in Hong Kong.

These interviews took place not too long after the 2014–15 student protests and 'occupy Central' movements in Hong Kong. These highly charged political events reflect a growing sense of concern over the increasing role and influence of Beijing in Hong Kong; for many there is a real concern that the rights, freedoms and autonomy of the HKSAR are being eroded. Many of these students took part in these protests and are vocal about the importance of maintaining a clear Hong Kong identity; resistance to and through language is one way in which this appears to be taking place. For many of these students, and others whom I have spoken to in classes, using Mandarin is symbolic of Beijing's influence and as such, they actively avoid using it. The interviews with these students support Van der Walt's (2013) assertion that

> individual circumstances and personal beliefs are important conditions for making use of different languages in academic contexts, and for acknowledging their use. (p. 114)

Linked to this, all of the students describing their languages and language use were emphatic about the importance of Hong Kong English and about the local practice of 'mixing' English with Cantonese. For all of the students this practice seemed to be very much a part of their sense of self and code-mixing was a key index of being a Hong-Konger. The students did not talk of code-mixing in Cantonese and Mandarin; this is similar to Gu's (2013) study of Mainland Chinese students studying in Hong Kong in which she found that Hong Kong students

> feel reluctant to include Putonghua code-switching in their daily communication, perhaps partly to due their dis-identification with mainland China and their desire to maintain a Hong Kong identity that [is] distinct from a more generic Chinese identity. (p. 230)

Students' Perceptions of Their Languages

All of the student interviewees were asked whether they considered themselves to be bilingual and/or multilingual. What was interesting in the answers, given the complexity of the language worlds they inhabit, was a distinct hesitation from all of them in regard to describing themselves as bilingual (and more so in relation to being multilingual), even though they all regularly interact in and through two or more languages. When asked to discuss this further, most of them offered a very measured description of their bilingualism and the following is typical of the explanations they offered:

> I don't see myself as a multilingual person, I am just a bilingual. I speak of course Cantonese and also English very well, very fluently. I have learnt to speak Mandarin but not very, I mean not a very good proficiency, so I would say if talking about multilingual I would say I do not speak Mandarin, I would use proficiency to distinguish whether I can speak that language or not so I would say I am a bilingual not a multilingual.

Such reflections on their languages are important not only in terms of gaining an insight into how they understand their own linguistic resources, but also in terms of understanding how policy and everyday discourses of Hong Kong are reflected in their comments and descriptions. For most of these students there was a sense that to be bilingual you have to have equal competence in the languages, which as highlighted earlier, is very much in keeping with the dominant policy of Hong Kong. Only one student confidently described himself as multilingual and for him the criteria was using the language on a daily basis, rather than proficiency.

Inside/outside school

All of the students recognised shifts in terms of which language they used and when they used them, with the clearest distinction being that between 'in-school' and 'out-of-school'. Some students expressed this as a percentage – for example that on a non-school day they felt they spent 90 to 95% of the day interacting in Cantonese, whereas on school days they thought it might be between 60 to 70% Cantonese. All interviewees, except one, felt that the language they used the most was Cantonese. It was regarded as the language used for everyday conversations and interactions in and around Hong Kong. It was also described as being used for reading magazines, newspapers and social media and for some forms of writing, particularly social media and instant messaging. It was also seen as the language mostly used in classes between peers. The following quote from one of the interviewees captures this well:

> I use English but only in an academic field or in school, in class; but most of the time if I go for let's say, transportation or trading in supermarket or something, erm or asking someone a question in the street, definitely Cantonese because it is … the context, the language context of Hong Kong I think.

With ten of the students the discussion moved to the use of English or Cantonese in classes at university and all the students held a similar view in terms of the role of Cantonese in this context. The students all said that they would listen to the lecturer/teacher in English and any written materials, presentation slides and textbooks used in classes would likely be in English (unless it was a language class), but that discussion amongst peers would mostly take place in Cantonese. The students said that in classes they would not expect anyone other than the teacher to address them in English. If their classmates asked them questions in English, they said they would find this 'strange' and would most likely respond in Cantonese. However, three caveats were given as reasons as to when they would use English to address their peers. The first was if they were working in a group with someone who did not speak Cantonese. Although the classes that these students participate in are predominantly made up of Cantonese students from Hong Kong, there are increasing numbers of international and exchange students whose first language is not Cantonese in classes. In my own undergraduate classes for example, in classes of between 30 to 55 students it was not uncommon for there to be 3 to 5 students who did not speak Cantonese. These students may be from Mainland China, Korea or Singapore as well as a range of European and North American contexts.

The second caveat was if the teacher came up to their group and listened to their conversations. The students said this switch would happen regardless of the language background of the teacher. Across Hong Kong 'internationalisation' is an agenda that is increasing the number of international faculty on campus. At the same time, however, there are significant numbers of faculty from Hong Kong as well as Cantonese speaking faculty from other backgrounds so in this sense there is a good chance that many of the professors these students have will be Cantonese speakers. The third, and most commonly cited, reason for switching into English would be when they did not know how to express ideas and concepts in Cantonese, or when they only knew the words in English (see below). An important point here is that there was a clear sense for these students that talk in classes was something that was predominantly done through Cantonese rather than English. By comparison, writing and reading appeared to be largely done through English. This is echoed in the following quote from a student when I asked her if she used Cantonese for writing essays or at any stage during the essay writing process. Although Cantonese was what she considered to be her mother tongue, and the language she used most often, her answer to my question about writing is very clear: 'No way. I could never write my essays in Cantonese. I only know how to do it in English'.

Different languages for different purposes

Whilst the students all seemed to be able to move in and out of the languages with relative ease in speaking, the languages used to achieve tasks through writing appeared to be more sharply defined. In this regard, Cantonese was no longer the default language in which tasks were achieved; instead the preferred language for academic writing and reading was English. From the responses to the interview questions, two factors emerged as the main reasons for operating in English for these tasks. The first factor was linked to whether or not the students felt they had the sufficient resources and/or experience to achieve the tasks in a language other than English; for example:

> I would write in English because I don't know the terms in Chinese [...] like I took Chemistry when I was in Cert Level and I know all the elements in English but I don't know their names in Chinese.

Many of the students talked about how they were in some ways 'restricted' to using English to communicate much of their subject knowledge, as they simply did not know, or had not studied these subjects in Cantonese. All of the students said that for some subjects it was almost impossible for them to even think about those subjects in Cantonese because they had only learnt to think about them in English.

A second key factor that emerged as a rationale for a preference appeared to do with experience and efficiency. It was simply easier for them to operate in English, as this is the medium which they had the most experience of using in academic literacy contexts. At secondary school, and at university, most of them had not been required to read or write academically in Cantonese. Some felt that they simply would not be able to do it and others felt that the effort required to do it in Cantonese would be too high. In this sense, it is not the university MOI that is shaping their practice but the MOI of their previous learning experience. A different student in the same interview provided the following rationale:

> I would say that the last time I really used Chinese to do an assignment, that will be er a Chinese lesson that teach me Chinese story writing in secondary school; but apart from this course most of the time 99% of the time English is what I used.

A key point in understanding this final example is that the student was from a CMI secondary school. Of the 13 students I interviewed, ten of them experienced some of their secondary schooling prior to the 2010 fine-tuning policy so they talked about their schools being EMI or CMI. Five of the students attended CMI schools and all of these students had similar experiences in that although they were at an officially CMI school, they experienced most of their secondary schooling in English. One student explained this as their school wanting to 'do the best they could and get the students ahead'; as a result their school had focused a great deal on the use of English. All five of the students attending CMI schools had similar stories and in many ways were the students who appeared to have the strongest affinity with English. When I asked them to explain this further, they said that CMI schools were thought to be inferior to EMI schools and as a result there was pressure on these schools to produce students who were good at English.

The student comments closely reflect the recent policy history of Hong Kong, in terms of policy rhetoric and public opinion about the differences between EMI and CMI schools. What is interesting though is the degree to which these students' comments challenge the perception of these labels, and raise questions about the everyday language practices of what are, in popular terms, considered to be 'inferior' schools. A common assumption is that students who study at EMI schools will have better English language and literacy than students who study at CMI schools, who will have better Chinese language and literacy. From the interviews with the students this division was not necessarily evident. As the comments above suggest, the students who had attended CMI schools were not as confident in their academic Chinese language and literacy skills as they were with their English. The students' experiences not only highlight the prestige that surrounds English and the pressure on schools to enable students to acquire it but also pose something of a challenge to the everyday assumptions about what takes place in CMI and EMI schools.

The data that follow are taken from one interview involving three female participants. All of them are ethnically Chinese and claim Cantonese as their mother tongue. They are all close friends and share many classes together. Two of the girls studied at EMI[4] schools and the third studied at a CMI school. What is interesting in their accounts is that the MOI of their schooling does not necessarily shape their language use in the way that current, and indeed, previous language policy would necessarily foresee. One of the students gave the following account of how she recalled learning Mandarin and English:

> at Kindergarten and primary school, we would have a Mandarin textbook, different chapters, know how to greet someone, what to say to order food that sort of thing. After primary school my school didn't teach me Mandarin. The way I can access to Mandarin will be like TV, I will automatically learn something about Mandarin instead of like for learning English I have a to have a very systematic way of going to school, doing grammar exercise but for Mandarin, because the Mandarin system is quite close to Cantonese the most difficult thing is basically the pronunciation, so it is not a very big problem.

Although attending different schools, the other two students also seemed to find this a familiar and easily identifiable experience. A point of interest here is that this student was the one who had attended a CMI school and the expectation, given the mandate of CMI schools might be that Mandarin would have featured more prominently in her experience as a medium of instruction and production. The experiences of these students reflect how the schools they attended took up and responded to the government's language policy. The comments not only reflect these localised responses to policy, but they can also be understood as reflecting local attitudes towards Mandarin and the value the students may ascribe to learning it.

I went on to ask them what language they felt they mostly used, or found easier, to write academic essays and assignments. In the first response the student makes an interesting distinction between reading and writing:

> For me, I would prefer writing essays in Chinese ... actually both are alright, but for reading academic essays or for something different from newspapers I would prefer Chinese because you know the terms inside those academic essays and readings are really difficult so you have to

check everything in the dictionary word by word and it takes me time. So I prefer reading in Chinese and writing in both languages.

The second student responded by saying:

I can write in both languages but I guess mostly English seems a bit comfortable than writing in Chinese but I don't know why, but sometimes I mix the two languages together.

[the others laugh at this and ask her when and how she does it]

when I am taking notes like when I have, when I have my [redacted] class [...] sometimes I write in like English but then I find it very long so I just change into Chinese. When I watch, when I want to mark down some examples then I will write in Chinese because I find it easier to read when I do my revision because I just listen to what the professor say and I copy and write down. So if it is an important point, I will write it in English, but if I have to mark down the example and you know that example will appear in the exam, I just write in Chinese for my reference.

Both of these comments were made by the two students attending EMI schools.

On thinking more about the question two of the students had the following interaction in which we can begin to get a clearer insight into the ways they understand the source of these literacy practices. The first comment is from the student who went to a CMI school:

You know the patterns and the styles of writing it doesn't mean that I am more able to use English than Cantonese of course there are also some technical terms in English that I don't know but because there is the essay style [...] I have already develop[ed] quite a habit of writing in English [...] if I have to write Chinese, it would be a contrast that would make me a little bit uncomfortable because I just I don't know the best way of expressing my idea in Chinese in writing.

The second student, from an EMI school, responded as follows:

Yes I agree, but more than that it is because we have Cantonese or Chinese as a mother tongue and it seems that we take it for granted and no one specifically teach us how to write perfectly in Chinese. The structure is somehow not normally taught and we- personally I think if we write in Chinese we need to really write pretty, in a fancy way because Chinese is a really complex language and you are not taught with the really formal or the beautiful structure. Whereas for English this is our second language and we are taught with the structure, the genre, all that so we are such more familiar with the writing style. But for Chinese we definitely we are taught some of the structures of how to write but we not really taught to write a really professional way for our essays or assignments.

What we begin to see here is that, for these students, there is no necessary correlation between the stated MOI of their secondary schooling, and the languages they make use of in the course of producing their work at University. In most cases, the students interviewed here tend to engage in language and literacy practices that almost run counter to what policy and local expectations might be, in that students who attended CMI schools were not necessarily more confident users of Chinese and *vice versa*. The student comments go some way in highlighting the complex relationships that these young people have with their different languages. Their comments begin to reveal the ideologies that shape, inform and determine their day-to-day language and literacy practices.

Codes, choices and the construction of identities

Although the previous discussion suggests that for certain tasks and/or activities the students have limited choice over the language in which these activities are taught and assessed, this is not necessarily characteristic of their general language practices. The discussions showed that the students have a great deal of agency in their choice of languages, and in the ways they choose to make use of these resources to communicate with peers and teachers in class, to prepare for classes and to do assignments. In one of the interviews one female respondent said that she uses only English in her academic written work and does not like to use Cantonese. When I asked her why, she replied, 'I don't like to jump the languages'. This prompted the following reflections from two of the other interviewees about the languages they used. One agreed and said that it was 'better' to stick to just one language and that she chose to use English all of the time for her academic writing as she felt that this was the best way to practise and to improve her language skills. She went on to say

> you have to deal with English; so the better you are, the better you handle with English, the better you are able to write in English; so I think this is also one way of training.

Other students, although they shared a similar perspective on English, also said that they made sure to sometimes write in Chinese. For these students it was a conscious act, and a deliberate way of trying to practise using their Chinese. They said they mostly used Chinese for their notes, or to annotate the English notes/texts they had written. What was particularly interesting is that one of the students said he only made annotations on his notes/texts by hand because he could not type in Chinese and therefore it was not an option for him. Another participant in the interview agreed with this sentiment and said that the only reason he could type in Chinese was because he had made a conscious effort to practise this outside of school. The student said that the main way he practised was not in his academic work but through texting and other social media. He said that without this conscious effort, he would not be able to type in Chinese.

Discussion

In focusing on the languages used in the context of their studies, perhaps one of the most interesting, although not unexpected, findings is the range of experiences and approaches the students have in terms of what resources they use to carry out certain tasks and why. These young adults clearly make choices about which languages they use in their reading and writing both in an academic context and in their day-to-day lives. These choices are very much individual and dependent upon a broad range of circumstances and experiences. Some of the students actively read and write in both Chinese and English in order to 'maintain' both languages, whereas some have made choices to keep the languages 'separate'. Others have not constructed such delineations and present themselves as drawing upon whatever language helps them to achieve the required outcomes most efficiently and effectively. What we see then is not a clearly defined set of common approaches or experiences, but a rich and diverse set of individual practices in which these young adults have a significant amount of agency. Canagarajah (2013: 1) offers a helpful perspective for understanding this when he says:

> Language resources always come into contact in actual use and shape each other. From this perspective, we have to consider all acts of communication and literacy as involving a shuttling between languages and a negotiation of diverse linguistic resources for situated construction of meaning.

As a teacher in this context, an interesting question for me is whether, given the policy focus on proficiency and trilingualism, these young adults would be recognised as 'successful'? The dominant policy position has been one that has constructed languages as separate, discrete entities that bilinguals can learn and take up in equal ways. From this perspective, success can be measured by how well the languages are used, and the extent to which mixing or switching is avoided. By this definition the broad range of competencies and experiences reflected in the students I have interviewed suggests that maybe they would not be attributed the label 'proficient' as their language and literacy skills are not 'equal' in all languages. If, however, we adopt a translingual framework that

> sees writing, writer identity, language forms used, and writer competence as always emergent, and hence writer agency as both always in operation and always in development. (Lu & Horner, 2013: 26–27)

then what we have is a set of highly skilled and highly competent multilinguals who make effective use of the resources they have.

Whilst there was great variation in the experiences of these students, there was also significant commonality. The overriding sense from the students was that they understood the variations in language practices amongst themselves as markers of what it means to be a university student in Hong Kong. For these students the ability to use both Cantonese and English and to 'shuttle' between them was evidence of being an educated Hong Konger. Underpinning this was the sense of power that came from the position of being able to choose which language to use, and what identity to construct and present in the process.

Choice was particularly relevant in relation to the use of Mandarin. Many of the students felt very strongly that the use of Cantonese and English, and in particular code mixing, were key features of Hong Kong life, and therefore essential in ensuring a distinct Hong Kong identity *vis-à-vis* Mainland China. Many felt very strongly about the use of Mandarin to the extent that they said they did not like to use it. Many of these young people had taken part in the student protests in Hong Kong and resisting using Mandarin was very much linked to the idea of autonomy from China. Many felt that the use of Mandarin was increasing in Hong Kong and that both Cantonese and English were therefore important markers of local identity. Many people who I spoke to at the time felt that the 2014 to 2015 protests and increasing tensions between Hong Kong and China would increase the use of Cantonese and code-mixing in schools and society more widely. They felt that this practice would only strengthen over the next few years as the future of Hong Kong is negotiated with China. As Leung and Street (2012) remind us,

> teaching and learning are unavoidably situated in a wider context of social norms and practices, curriculum affordances and constraints, and institutionally induced relationships, and at the same time, all the participants in the classroom activities are themselves social actors investing in particular social and cultural choices. (p. 3)

It is perhaps then this sense of choice that needs to be understood further and which needs to inform future language policy.

Notes

(1) Cantonese is used in Hong Kong and the Guandong province of China whereas Mandarin (also called 'Putonghua') is used in Mainland China. Cantonese and Mandarin, whilst belonging to the same family of Sinitic languages, are linguistically quite distinct. For example, although both are tonal languages, Cantonese has nine tones whereas Mandarin has five; the two languages, whilst sharing some similarities in form, are not mutually intelligible. In this chapter I use the term 'Mandarin' rather than 'Putonghua', as this is the term that was used most frequently by the interviewees.

(2) Cantonese, in Hong Kong and elsewhere, is written using the traditional Chinese script whereas Mandarin is written using the simplified Chinese script. Whilst the overall grammar of the two languages is similar, the scripts are quite different and may not be mutually intelligible for users of each. Anecdotally my students have suggested that it is easier for traditional script users to understand simplified Chinese than vice versa. Unless explicitly stated otherwise, when the term 'Chinese' is used in this chapter it is indexing Cantonese.

(3) 'Chinese' here is referring to Spoken Cantonese and traditional written Chinese. Some formal study of Mandarin as a specific curriculum subject would also take place.

(4) Many of the students attended secondary school prior to the implementation of the fine-tuning policy and the CMI/EMI distinction is still widely used to describe different schools.

References

Canagarajah, S. (2006) Toward a writing pedagogy of shuttling between languages: Learning from multilingual writers. *College English* 68 (6), 589–604.

Canagarajah, S. (2013) *Literacy as Translingual Practice: Between Communities and Classrooms.* London: Routledge, Taylor & Francis.

Census and Statistics Department (CSD) (2011) *Thematic Report: Ethnic Minorities.* Census and Statistics Department Hong Kong Special Administrative Region.

Census and Statistics Department (CSD) (2013) *Thematic Household Survey Report No. 51: Use of Language in Hong Kong.* Census and Statistics Department Hong Kong Special Administrative Region.

Education Bureau (2009) *Fine-Tuning the Medium of Instruction for Secondary Schools.* (Education Bureau Circular No. 6/2009). Hong Kong Special Administrative Region.

Education Bureau (2015a) *Language Learning Support.* See http://www.edb.gov.hk/en/edu-system/primary-secondary/applicable-to-primary-secondary/sbss/language-learning-support/featurearticle.html (accessed January 2015).

Education Bureau (2015b) *Programme Highlights on Primary Education.* See http://www.edb.gov.hk/en/edu-system/primary-secondary/primary/highlights/index.html

Evans, S. (2000) Hong Kong's new English language policy in education. *World Englishes* 19 (2), 185–204.

Ferguson, G. (2003) Classroom code-switching in post-colonial contexts: functions, attitudes and policies. In S. Makoni and U. Meinhof (eds) *African and Applied Linguistics. AILA Volume Review Volume 16* (pp. 38–51). Amsterdam: John Benjamins.

García, O. (2009) *Bilingual Education in the 21st Century A Global Perspective.* Chichester: Wiley-Blackwell.

Glenwright, P. and Wang, L. (2013) Trilingual paths: Cultures of learning and the use of Cantonese, English or Putonghua within a Hong Kong primary school. In L. Jin and M. Cortazzi (eds) *Researching Intercultural Learning: Investigations in Language and Education* (pp. 77–95). Basingstoke: Palgrave Macmillan.

Gu, M. (2013) Language practices and transformations of language ideologies: Mainland Chinese students in a multilingual university in Hong Kong. In H. Haberland, D. Lønsmann and B. Preisler (eds) *Language Alternation, Language Choice and Language Encounter in International Tertiary Education* (pp. 223–237). Dordrecht: Springer.

Horner, B. and Lu, M. (2012) (Re) Writing English: Putting English in translation. In C. Leung and B. Street (eds) *English: A Changing Medium for Education* (pp. 59–78). Bristol: Multilingual Matters.

Johnson, R. (1997) The Hong Kong education system: Later immersion under stress. In R. Johnson and M. Swain (eds) *Immersion Education: International Perspectives* (pp. 171–189). Cambridge: Cambridge University Press.

Lea, M. and Street, B. (1998) Student writing in higher education: An Academic Literacies approach. *Studies in Higer Education* 23 (2), 157–172.

Leung, C. and Street, B. (2012) Introduction: English in the curriculum – norms and practices. In C. Leung and B. Street (eds) *English: A Changing Medium for Education* (pp. 1–21). Bristol: Multilingual Matters.

Li, D. (2012) Linguistic hegemony or linguistic capital? Internationalization and English-Medium instruction at the Chinese University of Hong Kong. In A. Doiz, D. Lasagabaster and J. Sierra (eds) *English-Medium Instruction at Universities: Global Challenges* (pp. 65–84). Bristol: Multilingual Matters.

Li, W. and Martin, P. (2009) Conflicts and tensions in classroom codeswitching: An introduction. *International Journal of Bilingual Education and Bilingualism* 12 (2), 117–122.

Lin, A. (1996) Bilingualism or linguistic segregation? Symbolic domination, resistance and code-switching in Hong Kong Schools. *Linguistics and Education* 8 (1), 49–84.

Lin, A. (2012) Genre-based pedagogical approaches to L2 English content classrooms. In C. Leung and B. Street (eds) *English A Changing Medium for Education* (pp. 79–103). Bristol: Multilingual Matters.

Lu, M. and Horner, B. (2013) Translingual literacy and matters of agency. In S. Canagarajah (ed.) *Literacy as Translingual Practice: Between Communities and Classrooms* (pp. 26–39). London: Routledge, Taylor & Francis.

Luk, G.N.Y. and Lin, A.M.Y. (2015) L1 as a pedagogical resource in buidling students' L2 academic literacy: Pedagogical innovation in the science classroom in a Hong Kong school. In J. Cenoz and D. Gorter (eds) *Multilingual Education: Between Language Learning and Translanguaging* (pp. 16–35). Cambridge: Cambridge University Press.

Morrison, K. and Lui, I. (2000) Ideology, linguistic capital and the medium of instruction in Hong Kong. *Journal of Multilingual and Multicultural Development* 21 (6), 471–486.

O'Halloran, S. (2000) English medium secondary schools: Privileged orphans in the SAR. *Intercultural Communication Studies* X (2), 145–158.

Perez-Milans, P. (2014) Bilingual Education in Hong Kong: History, challenges and directions forresearch. *Working Papers in Urban Language & Literacies* Paper 139.

Poon, A.Y.K. (2000) Implementing the medium of instruction policy in Hong Kong schools. In D. Li, W.K. Tsang and A. Lin (eds) *Language Education in Post-1997 Hong Kong* (pp. 148–178). Hong Kong: Linguistic Society of Hong Kong.

Safford, K. and Costley, T. (2006) 'I try to open my ears': Experiences and strategies of students learning English as an Additional Language and studying for higher education. *NALDIC Occasional Paper* 20.

Safford, K. and Costley, T. (2008) 'I didn't speak for the first year': Silence, self-study and student stories of English Language learning in mainstream education. *Innovation in Language Learning and Teaching* 2 (2), 136–151.

Swain, M., Kirkpatrick, A. and Cummins, J. (2011) *How to Have a Guilt-Free Life Using Cantonese in the English Class: A Handbook for the English Language Teacher in Hong Kong.* Hong Kong: Research Centre into Language Acquisition and Education in Multilingual Societies, Hong Kong Institute of Education. http://www.ied.edu.hk/rcleams/handbook/handbook.pdf (accessed 16 December 2016)

Tollefson, J.W. and Tsui, A.B.M. (eds) (2004) *Medium of Instruction Policies: Whose Agenda? Which Agenda?* Mahwah, NJ: Lawrence Erlbaum.

Van der Walt, C. (2013) Active biliteracy? Students taking decisions about using languages for academic purposes. In H. Haberland, D. Lønsmann and B. Preisler (eds) *Language Alternation, Language Choice and Language Encounter in International Tertiary Education* (pp. 103–125). Dordrecht: Springer.

Yang, A. and Lau, L. (2003) Student attitudes to the learning of English at secondary and tertiary levels. *System* 31, 107–123.

3 Academic Biliteracy in College: Borderland Undergraduate Engineering Students' Mobilization of Semiotic Resources

Alberto Esquinca, Erika Mein, Elsa Q. Villa and Angélica Monárrez

Introduction

In an increasingly globalized world, students throughout the world are seeking college degrees in other countries, particularly advanced degrees. Global flows of students are expected to continue to grow: Altbach and Knight (2007) estimate that by the year 2025 as many as 15 million students will be studying abroad, with English-speaking nations, particularly the US, providing the bulk of services. In particular, most, if not all, US universities offering engineering undergraduate and graduate degrees in the US have a growing population of international students in their programs (Sana, 2010).

Global flows of students have an undeniable impact on language and communication, with increasing numbers of people communicating across social, cultural and linguistic boundaries (Heller, 2010). However, little is known about the experiences of bi-/multilingual students in the US at the postsecondary level (Kanno & Cromley, 2013; Oropeza *et al.*, 2010).

Scholarship on globalization has tended to focus on the spread of one language, English, some with a strong critique (Phillipson, 1992) and others more positively (Crystal, 1997); Pennycook (2001) insists on the need to examine the spread of global English from an historical perspective that contextualizes language studies and avoids essentialist views of language, culture and identity. Globalization has also forced language scholars to

41

reconsider the very notion of language. For instance, scholarship on language ideologies suggests that boundaries between languages are ideologically constructed. According to Pennycook (2011), globalization demands a reconceptualization of the notions of language, bilingualism and multilingualism, and encourages researchers to question whether it is useful to think of 'languages as separate, distinguishable, countable entities' (p. 515).

As scholars such as Canagarajah (2013) and García and Li (2014) have argued, 'languaging' is an active, dynamic process in which bi-/multilingual writers draw on various semiotic resources to construct and enact ways of being. A focus on dynamic semiotic activity considers language as one of several resources, with movement across languages, registers and modalities receiving special attention. From a resource-oriented perspective, a view of *translanguaging* considers the dynamic and mobile resources bi-/multilingual users bring to every communicative act.

Set in a place of constant flows of people, material resources and communicative interactions on the Mexico–United States border, this chapter provides an ethnographic account of academic biliteracy among transborder *(transfronterizo)* students in a US engineering program. Countering deficit notions of 'English Language Learners' – and indeed of 'bilingual' – we highlight and examine the literacy practices of students as they author and critique a multimodal text, an electronic portolio (ePortfolio). We show how participants draw on multiple semiotic resources in the text and in interaction around the text, i.e. the continua of biliteracy (Hornberger & Skilton-Sylvester, 2000). While recognizing that 'English' and 'Spanish' are social constructions, we highlight the ways that participants use face-to-face communication to 'write' or design multimodal texts.

Theoretical Perspective

Whereas traditional linguistics conceptualizes grammar as a code or a set of rules, Halliday (1978) proposed that language is primarily a resource for making meaning. Other signs have meaning potential as well, but language is the best tool we have to make meanings; we use the tool called language to construe reality and enact social relationships. In Spanish and other Romance languages, for instance, second-person pronouns (in Mexican Spanish, *tú* and *usted*) are ways to index social hierarchies, so that the choice of one or the other is meaningful in relation to its alternative. Choosing the pronoun *tú* over its more formal counterpart *usted* means that the speaker construes a particular kind of social relationship with her interlocutor (the nuances of which depend also on the variety of Spanish being used). Webster (2009) draws on Halliday's work to suggest that by treating language as a system of meanings, evolved from social encounters, we can conceptualize how people actively create meanings by exchanging symbols in a shared situational context. A context of situation is composed of three dimensions: *field*, or the topic at hand in a situation; *mode*, the role language takes in the situation; and *tenor*, the social relationship between participants in the situation (Eggins, 2004).

Van Leeuwen (2005) extends Halliday's insights to frame multimodal communication within social semiotics, as part of the human ability to make meaning. From a social semiotic perspective, language is one of a host of semiotic tools and actions, which can include the materials and artifacts used to communicate. Resources can be physiological (voice, facial expression) as well as technological (paper and pencil, computers and software), and can be (re)configured and (re)combined:

> Semiotic resources have a meaning potential, based on their past uses, and a set of affordances based on their possible uses, and these will be actualized in concrete social contexts where their use is subject to some form of semiotic regime. (van Leeuwen, 2005: 285)

Writing about principles of multimodal communication, Kress (2009) notes that, though cultural configurations vary, certain principles of sign-making apply. Specifically,

> *signs are motivated conjunctions of form and meaning*; that conjunction is based on *2) the interest of the sign-maker*; using *3) culturally available resources*. (p. 10, emphasis in the original).

The idea of dynamically drawing on multiple semiotic systems, including language, to construe and convey meaning has gained traction in recent years. Swain (2006) notes that the term *languaging* can convey 'an action – a dynamic, never-ending process of using language to make meaning' (p. 96). García and Li (2014) note that

> language can never be accomplished; and thus languaging is a better term to capture an ongoing process that is always being created as we interact with the world lingually. (p. 8)

Similarly, Blommaert and Rampton (2012) assert that a focus on languaging, as action,

> puts situated action first. It sees linguistic conventions/structures as just one (albeit important) semiotic resource among a number that are available to participants in the process of local language production and interpretation, and it treats meaning as an active process of here-and-now projection and inferencing, ranging across all kinds of percept, sign and knowledge. (p. 13)

Current sociolinguistic approaches to globalization have traced the ideological roots of monolithic conceptions of language and have often abandoned an adherence to the notion of distinct languages. Canagarajah (2013) traces the concept of distinct languages to 19th century notions from the Romantic era, which posited that a language bore essential elements of a community, making that community the legitimate owner of the language and delegitimizing others. Such conceptualization, Canagarajah proposes, also posited languages as separate from one another – to keep them pure from contamination by outside elements. Similarly, Blommaert and Rampton (2012) argue that

> [i]n differentiating, codifying and linking 'a language' with 'a people', linguistic scholarship itself played a major role in the development of the European nation-state as well as in the expansion and organisation of empires. (p. 10)

In characterizing the complex language dynamics associated with 21st century globalization, García (2009) put forth the notion of 'dynamic bilingualism' to emphasize the ways in which

> language practices are multiple and ever adjusting to the multilingual multimodal terrain of the communicative act. (p. 53)

From this perspective, bilinguals' fluid movement across languages (and varieties and modalities) for the purposes of meaning-making is taken as a given. Languages are not seen as separate entities; translanguaging is the norm rather than the exception. García (2009) defines translanguaging as the

> multiple discursive practices in which bilinguals engage in order to make sense of their bilingual worlds. (p. 45)

Drawing on the work of García and others (see Baker, 2003; Creese & Martin, 2003), Hornberger and Link (2012) emphasize the pedagogical implications of translanguaging as a means of drawing on bi-/multilingual students' full communicative repertoires in order to foster meaningful educational experiences. In particular, they argue that translanguaging practices pave the way for teachers and students

> to access academic content through the linguistic resources and communicative repertoires they bring to the classroom while simultaneously acquiring new ones. (p. 268)

As a way of framing translanguaging practices in the classroom, we propose the use of the continua of biliteracy, where biliteracy is defined as communication in two or more languages around writing (Hornberger, 2003; Hornberger & Skilton-Sylvester, 2000). The continua highlight students' biliterate development across multidimensional, nested continua that include context, content, media and development. For the purposes of the present study, the context and development continua are particularly relevant. The *context* dimension of the continua emphasizes the movement between micro and macro levels of analysis; between oral and literate channels of communication; and between multilingual and monolingual contexts. The (individual) *development* dimension highlights the continual movement in literacy development, often in a non-linear fashion, between reception and production; oral and written; and L1 and L2. In our analysis, we provide micro-instantiations showing how students move along these continua to make meaning in an ePortfolio development activity.

Methodology

The results highlighted in this chapter branch out from a large-scale study funded by the US Department of Education, which explored the experiences of Latino/a undergraduates in an engineering leadership program. The program took place at a Hispanic-serving university located in the Paso del Norte border region of Texas, which has one of the lowest median incomes in the state (Texas Higher Education Coordinating Board, 2011). The student population is comprised of more than 23,000 students, and approximately 55% of these students are the first member of their family to pursue a college degree. The university is located in a bilingual community where Spanish is spoken in the majority (74%) of households (US Census Bureau, 2010). The larger study drawn from in this chapter was a mixed-methods study taking place during a 3-year period (2011 to 2014); ethnographic data from within this larger study were collected over the period of three semesters: Spring 2012, Fall 2012 and Spring 2013.

Participants

The large-scale study included 51 Latino/a undergraduate engineering students (24 females, 27 males), many of whom are *transfronterizo* students. The term *transfronterizo* indicates that students cross the US–Mexico border on a regular basis and their lives connect two social, cultural and linguistic worlds (Relaño Pastor, 2007). Transfronterizo students represent part of the population of transnational students in the United States whose life experiences and communicative practices span across borders (Jimenez *et al.*, 2009; Warriner, 2007). This chapter focuses on 12 transfronterizo students who participated in the large-scale study. Out of 31 participants who completed our survey, 14 participants reported Spanish as their primary language and five (5) reported it to be English. The remaining 12, who are the focus of this chapter, reported both English and Spanish as their native languages. Half of these participants were in their third year of study, and the other half were in their second year of study in engineering.

Data collection

During data collection and analysis, an ethnographic orientation was adopted in order to document and understand the communicative practices of students in the context of an engineering leadership program. To explore how participants make meaning of their experience, ethnography seeks insider accounts (Hammersley & Atkinson, 2007) derived from immersion in the everyday interactions and experiences of the participants (Emerson *et al.*, 2011). The research team consisted of two literacy/biliteracy researchers and two mathematics education doctoral students; the researchers were immersed in the context of the engineering leadership program to be able to observe and describe the communicative practices of the participating students.

The main data sources for the study focused on in this chapter included: (1) an online survey about background information related to students' languages and academic support that relied on self-reported language use (see Gunnarsson *et al.*, 2015 for a discussion of self-reported data); (2) participant observation in weekly or bi-weekly engineering leadership workshops, some videotaped; (3) focus groups with all student participants from the engineering leadership program; and (4) in-depth interviews with focal transfronterizo participants.

The research team accumulated a total of 54 hours of workshop observations during the three-semester period and took fieldnotes on all observations. Four focus groups were conducted as follows: May and December 2012, and March and May 2013; focus groups lasted between 30 and 60 minutes. Initial individual interviews were conducted with 12 focal transfronterizo/a students in the language chosen by the interviewee (usually Spanish) and lasted between 40 to 70 minutes. One follow-up interview was conducted with six of the 12 transfronterizo/a focal students who were chosen because they had completed all of their K-12 schooling in Mexico. These follow-up interviews also lasted between 40 to 70 minutes. The interviews covered various topics, including students' experiences in their engineering studies in general and in the engineering leadership program specifically. Moreover, the interviewees shared their language and literacy practices embedded in coursework, key learning experiences, and people who had influenced their paths into engineering.

Data analysis

To make sense of the communicative practices of undergraduate students in the engineering leadership program, data was interpreted through theories of biliteracy and translanguaging. In particular, we draw on the continua of biliteracy to provide an account of biliteracy in college in a particular context – a US/Mexico border university. We focus on interactive ePortfolio sessions – giving and receiving constructive feedback – to show how participants draw on their linguistic resources dynamically. The literacy event we identified was the interactive presentation/peer critique. It centered on an individual's ePortfolio, and consisted of an author presenting his/her ePortfolio, and then receiving and responding to peers' critique. Since each ePortfolio was different, all events were similarly unique.

Findings

Contexts of biliteracy

The study is set in a US/Mexico borderland context in which Spanish and English are not weighted the same. Understood in a continua of biliteracy framework, macro-micro contextual factors reflect 'the tendency to weight power towards the macro, literate and monolingual ends of the continua' (Hornberger, 2003: 101). The existence in bilingual communities of different domains associated with different languages reflects this unbalanced weighting at the macro level (Hornberger, 2003). In the bilingual university community we studied, members establish domains of language (Fishman, 1965) that reflect these macro-level weightings, and responses to our survey reflected this relationship. The information we gathered included questions about what language was used with whom and in what context.

Table 3.1, which summarizes our findings, shows that students reported exclusively using Spanish in the family domain, whereas they reported using both Spanish and English in the education domain – including with classmates and study group peers. Significantly, they reported using exclusively English in the education domain when the interlocutor is a professor. Thus, for the education domain both Spanish and English are used, depending on the addressee. If the addressee is a friend, the participants use either Spanish or English; but when the addressee is a professor, the expectation is that only English is used. These responses suggest that if a bilingual student encounters a faculty member, they would switch to English even if both interlocutors are bilingual. For instance, in addressing the first author of this chapter, a faculty member, participants would use English even after learning that he is bilingual and also a transfronterizo. In our observations, members of the research team – including two bilingual faculty members from another college – were indeed addressed in English by participants in the study.

Table 3.1 shows that in the Education domain both languages are used, not only English. An engineering topic would not mean a switch into English; however, a professor as addressee might trigger a switch into English.

Table 3.1 Domains of language use

Domain	Addressee	Setting	Topic	Language
Family	Parent	Home	School	Spanish
Education	Classmates	Classroom	Engineering	Spanish/English
Education	Study group peers	Study groups	Engineering	Spanish/English
Education	Professor	School	Engineering	English

Participants also reported using both languages with classmates and study group peers, (presumably other bilinguals).

Table 3.1 also suggests that Spanish was often used in everyday, face-to-face communication. This finding was consistent with observations and focus groups. Indeed, in the more than 50 hours of engineering leadership workshops that we observed, students used Spanish as often as English. We observed students participating in workshops by listening attentively to English instructions or asking questions in front of the whole class in English, while engaging in small group interactions primarily in Spanish.

What Table 3.1 does not reflect, however, is participants' fluid use of their full linguistic repertoire. Participants often translanguaged in the context of the engineering leadership workshops, which we will discuss later in this chapter. Some participants explicitly acknowledged the use of both languages, explaining their choices with references to fluidity. In an initial interview, Adriana, a sophomore industrial engineering major who has been studying in the US all of her life, said the following:

> I think most of the time [my peers] initiate like talking in Spanish so I just go along with it since I'm able to talk in both languages. I just go along with it and I think with my other friends most of the time they also like start talking about it in English so I just go along with it too.

As part of their participation in new ways of being, engineering students developed new ways of languaging. A number of students, including participants who graduated from US high schools, reported feeling that academic English was a major challenge for them. For instance, in a personal interview, Adela (a sophomore civil engineering student who came to the US in fifth grade) stated that academic English was *the* most challenging aspect of university studies, as opposed to engineering content.

Even students who stated that they consider themselves to be equally fluent in both languages recognized that languaging in academic English was a major challenge. Pablo stated that reading assignments were especially difficult, adding that he found some of the engineering courses to be theory driven. He noted that he used internet searches to make sense of the technical terminology in English.

In an initial interview, Amelia (a freshman industrial engineering major who had recently arrived from Monterrey, Mexico) noted that mathematics was especially difficult in a new language:

> I have never had classes in English in math, and it was all so hard for me; but the first time I was also like crying at home.

She added that she drew on meaning making resources including dictionaries. She also noted that the practice of asking a question in front of the math class was a milestone for her: new languaging practices emerge in relation to the known ones (García & Li, 2014). These findings suggest that languaging resources are deployed in a context where macro-level influences constrain their use, including the choice of only one language (English) to address certain known bilingual audiences (faculty).

Mobilizing linguistic resources in Spanish

Engineering topics, according to participants, were discussed in both languages; that is, academic interactions took place using participants' full linguistic repertoire. Students reported using Spanish often to communicate among themselves, and this communication took place both inside and outside the classroom space. Regardless of the high school they had attended, students reported that much of their current study sessions took place in Spanish. For instance, Karina, a student who considered herself strongly English dominant, nonetheless reported using translanguaging often in interaction with *transfronterizo* study partners.

Another student, Pablo, who had attended high school on the United States side of the border, had study sessions only in Spanish and reported learning academic Spanish terms from them (e.g. *coseno* for cosine). Luis, a US-educated student who was about to start an internship with NASA, noted that academic Spanish would allow him to leverage economic and professional opportunities, i.e. that it would make him more marketable. Paola, a *transfronteriza* student who visited factories in Mexico to make professional contacts, noted that she expanded her knowledge of Spanish through these connections. She gave the examples of *pistón* (piston) and *cilindro* (cylinder) as words she had learned in her factory visits. Having sketched the broader linguistic, disciplinary and professional context of these students' biliteracy from the survey and interview data, in the following sections we elaborate on participants' languaging practices in the education domain.

Designing and critiquing a multimodal text: The ePortfolio

The funded engineering education initiative at the center of this research (Hispanic Engineering Leadership Institute – HELI) was meant to provide opportunities for underrepresented Latinos to enter and persist in engineering.

One of the goals of this co-curricular program was for students to gain awareness of and mastery in interpersonal teaming skills, and to help them secure
undergraduate research positions, internships and, eventually, jobs in engineering. To support them in that search, they were asked to begin to develop a
professional document that would grow and change as they learned in the engineering program and in their service learning activities. This mechanism would
help them become more aware of their learning, and more conscious of the
importance of documenting their activities throughout their university career.

Participants were asked to develop an ePortfolio to fulfill that purpose
using iBooks Author software. Participants were not specifically asked to
choose a language to write the ePortfolio, but the sessions were conducted in
English by co-author Villa, who directed HELI. The following support was
provided by engineering education faculty for students: guidance on choosing and using software to create the ePortfolio; access to a computer lab
assistant, Andrea[1], to provide guidance on how to use that software; monthly
sessions to support creation of the ePortfolio; examples of ePortfolios from
other students; suggestions of content to include in their ePortfolio; and a
stipend. As part of the portfolio development process, students were invited
to reflect on their learning, gather evidence of their learning, organize the
information and construct their individual ePortfolios.

To support the design of individual ePortfolios, monthly one-hour sessions were organized during one semester and took place at a university
computer lab. At these sessions, students wrote, designed and received feedback on their progress from their peers and from the main facilitator, co-
author Villa. Although not all participants in the institute were able to attend
every session, they were able to access the other resources throughout.

Attendance at the sessions was also useful for students because software
issues were quickly resolved. Andrea, the computer lab assistant, quickly
dealt with issues with the iBooks Author software since she was experienced
with iOS (ePortfolios could be displayed on iPads during job fairs) and was
able to lead students in using the software. For example, at the mandatory
first session, she covered basic issues, such as using the software. Students
were asked to download the software, which required them to enter their
iTunes account information. Although most students were able to do this
without any problem, some did not have an account. Others, like Amelia,
had other issues: 'I have the Mexican iTunes – I can't use it'; calmly, Andrea
guided Amelia to create a US store account. Others were confused about how
the ePortfolio would be published. One of the instructors and a number of
students asked how the work could be saved; Andrea clarified that the publication was an iBook, which could be read on an iPad. The publication could
also be saved as a PDF, although this would lose video and audio content.

Participants designed their texts drawing on multiple modes (New London
Group, 1996): a mix of text, image, color and gestural participation on the
screen. Adela designed a 32 'page' third draft (earlier drafts were 22 and 28

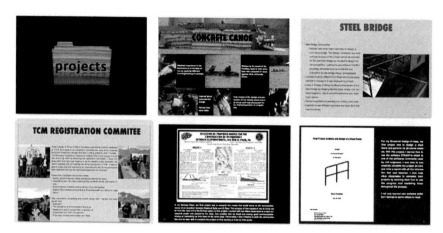

Figure 3.1 Adela's ePortfolio

pages, respectively). An excerpt is screen captured in Figure 3.1 to show the dynamic use of multiple meaning-making systems. In the excerpt, we see Adela's inclusion of photographs (second and third slides) to highlight her participation in engineering design competitions, photographs in which she is pictured wearing a hard hat with other engineering students (fourth slide), her co-authorship of an academic poster (fifth slide), and her design of a steel frame (sixth slide). The excerpt shows how she balanced images, color, font and text to convey the image of a successful engineering student.

Designing ePortfolios required extensive time for planning, gathering information, working on the computer and discussing with peers. For example, one two-hour session was designated for students to offer each other critique on their ePortfolios before turning in a first draft; co-authors of this chapter collaborated to develop the day's agenda. The two hours were spent on the following activities: a trust-building exercise, forming groups to decide on evaluation criteria, self-selecting into groups, giving critique and reporting to the whole group.

Small group members discussed these activities in English and Spanish: two out of the three groups used mainly English, and one used both languages. However, even if the group had selected a language (probably because one or more participants was monolingual or was perceived to be so), participants switched into the other language depending on the interlocutor. The excerpt below shows how Andrés switches into English to address Dr Villa then switches back into Spanish to address Amelia.

Andrés: (*to Dr Villa*) So we are going to go over each other's portfolio؟
Villa: Yeah you're going to go over, she is going to share her portfolio with you (*Amelia opens computer*) and then she is going to look at yours and then based on the criteria…

Amelia: (*Looks at screen*) Okay
Villa: If you have any questions, you're not sure (trails off)
Andrés: Oye ¿cómo se guarda? (*Hey, how do you save it?*)
Amelia: No sé. O sea lo sé guardar así pero en PDF no, no sé como.
(*I don't know. I mean, I know how to save it as a PDF, but I don't know how [in this format]*).
Andrés: Es que yo lo quise guardar como así nomas le das save. (*Because I tried to save it, but you just click on* save.)

Similarly, bilingual participants in ePortfolio sessions used both languages fluidly. They used translanguaging with ease to accomplish writing tasks, such as the design of multimodal texts. The use of translanguaging in small groups can be understood within a continua of biliteracy framework. At the macro-level, there are constraints that trigger a switch into English. However, at the micro-level, students used both languages fluidly with each other, as is shown in the following section.

Interplay of semiotic resources in commentary about design

Micro-level (process) interactions often remain hidden when the focus of analysis remains at the macro level (written product). During workshops, students drew on a variety of semiotic resources to comment on each other's work. They used languages, gestures, and the shared computer screen as resources to elaborate with each other.

Embodied interaction in which students participated in shared meaning making was observed as students commented on each other's designs. Students spoke to each other in full view of a shared screen as students pointed and read each other's designs. Through these embodied interactions, utterances were meaningful.

The following example shows how students drew on a full range of semiotic resources to communicate, even in the absence of absence of a necessary software-related word, in the excerpt below. The interaction below took place as Josué finished presenting his portfolio to Mario and Eduardo. At one point, Josué struggled to find a word related to iBooks software. However, he did not ask his peers for the word directly. Instead, he chose to employ a gesture as he continued to present his plans for the design of the ePortfolio. In lines 544, 548 and 550, he made a sweeping motion across the screen to convey his design plans. With each sweeping hand motion, his peers provide terms. Thus, in line 545 Mario suggests 'una lista' (*a list*), in line 549 Mario next offers 'slide show', and in line 552 finally Eduardo offers 'gallery', which Josué ratifies with 'exactamente' (*exactly*) in line 553. The final turn in this excerpt, which acts as a cue for the end of the exchange, is Josué's minimization of the ePortfolio screen. Gestures serve as a way to cue others for help and to open and close (line 555 below) an interaction.

542	**J:**	En honors pos quería poner por ejemplo lo del Presidential Scholarship¿ y luego pues todos lo de, los Dean's List ya ves que nos dan uno cada semestre¿	
		(In honors *I wanted to include the* Presidential Scholarship, *for example¿ And then all of the* Dean's List. *You know how they give us one every semester¿)*	
543		Habia pensado en escanearlos y luego ponerlos aquí *(I was thinking of scanning them and then putting them here.)*	J points to screen
544		pero no ponerlos aquí como de así *(but not putting them here like)*	J points to screen, makes sweeping hand motion
545	**M:**	Una lista *(A list)*	
546	**J:**	Sí, aja *(Yes, right.)*	J points to screen
547		no tener así como una lista pero tener así por ejemplo *(Not having them like a list but having something for example)*	J points to screen
548		aquí uno y luego si le das click puedes … No sé. *(you have one here and then you* click, *you can … I don't know.)*	J makes sweeping hand motion
549	**M:**	Como un slide show *(Like a* slide show*)*	
550	**J:**	Sí *(Yes)*	J: sweeping hand motion
551		pero que no estén aquí todas las fotos *(but not all of the pictures here)*	J points to screen
552	**E:**	Es un gallery. *(It's a* gallery.*)*	E points to J's screen
553	**J:**	Aja un gallery exactamente, una de estas cositas que esta aquí. *(Yes, a* gallery, *exactly, one of the little things which are here.)*	J opens menu and whistles
554		Y luego ya después de eso. *(And then after that.)*	J changes screen display
555		eso fue todo lo que hice en el, en el eportfolio de aquí *(that's all I did in the, in the ePortfolio here.)*	J minimizes screen and portfolio disappears

The above interaction is representative of the interactions that were observed during that workshop. These embodied interactions included semiotic resources that

> participants themselves attend to, and treat as relevant, as they build action within interaction together. (Streeck *et al.*, 2011: 4)

Interactions around the computer displays of ePortfolios were embodied in the sense that speech was only one aspect of the interaction. Movements, images and words on the screen were crucial for the interaction to occur.

Discussion and Conclusion

In this ethnographic account of academic biliteracy practices in a specific globalized context, an engineering program in the US/Mexico border, our survey and interview data suggest that participants are fully aware of the value, utility and meaning of their languaging resources. In this borderland context, our findings suggest that participants are moved to continuously build their repertoire to add on new meaning-making resources. In most cases it means adding languaging resources in English; for some, whose trajectories has led to abandoning Spanish languaging resources, the space allows for opportunities to recover them instead.

We used a translanguaging lens to draw attention to the tenuous and porous dividing line between languages. We show how participants used languaging resources to traverse the mode continuum as they talked in one language (Spanish) to discuss a text written in another language (English). In this sense, translanguaging was used to accomplish a specific communicative purpose, the development and critique of electronic portfolios. In their embodied interactions, they drew on multiple semiotic resources, including words from multiple languages and styles, movement, as well as words and images on the screen. Similarly their designed ePortfolios drew on multiple semiotic resources, including color, photographs, logos, and different sized fonts.

In addition, we draw on a theory of language and multimodality as social semiotic to account for the situated, multi-semiotic character of the literacy events we documented here. Acts of meaning are co-constructed in particular contexts across languages and across semiotic systems. A concrete social context affords a range of potential meanings, but past uses can constrain this range. In Adela's ePortfolio we can see how her design choices work to portray herself as a member of academic, personal and professional networks. This design conveys a socially desirable identity that situates her as a successful engineering student and as an employable engineer.

The intended audience for the ePortfolio was potential employers; the text in the ePortfolios was written in English, a language students predicted would be appropriate for potential employers. This choice is congruent with the language choices students reported in surveys (see Table 3.1). While their bilingualism could reasonably be a quality that recruiters would be interested in, students chose not to include any material in Spanish. Bilingualism was mentioned, however, in a number of student resumes. While the use of Spanish was not seen in the final products, translanguaging was observed in authoring and discussing the texts.

By drawing attention to a particular activity, discussion around text, we intend to highlight the highly situated nature of cognition and learning. Participants designed their message for specific purposes, but perhaps most importantly, they drew on the range of cultural and linguistic tools at their disposal to achieve that end. Participants in this study were able to draw on a range of meanings as a function of their participation in a range of learning experiences both inside and outside classrooms. Providing co-curricular opportunities for students, especially underrepresented and language minoritized students, to develop disciplinary and professional identities is critically important and should be a policy priority not only in engineering education but across the disciplines.

By highlighting the highly situated nature of learning activity, we also wish to counter deficit perspectives on students from non-dominant communities that would frame many of our participants (and students like them) as deficient. Deficit perspectives typically frame students from working class backgrounds as lacking 'standard' English, in need of remediation or at-risk of failure. Instead, we propose that meaningful interactions mediate cognition and identity development. Our participants were able to author their texts and their ePortfolios, texts that index their incipient professional identities, when given the opportunity and support to do so. It suggests that other students might also benefit from these learning activities and supports.

As educators, we also wish to highlight the value of drawing on multiple points along the continua of biliteracy for full expression and development (Hornberger & Link, 2012). Other educators might consider ways to incorporate opportunities for full expression of languaging resources, such as through the creation of hybrid communicative spaces that invite the non-stigmatized use of multiple languages and registers (Gutiérrez et al., 2000). In particular, educators interested in sociocultural views of situated cognition (Lemke, 1997) might consider the ways in which students' lived experiences influence their future learning, in order to use these experiences as a springboard for learning disciplinary content. Ultimately, access to high-quality educational opportunities that value students' full linguistic repertoires is a question of equity, and efforts must be made at all levels – from policy to practice – to provide and sustain such opportunities for students.

Note

(1) Andrea is also an engineering student who participated in this Institute.

References

Altbach, P. and Knight, J. (2007) The internationalization of higher education: Motivations and realities. *Journal of Studies in International Education* 11 (3–4), 290–305.

Baker, C. (2003) Biliteracy and transliteracy in Wales: Language planning and the Welsh national curriculum. In N. Hornberger (ed.) *Continua of Biliteracy: An Ecological Frame Work for Educational Policy, Research, and Practice in Multilingual Settings* (pp. 71–90). Clevedon: Multilingual Matters.

Blommaert, J. and Rampton, B. (2012) Language and superdiversity. *MMG Working Paper* (Vol. 12): Max Planck Institute for the Study of Religious and Ethnic Diversity.

Canagarajah, S. (2013) *Translingual Practice: Global Englishes and Cosmopolitan Relations.* New York: Routledge.

Creese, A. and Martin, P. (eds) (2003) *Multilingual Classroom Ecologies: Inter-Relationships, Interactions and Ideologies.* Clevedon: Multilingual Matters.

Crystal, D. (1997) *English as a Global Language* (2nd edn) Cambridge: Cambridge University Press.

Eggins, S. (2004) *An Introduction to Systemic Functional Linguistics* (2nd ed.) New York: Continuum.

Emerson, R.M., Fretz, R.I. and Shaw, L.L. (2011) *Writing Ethnographic Fieldnotes.* Chicago: University of Chicago Press.

Fishman, J.A. (1965) Who speaks what language to whom and when? *La Linguistique* 1 (2), 67–88.

García, O. (2009) *Bilingual Education in the 21st Century: A Global Perspective.* Malden, MA: Wiley-Blackwell.

García, O. and Li, W. (2014) *Translanguaging: Language, Bilingualism and Education.* London: Palgrave Macmillan.

Gunnarsson, T., Housen, A., van de Weijer, J. and Kälkvist, M. (2015) Multilingual students' self-reported use of their language repertoires when writing in English. *Apples: Journal of Applied Language Studies* 9 (1), 1–21.

Gutiérrez, K., Baquedano-López, P. and Tejeda, Ñ. (2000) Rethinking diversity: Hybridity and hybrid language practices in the third space. *Mind, Culture, and Activity* 6 (4), 286–303.

Halliday, M.A.K. (1978) *Language as Social Semiotic: The Social Interpretation of Language and Meaning.* Baltimore, MD: Edward Arnold.

Hammersley, M. and Atkinson, P. (2007) *Ethnography: Principles in Practice.* New York, NY: Routledge.

Heller, M. (2010) Language as resource in the globalized new economy. In N. Coupland (ed.) *The Handbook of Language and Globalization.* Malden, MA: Wiley-Blackwell.

Hornberger, N. (ed.) (2003) *Continua of Biliteracy: An Ecological Framework for Educational Policy, Research, and Practice in Multilingual Settings.* Clevedon: Multilingual Matters.

Hornberger, N. and Link, H. (2012) Translanguaging in today's classrooms: A biliteracy lens. *Theory into Practice* 51 (4), 239–247.

Hornberger, N. and Skilton-Sylvester, E. (2000) Revisiting the continua of biliteracy: international and critical perspectives. *Language and Education* 14 (2), 96–122.

Jiménez, R., Smith, P. and Teague, B.L. (2009) Transnational and community literacies for teachers. *Journal of Adolescent & Adult Literacy* 53 (1), 16–26.

Kanno, Y. and Cromley, J.G. (2013) English language learners' access to and attainment in postsecondary education. *TESOL Quarterly* 47 (1), 89–121.

Kress, G. (2009) *Multimodality: A Social Semiotic Approach to Contemporary Communication.* New York: Routledge.

Lemke, J.L. (1997) Cognition, context, and learning: A social semiotic perspective. In D. Kirshner and J.A. Whitson (eds) *Situated Cognition Theory: Social, Neurological, and Semiotic Perspectives.* New York: Routledge.

New London Group (1996) A pedagogy of multiliteracies: Designing social futures. *Harvard Educational Review* 66 (1), 59–92.

Oropeza, M.V., Varghese, M.M. and Kanno, Y. (2010) Linguistic minority students in higher education: Using, resisting, and negotiating multiple labels. *Equity & Excellence in Education* 43 (2), 216–231.

Pennycook, A. (2001) *Critical Applied Linguistics: A Critical Introduction.* Mahwah, NJ: Lawrence Erlbaum Associates.

Pennycook, A. (2011) Global Englishes. In R. Wodak, B. Johnstone and P. Kerswill (eds) *The SAGE Handbook of Sociolinguistics.* Thousand Oaks, CA: SAGE.

Phillipson, R. (1992) *Linguistic Imperialism.* Oxford: Oxford University Press.

Relaño Pastor, A.M. (2007) On border identities: 'transfronterizo' students in San Diego. *Diskurs Kindheits- und Jugendforschung* 2 (3), 263–277.

Sana, M. (2010) Immigrants and natives in US science and engineering occupations, 1994–2006. *Demography* 47 (3), 801–820.

Streeck, J., Goodwin, C. and LeBaron, C. (2011) Embodied interaction in the material world: An introduction. In J. Streeck, C. Goodwin and C. LeBaron (eds) *Embodied Interaction: Language and Body in the Material World.* New York: Cambridge University Press.

Swain, M. (2006) Languaging, agency and collaboration in advanced second language proficiency. In H. Byrnes (ed.) *Advanced Language Learning: The Contribution of Halliday and Vygotsky* (pp. 95–108). New York: Continuum.

Texas Higher Education Coordinating Board (2011) Report on student financial aid in Texas higher education for fiscal year 2010. See http://www.thecb.state.tx.us/reports/PDF/2337.PDF?CFID=16584213&CFTOKEN=62401137

van Leeuwen, T. (2005) *Introducing Social Semiotics.* New York: Routledge.

US Census Bureau (2010) El Paso Statistics. State & Country Quickfacts. See http://quickfacts.census.gov/qfd/states/48/4824000.html (accessed June 2015).

Warriner, D.S. (2007) Transnational literacies: Immigration, language learning, and identity. *Linguistics and Education* 18 (3–4), 201–214.

Webster, J. (2009) Introduction. In J. Webster (ed.) *Bloomsbury Companion to Systemic Functional Linguistics.* New York: Continuum.

4 Translanguaging in University Literacy Practice: Bilingual Collaboration Around English Texts

Catherine M. Mazak, A.J. Rivera and
Lauren Pérez Mangonéz

Introduction

Academic biliteracy in Spanish and English is taken for granted at Puerto Rican institutions of higher education. Even Puerto Ricans who have not been to college are clearly aware of the need to be able to read academic textbooks in English (Mazak, 2008). In fact, it is quite 'normal' and seldom interrogated to take a college course where the textbook is in English and the talk-around-text, exams and written assignments are in Spanish. This expectation of academic biliteracy leads to translanguaging practices (García & Li, 2014) in many Puerto Rican university classrooms. This chapter is a descriptive case study of one such classroom at a prestigious public university in Puerto Rico. Our purpose is to provide thick description of translanguaging practices specifically related to reading and writing that take place in our context, in order to contribute to the growing study of such practices and to facilitate cross-case comparison with other bi- and multilingual translanguaging contexts.

Biliteracies in Puerto Rico

English has been noted as the 'default' foreign language and one of the major keys to internationalization, leading to its (at times unenthusiastic) acceptance within the university setting (Cots, 2013). It should not be too surprising that academic biliteracy is expected in Puerto Rico, a context where everyday, non-academic life is dripping with text in English, though Spanish is the everyday language of communication. Facilitated by the colonial relationship with the United States and within a broader context of globalization, Puerto Ricans navigate a sea of English text as part of their daily lives (Mazak, 2007, 2008). These include such ubiquitous texts as computer interfaces, websites, business signs, federal government forms (such as the Free Application for Federal Student Aid (FAFSA) and federal tax forms, which some Puerto Ricans must submit), restaurant menus, the 'start' button on a printer, buttons on a microwave and instructions on over-the-counter medications among others (see Mazak (2006) for an extensive study). Though many Puerto Ricans do not *speak* English in their everyday lives (many, of course, do), everyone *interacts with English text* at some point during their day. At the same time, Puerto Rico has a very high literacy rate in Spanish. Thus, it is safe to say that most Puerto Ricans are, at some level, biliterate in Spanish and English.

The forces of both colonialism and globalization are also at work in university classrooms. Cots and Llurda (2011, cited by Cots, 2013) note that most bilingual professors see English as a key component for their 'survival' in the academic world – 'either [they learn] English or [they have] to leave' (p. 116). Further, to participate in the global research community they 'have no other option' than to learn English (Cots & Llurda, 2011, cited by Cots, 2013). Since many university professors in Puerto Rico studied and earned their graduate degrees at US universities, they enter Puerto Rican classrooms with deep content knowledge learned in English, yet most are quite aware of many students' preference for their professors to speak Spanish (Morales & Blau, 2009). This leads to an academic environment ripe for translanguaging.

Hornberger and Skilton-Sylvester (2000) point out that multilinguals do not simply use two languages, but deploy them across contexts and media in a constellation of communicative options, drawing on 'a range of communicative resources, rather than one or more fixed or mutually exclusive options' (see Introduction). The related concept of translanguaging is defined by García (2009) as the

> *multiple discursive practices* in which bilinguals engage in order to *make sense of their bilingual worlds.* (p. 45, emphasis in original)

These include academic biliteracy practices. García and Li (2014) further developed the pedagogical idea of translanguaging, describing a *translanguaging epistemology* that

> would be like turning off the language-switch on the iPhone and enabling bilinguals to select features from their entire semiotic repertoire, and not solely from an inventory that is constrained by societal definitions of what is an appropriate 'language'. (p. 23)

This translanguaging epistemology opens the door for the development of translanguaging practices in Puerto Rican university classrooms. Mazak and Herbas-Donoso (2014) interviewed and observed the classes of fifteen science professors at the University of Puerto Rico in Mayagüez. They found that professors had quite strong ideologies about English as 'the language of science' (p. 41) and had especially strong beliefs about the central nature of English texts in science. However, these same professors did not limit their classrooms to English only. Instead they employed various translanguaging practices in class. These practices included reading English texts and talking about them in Spanish (talk-around-text), reading texts in English and taking exams about those texts in Spanish, projecting slides in English while delivering a presentation orally in Spanish. Framing these results within Hornberger's continua of biliteracy (Hornberger & Skilton-Sylvester, 2000), Mazak and Herbas-Donoso (2014) found that

> The professors' discourse about the role of English in science shows that their beliefs tend toward the traditionally more powerful end of the continua of biliterate contexts. [...] However, what the professors actually did in their classrooms, as evidenced in the observations, operated on the traditionally less powerful ends of the context continua of biliteracy: the micro, oral, and bilingual. (pp. 45–46)

Thus, the relationship between Spanish and English literacies in Puerto Rican academia is quite complex, and out of this complexity translanguaging practices develop.

Methodology

To get an up-close look at the academic biliteracy practices in a university classroom, we conducted an ethnographic case study using classroom ethnography at the University of Puerto Rico at Mayagüez (UPRM) from January until May of 2014. UPRM is officially bilingual, and maintains an open language policy which allows professors the choice of how to use Spanish and English in their classrooms. The ethnography explored the translanguaging practices of a professor and her students in an Abnormal Psychology class where the professor enacted a *'flexible bilingual pedagogy'* (Creese & Blackledge, 2010: 112) or *translanguaging epistemology* (García & Li, 2014: 23). We chose this particular class because of previous work we had done with the professor, through which we became aware of her openness to the use of both her own and her students' bilingual repertoires in the classroom.

The class itself was designed for upper-level undergraduate Psychology majors and was delivered in 'hybrid' format, which meant that the class met face-to-face in a classroom on Tuesdays for one hour and fifteen minutes. The other hour and fifteen minutes of class time required for this three credit hour course was completed by viewing movies and completing assignments outside the classroom. The class met for 14 weeks and we completed nine classroom observations (every class meeting except for the first two classes and the three classes dedicated to taking exams). The class had a total of 29 students enrolled, though their participation and observation was inconsistent depending on their schedules and available time. Participation was voluntary, and students could opt out at any time. For this reason, every student did not complete all surveys or provide the same amount of work as samples for our review.

Data was collected by two of the co-authors of this paper, a US-born English professor who has learned Spanish in her nine years of living in Puerto Rico, and a Colombian graduate student enrolled in the Master's in English Education program, who holds certification in Spanish and English Teaching from her undergraduate university in Colombia. Both of us observed and audio-recorded the classes, taking field notes during the observations. In addition, we collected artifacts from the classroom including student assignments, teacher's PowerPoint presentations, students' PowerPoint presentations, and completed student examinations. Further, students answered two surveys about their attitudes toward Spanish, English and translanguaging which sought to gauge their espoused language ideologies. Short, informal interviews with the professor occurred at the beginning and end of every class. The graduate research assistant then transcribed the recorded data and compiled the field notes, audio recordings, and any relevant artifacts into detailed accounts of each class.

Alison, the professor

Alison (a pseudonym) is an associate professor of psychology. Her cheerful, caring disposition and enthusiastic, energetic demeanor encouraged students to attend and participate in class. Alison was always professional, but also used humor to engage her students. She employed movies and other popular culture media to help her students relate to the abnormal psychology material. Her pedagogy engaged students through a heavy emphasis on group work and discussion. She also required students to present and to incorporate engaging activities into their classroom presentations, such as psychological tests, physical exercises, and YouTube videos. It was not unusual for Alison's class to be engaging in beginner's Tai Chi routines in relation to a lesson on anxiety disorder, or singing along with a music video during a lesson about suicide and self-esteem. She required students to change their thinking by writing down three positive things that happened to them everyday. Always one to practice what she preaches, Alison, who encouraged students to exercise to battle stress, was an active marathon runner.

Born and raised in the United States, Alison had learned Spanish through extensive time living abroad, including a Fulbright in Colombia. An associate professor, she had won numerous awards for her teaching and research. Alison's academic bilingualism in English and Spanish was very well-developed. She was perfectly comfortable giving class in both English and Spanish, and corrected students' writing in both English and Spanish.

The students

Alison's students were upper-level undergraduate psychology majors. These students reflected the language backgrounds of most students at UPRM: they had graduated from high schools, both public and private, that ranged in quantity and quality of English instruction. As part of their undergraduate studies in Psychology, they were required to take four semesters of English classes; which classes they took depended on their standardized test scores at admission. The result of these varied educational backgrounds was a variety of English language proficiencies. On the surveys, students self-reported their comfort with the two languages; their responses, on a one to four scale (with 1 indicating low confidence/proficiency and 4, high confidence/proficiency), can be seen in Table 4.1.

Thus, with only two exceptions, students in the class felt (fairly) confident in extended conversations in both languages.

The classroom

The class observed was typical in that it used an English textbook and many written materials in English. However, it was atypical because of Alison's openness to bilingual classroom practices. The UPRM's language policy is quite open; the course catalogue calls the university 'bilingual', and then simply goes on to state that it is left to the professor's discretion as to which language to use for classroom activities. Nevertheless, students are

Table 4.1 Self-reported student language comfort

Rating	Number of Students (Spanish)	Number of Students (English)
1 – Only know some words and expressions	0	0
2 – Confident in basic conversations	1	1
3 – Fairly confident in extended conversations	5	10
4 – Confident in extended conversations	23	14

assumed to have a 'working knowledge of the English language' (Undergraduate Course Catalogue, n.d.: 69). In this sense, the classroom under study here is an example of how this policy is taken up by a bilingual professor with her bilingual students at a purportedly bilingual university in Puerto Rico. Other professors at the same university, with other combinations of language resources, subject matter, and students undoubtedly enact this policy differently.

Alison enacted a translanguaging epistemology in her classroom. English and Spanish co-existed easily and without tension in her pedagogy. Alison used both Spanish and English most of the time in both her speaking and her PowerPoint slides. By using both the English and Spanish key terms for abnormal psychology concepts, and giving explanations in both English and Spanish, she emphasized the most important content information throughout the course. This may have acted to solidify the content material for her bilingual students, while simultaneously modeling a fluid academic bilingualism that could serve them well in their further studies and their professional lives as psychologists.

Class materials and texts

The textbook, worksheets, and exercises which the professor frequently adapted from materials related to the textbook were written entirely in English. The textbook was the *DSM-5* (American Psychiatric Association, 2013), which is the US standard for psychiatric diagnosis. Alison also often drew exercises and cases from the textbook *Understanding Abnormal Behavior* (Sue *et al.*, 2015). Both of these texts are in English and intended for a US audience. In addition, the movies that students were assigned to watch as part of the hybrid nature of the course (for example, *Silver Linings Playbook* and *The Perks of Being a Wallflower*) were Hollywood movies which students generally watched in English with Spanish subtitles. As a result, students were required to engage with materials produced solely (the textbook) and partly (the movies) in English, in addition to the more bilingual written resources (PowerPoint presentations) which Alison created herself.

Translanguaging and Academic Biliteracies in the Classroom

This psychology classroom was filled with many types of translanguaging practices, which will be reported on elsewhere (Carroll & Mazak, forthcoming). Here we focus on translanguaging practices particularly related to writing, both in students' actual writing and in their talk around texts. As we have already mentioned, Alison used a bilingual pedagogy during class.

+
*Depression & Mania = *Bipolar
(*Depresión y manía = Bipolaridad)

- Mania: Elevated mood state, including increased energy, changes in mood.
  - Manía: Un animo elevado, incluyendo energía alta y cambios en su estado de animo

- Depression: Alternates with Mania and Hypomania
  - Depresión: Se ve en cíclos con manía e hipomanía

Figure 4.1 Translanguaging on a presentation slide

The slide shown in Figure 4.1 was typical of her PowerPoint presentations in using both Spanish and English, in this case in a 'co-languaging' approach (García, 2009: 303).

Alison's PowerPoints often looked like Figure 4.1, with information appearing in both languages. English was not always first; sometimes Spanish was. There were also times when she did not translate exactly but rather used one language or the other to further explain the content. However, the majority of the slides included both Spanish and English. We include this example to establish that bilingual texts (in this case, the slide) were both sanctioned and created by the professor. In fact, students saw bilingual texts modeled by Alison in every class. By mentioning this, we intend to set the stage for interpretation of the bilingual texts that students created during her class as they reflected her model of bilingual text creation.

Students' bilingual talk-around-text

Figure 4.2 shows an interaction between two students as they debrief a written assignment. The students had completed the assignment for homework and were tasked with reviewing their answers in small groups in order to double-check their responses before turning in the assignment for points. The worksheet itself was written in English, photocopied from an English textbook. The worksheet was titled 'Stressors, thoughts, stress reactions, and coping by students'. As often happened, some students chose to translanguage in their written assignments by completing their answers to the English prompts in Spanish; others wrote their answers in English. However, since the 'default' language of everyday talk in Puerto Rico is Spanish, the students negotiated and shared their written responses mainly in Spanish.

Since Student 1 (S1) had written her responses in English, the conversation between her and Student 2 (S2) involved translanguaging. Some surveys of UPRM students in the past have noted a lack of confidence in students' speaking in English throughout their undergraduate careers (Morales & Blau, 2009). Translanguaging can be (and is) used as a clarifying tool for the sake of the students, often of their own accord. As Moore *et al.* (2013) note, even when English is favored (here implicitly via course work and texts), its use is 'locally conditioned by participants' assessments of their own competence and possibilities' (p. 80). In this case, based on these personal assessments one student has written her response in English and one in Spanish; their conversation involves translanguaging as they each bring their particular linguistic repertoires to the activity.

For the sake of clarity, in Figure 4.2, we have added *italic* English-language translations after each line of Spanish text. **Bold** type indicates parts of the conversation which are referred to in the discussion which follows.

Each student had a copy of the assignment sheet and had filled it out prior to arriving in class. Alison asked students to form small groups to compare their work. The worksheet was written in English. Students had to fill out the sheet with common 'stressors' and 'stress-related thoughts.' Students 1 and 2, both female, began by talking about an item on the worksheet that asked them to list 'The most common stressors facing students.' S1 had filled out her worksheet in English; S2 had filled out her worksheet in Spanish.

1	**S1:**	Sí. Este, **los pensamientos yo los puse en inglés, so te los voy a leer**. Dice [*Yes. Umm,*
2		*the thought I put in English,* so *I'm going to read. It says]:* "I did not do a good job, I am not
3		good for this, I don't understand as well as others, I don't work hard enough, I should have
4		tried more". (there is a brief interruption) Este *[Umm]* … "I'm afraid to admit I'm wrong, I
5		ask too much, I don't want to ask because it's a stupid question, I don't know how to
6		organize myself, not feeling good enough."
7	**S2:**	Yo lo puse **a lo puertorriqueño** (laughs) [Inaudible] primero: 'me jodí'. *[I put it Puerto*
8		*Rican style: 'I'm screwed']*
9	**S1:**	Ajá. *[ah-ha]*
10	**S2:**	Ese momento en el que cuando tú dices 'me jodí', eso ya… *[That moment when you*
11		*say, 'I'm screwed,' that's it.]*
12	**S1:**	You got it.
13		[…]
14		(The students are briefly interrupted by the professor, who gives them a handout. They
15		move on to the next section of the worksheet titled "Stress Reactions"; The instructions
16		say, "List ten or more stress reactions common in the life of college students.")
17	**S2:**	Ok. Este… *[Ok, Umm…]*

Figure 4.2 Students review their worksheet answers

18	**S1:** Stress reactions.

19   (The professor reminds the class of the time: "¡Tres minutos! Three minutes!")

20   **S1: Este... [Umm..] "Stomach pain, crying, bad attitude, acne, tension headaches, chest**
21   **pain..."**

22   **S2: Sí. [Yes]**

23   **S1:** ... "Shoulder/back spasms, insomnia, stress eating y depression".

24   **S2: Sí. La única diferente fue hiperventilar, yo hipervento.** [Yes. The only difference was
25   hyperventilate, I hyperventilate.]

26   **S1:** Ah, de verdad. [Oh, really]

27   **S2:** Este... [umm]

28   **S1:** Ay, qué horrible. [Oh, how horrible.]

29   **S2:** Sí. Cuando me... Me... Cuando yo estoy... [Yes. When I... I... When I'm] (simulates
30   hyperventilating) me desespero. [I get desperate.] "Hiperventilo" fue lo único diferente...
31   "Llorar", lo mismo. Dolor de cabeza, insomnio, ansiedad, irritabilidad... Pérdida de apetito,
32   desesperación. ["Hyperventilate" was the only different one... "Cry," the same. Headache,
33   insomnia, anxiety, irritability... Loss of appetite, desperation.]

34   **S1: Tu dijiste 'pérdida de apetito' y yo puse 'stress eating'. Yo como cuando tengo estrés.**
35   [You said 'loss of appetite' and I put 'stress eating.' I eat when I'm stressed.]

36   [...]

37   (They move on to the next section, which asks them to list the three most common stress
38   reactions.)

39   **S1: Este... para mí los más common stress reactions es este, bad attitude, el chest pain y**
40   **el depression.** [Umm... for me the most common stress reactions is umm, bad attitude,
41   chest pain and depression.]

42   **S2: El mío más común es llorar, la desesperación y la irritabilidad. Eso sí.** [My most
43   common is crying, desperation, and irritability, yes.]

44   (The last section of the worksheet is titled, "Coping Methods." Again, it asks them to "List
45   ten or more coping methods that college students use to respond to stress.")

46   **S1: Got it. Coping methods: praying, going to the movies, going out, hang out with**
47   **friends, running or exercising, talking with friends, cooking, shopping, writing, and**
48   **reading books you like.**

49   **S2: En verdad es todo lo mismo. Lo único que hay de diferente es window shopping, que**
50   **yo digo como que 'vámonos de window shopping' aunque no compremos nada.** [Really
51   it's all the same. The only one where there is a difference is window shopping: I say like
52   'let's go window shopping' even though we don't buy anything.]

53   **S1:** Sí. En verdad yo cuando digo "shopping" es como que ir, y ver... Yo digo que la gente
54   que trabaja me tiene que odiar porque yo me pruebo todo lo de la tienda y me voy sin
55   nada. [Yes. Really when I say 'shopping' it's like go and look... I always say that the people
56   who work there must hate me because I try on everything in the store and I leave with
57   nothing.

58   **S2:** Y no compras nada. [And you don't buy anything.]

59   **S1:** Es simplemente por entretenerme. [It's simply for entertainment].

Figure 4.2 *Continued*

In Figure 4.2, the students work together to compare and contrast their written answers. However, since S1 has answered her worksheet in English, their negotiation of their written work is done bilingually. In line 1, S1 lets S2 know that her writing is in English: 'los pensamientos yo los puse en inglés, so te los voy a leer. Dice ... *[The thoughts I put in English, so I'm just going to read them. It says ...]*'. By setting up her English talk, S1 acknowledges that the 'default' language of their conversation is Spanish. Her use of the English connector 'so' also indicates her comfort with translanguaging. This use of English does not seem troublesome to S2, who highlights that her own writing is 'a lo puertorriqueño' [Puerto-Rican style], i.e. not only in Spanish but using a very particular vernacular phrase, 'me jodí' ['I'm screwed'] to describe her thoughts (line 11). In doing so, she highlights the contrast between S1's longer, somewhat more eloquent list of stress-related thoughts in English (I did not do a good job, I am not good for this, I don't understand as well as others, I don't work hard enough, etc.) and her own very succinct and colloquial 'me jodí'. Thus, S2 demonstrates her meta-linguistic awareness of the conventions of academic biliteracy that are circulating in the classroom. By contrasting her written Spanish answer to S1's use of written English and calling her own the 'Puerto-Rican style', she shows she is aware that her own answer is not considered as academic as her partner's written English answers.

The students continued their pattern of sharing as they work through the worksheet in line 21. S1 shared her list of stress reactions in English, and S2 agreed. In line 24, S2 added, 'Sí. La única diferente fue hiperventilar, yo hiperventilo' [Yes, the only difference was 'hyperventilate', I hyperventilate]. The rhetorical structure they were using was a list, and it is clear that the language of the list was not relevant for these students; rather what was most important is the content. In line 34 they came to a conflict they must resolve. After listening to S2's extended list in Spanish, S1 said, 'A mí ... Tu dijiste 'pérdida de apetito' y yo puse 'stress eating'. Yo como cuando tengo estrés' [To me ... you said 'loss of appetite' and I put 'stress eating.' I eat when I have stress]. Again, the fact that 'pérdida de apetito' is in Spanish and 'stress eating' is in English is not at issue, but rather, the two students were completely focused on content. The next several turns were dedicated to an elaboration of their individual differences when it comes to appetite and stress.

The students were beginning to run out of time (the professor had given them a 3 minute warning some time ago, in line 20) so they started to move more quickly through the worksheet. Their next task was to identify the three most common stress reactions. S1 slightly altered her translanguaging practice and instead of directly reading her list from the paper, she integrated it more deeply into her Spanish sentences, saying, 'Este ... para mí los más common stress reactions es este, bad attitude, el chest pain y el depression [Umm ... for me the most common stress reactions is umm, bad attitude, chest pain and depression' (line 39). Notice how her list took on Spanish articles, and how 'common stress reactions' becomes a chunk, as shown by S1's use of the singular verb 'es' rather than the plural 'son'; 'chest pain' is used similarly, preceded by the Spanish determiner 'el'. S2 was all business with her answer, which closely parallels the form of S1's list, but all in Spanish: 'El mío más común es llorar, la desesperación y la irritabilidad' [My most common is crying, desperation, and irritability (line 42).

In line 47 the two students continued to the last part of the worksheet, 'coping methods'. S1 confirmed S2's previous turn in English, 'Got it', and said, 'Coping methods' to signal their movement to the next question. She read her list in English: 'Praying, going to the movies, going out, hang out with friends, running or exercising, talking with friends, cooking, shopping, writing, and reading books you like'. S2 confirmed the similarity with her list by saying, 'En verdad es todo lo mismo' *[Really it's all the same]*. Then she brought up another contrast that lead to a negotiation: 'Lo único que hay de diferente es window shopping, que yo digo como que 'vámonos de window shopping' aunque no compremos nada' *[The only difference is window shopping, that I say like 'let's go window shopping' even though we don't buy anything]* (line 50 to 51). S2 differentiated 'shopping' from 'window shopping', and used the English term to do so. 'Window shopping' does not have an equivalent term in Spanish and is often used in its English form by Puerto Rican Spanish speakers. This contrast leads to several turns of discussion about window shopping, including S1 clarifying that when she wrote 'shopping' she really meant 'window shopping'.

As established earlier, students in this class were used to bilingual texts, as they saw them modeled by Alison, particularly in her PowerPoints. They were also very much aware of Alison's flexible bilingual pedagogy, and knew that just because the written assignment's prompts were in English, they were not obligated to respond to those prompts in English. Thus, when charged with negotiating their written answers to the assignment, students themselves adopted both translanguaging practices – they seamlessly integrated Spanish and English into their talk-around-text – and also translanguaging attitudes or ideologies. Their acceptance of both Spanish and English in both talk and text was demonstrated in their conversation, which after S1's initial comment focused solely on content. In fact, both students brought all their linguistic resources to bear on this in-class literacy task and they engaged quite strongly and directly with the content of the worksheet, showing how accepted these particular academic biliteracy practices are in this classroom context.

Students' translanguaging on written exams

The final exam for the class was based on descriptions of ten cases taken (like the worksheet discussed in Figure 4.2) from a textbook written in English. For each case, students had to answer four questions, for a total of 10 points. The questions appeared in English as seen in Figure 4.3.

Students were allowed to bring with them an index card with notes and to use this during the exam. We collected both the exams and the index cards in our data set.

Of the 29 exams that we collected, 15 were answered only in English, and the remaining 15 showed translanguaging. Of the translanguaged exams, most followed the pattern of using Spanish with some key words in

> Questions (10 points/each):
>   1) Differential diagnosis: What are THREE possible diagnoses for this patient? (2 points)
>   2) Actual diagnosis: What is the FINAL diagnosis for this patient (as per the DSM-5)? Why was this diagnosis indicated instead of the other two diagnoses in #1? That is, justify this diagnosis over the others (4 points)
>   3) What are TWO research-proven interventions you can use for this client? (2 points)
>   4) What are two questions that you should ask to better understand this client – in terms if diagnosis and/or intervention? (2 points)

Figure 4.3 Final exam instructions

English (like the names of the diagnosis), but some others (as described below) mixed languages considerably more. The exams written in only English comprised an initial diagnosis, final diagnosis, arguments and questions all in English. In addition to the fact that the exam prompts were exclusively in English, the experience of having studied technical vocabulary mostly in English (both in the textbook and the DSM-5) could have also influenced this choice. In addition, the exam asked for a final diagnosis 'as per the DSM-5', so students may have felt compelled to use English rather than Spanish, at least when answering this question. The index cards attached to those exams are almost exclusively in English, too, and appeared to be copied mostly from the diagnoses in the textbook (which is in English).

The other exams incorporated various written translanguaging practices. The initial and final diagnoses are almost all in English; the arguments, however, are almost exclusively in Spanish except for a few technical vocabulary items in English, quotes from the cases and misspellings which show knowledge of both languages (i.e. 'hyperactividad' – a blend of English and Spanish spelling – instead of 'hiperactividad'). Most index cards included technical vocabulary in English, with several clarifying notes in Spanish, especially regarding possible treatments. In this way, the Spanish clarification was used to clarify or explain English text (similarly to how Spanish was used as talk-around-English-text in Figure 4.2 above). Students employed various translanguaging practices in their writing while answering their exams. An example of this can be seen in Figure 4.4 (underlining was added to examples by the researchers to highlight English use).

In Figure 4.4, both answers begin with English language headings: 'Final Dx' (with 'Dx' being an abbreviation for 'diagnosis') and 'Treatment', respectively. The response to question two is denser than that for question three in its explanation and defense of the diagnosis the student would give this particular patient. As seen in the answer, there are three specific points at which English words are incorporated.

The use of 'slower state' is particularly interesting since, in the same sentence, the student uses the Spanish-language equivalent of the word 'state' ('estado'). She clearly knew the correct Spanish term for the English

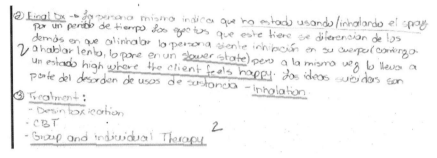

Figure 4.4 Translanguaging in a Final Exam response (example 1)

equivalent, but for whatever reason, opted not to use it. Whether this was conscious or not is unknown, but it shows a situation where the answer she gave makes sense for the bilingual reader. She conveys the information she needs to in order to get her message across, whether or not she sticks to one language in a 'neat' and conventional way. An additional example of this type of translanguaging can be seen in Figure 4.5.

In Figure 4.5, the student begins her answer with an English language statement of the diagnosis. Again, when outlining her probable treatment plan, she used an English term ('medications') and an English acronym ('CBT'). The translanguaging which can be seen in this student's written work is not easily predictable; while she uses a number of key terms and disorders in English, her translanguaging is not simply limited to this, as can be seen where she opened her answer with a full English sentence. She also (seemingly indiscriminately) used English terms and phrases in the middle of all Spanish-language sentences. The fact that this student used so much translanguaging on her final exam, which was a timed test in a finite period of time, shows that translanguaging can be useful for students pressed for time and needing to express the most information clearly and speedily.

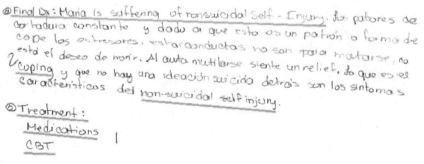

Figure 4.5 Translanguaging in a Final Exam response (example 2)

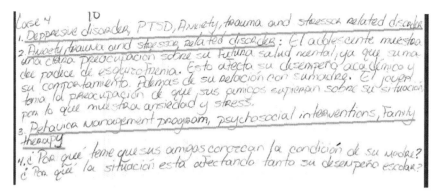

Figure 4.6 Translanguaging key terms

Other students mainly stuck to using key terms in English only, as seen in Figure 4.6. In each of this student's answers, she began with the English label and number (e.g. 'Case 1'). Further, each question, except for the last, contains English-language terms for disorders in her diagnoses. The first and third answers consisted exclusively of such terms, while the second started with a listing of terms, followed by a lengthy justification of the diagnosis given. These trends continued throughout the ten various cases on the exam, in an almost formulaic manner.

The samples here were chosen because they represent typical biliteracy practices in the translanguaged exams. As in Figure 4.2 in the previous section, there is a fluid yet academic use of both languages in students' answers. As suggested above, the amount of translanguaging may have increased due to the timed nature of the exam; students may have been compelled to answer in whatever language came to their minds first. However, this is not necessarily so as these written translanguaging practices quite predictably reflect the other kinds of bilingual writing and talk we found in class. What is clear is that students were quite skilfully able to bring all of their linguistic resources to bear on a task which had the purpose of making them demonstrate their content knowledge through writing. Again, the exam data shows the acceptance of a range of academic biliteracy practices in this course.

Discussion and Implications

The advantages of the biliterate translanguaging practices described here can be summarized in four points:

(1) *Making use of the available linguistic resources*: Both Alison and her students brought all of their linguistic resources to bear on the learning of

content material. Their written academic products were bilingual, which gave both Alison and students the opportunity to mobilize and develop their academic literacy in two languages.

(2) *Being aware of a bilingual audience and making shrewd choices*: Because of the flexible bilingual pedagogy Alison employed, students were aware that they could use their bilingual resources in ways that showed Alison their knowledge of the content material, especially on exams.

(3) *Focusing on content rather than language*: Classroom biliteracy practices focused on content – not language – and thus were appropriate for students' academic development as future psychologists in the bilingual context of Puerto Rico.

(4) *Using the first language that comes to mind in a time-limited test*: Without restraints on which language they needed to use in their answers, students were free to engage their biliteracy practices in completing a test under a time-limit. By taking away this extra layer of stress and grading the tests based on their content, Alison created a more valid testing environment – students answered in a testing situation using the same types of translanguaging that they were accustomed to using in the learning situation.

The study of academic biliteracies in Puerto Rico is particularly interesting given the ubiquitous role of English text in everyday life in this Spanish-speaking environment. This everyday interaction with English text in Puerto Rico becomes amplified in academia, where ideologies common in today's globalized academic marketplace about English as the language of science and the prominence of text in English are taken up (Tonkin, 2011; Phillipson, 2009, 2011). Cots (2013) indicates that some students, more so than instructors, may be wary of English as a potential 'predatory' language, which will usurp their native language as the main medium of communication in the academic context (p. 124).

In the particular classroom we studied, students employed a range of academic biliteracy practices, many of which were characterized by translanguaging. That is, they read texts, assignments, and exams in English, but talked about them using both English and Spanish, much as they used translanguaging in their written responses to English prompts based on the material that they had learned bilingually. Because the professor enacted a flexible bilingual pedagogy, such practices were 'normal' in her classroom. All participants in the classroom were allowed to bring all of their linguistic repertoires to bear – both orally and in writing.

By employing a flexible bilingual pedagogy, Alison modeled bilingual text creation for her students, as seen in Figure 4.1. Because text in Alison's classroom was allowed to be in both Spanish and English – an expectation that Alison not only modeled in her teaching materials but also told students was an acceptable practice – students created texts that combined Spanish and English. Though they may not have copied her exact model, students did adopt bilingual practices in their own academic text creation. Specifically, they tended to use English terminology and Spanish explanations (as in Figure 4.5). It could be argued that this translanguaging practice prepared them for their future careers as psychologists in Puerto Rico, which will require them to have a certain level of bilingual science literacy. For example, they were able to apply the key diagnosis terminology from the DSM-5 to their work, as they would have to do in English to insurance companies; but they could explain their diagnosis in Spanish, as they would most often have to do with their patients and possibly in their patients' records.

The framework used by Airey (2009) suggests that bilingual science literacy requires both the ability to work within science and the ability to apply science in society. This consists of control of both disciplinary languages of the students, though Airey's research determined that spoken language, in both the L1 and L2, was the least developed disciplinary resource at the students' disposal. By providing an outlet for students to build communicative competence in both the language they will need for scholarship and for communicating with bodies such as insurance companies (English) as well as the language they will very likely need for interacting with and explaining diagnoses and conditions to their patients (Spanish), Alison provided a unique opportunity for her students not only to grow as future psychologists, but to more fully develop their linguistic resources.

This case study has implications for other university content courses in bilingual settings. The examples shown here emphasize the students' clear focus on content, and on expressing their knowledge of that content in whatever way was most suitable for them. Airey (2009) also highlights the fact that students, in a context where they are explaining disciplinary terminology and concepts solely in English (their L2), tended to speak much slower, though the content of the explanation is much the same as if they were speaking in their L1. It may be good practice for the students to engage in explanation of the concepts in their L2; but in a situation where class time is limited and there is a wealth of content to be covered, demonstrating understanding of the concept may be more beneficial for the students' content learning. By allowing the students to engage in explanation of the given concept to demonstrate their understanding of said concept, the discussion is expedited and more information is able to be explored; misunderstandings are reduced, and students are arguably able to get more out of each class session.

In addition, the aforementioned examples show students' keen awareness of their bilingual audience, both when that audience was their fellow students (as in Figure 4.2) and when that audience was the professor (as in the exams). This gauging of others' language expectations and proficiencies is an important and critical meta-linguistic skill which will serve students well in their university lives and beyond. In this way, it could be argued that classes that operate under translanguaging ideologies are preparing students well to take on challenges in our increasingly globalized world.

References

Airey, J. (2009) Science, Language and Literacy: Case Studies of Learning in Swedish University Physics (Doctoral dissertation). Uppsala University.

American Psychiatric Association (2013) *Diagnostic and Statistical Manual of Mental Disorders* (5th edn). Arlington, VA: American Psychiatric Publishing.

Carroll, K. and Mazak, C. (forthcoming) Language policy in Puerto Rico's higher education: Opening the door for translanguaging practices. *Anthropology and Education Quarterly.*

Cots, J.M. (2013) Introducing English-medium instruction at the University of Lleida, Spain: Intervention, beliefs, and practices. In H. Haberland, D. Lonsmann and B. Preisler (eds) *Language Alternation, Language Choice and Language Encounter in International Tertiary Education* (pp. 106–127). New York, NY: Springer.

Creese, A. and Blackledge, A. (2010) Translanguaging in the bilingual classroom: A pedagogy for learning and teaching? *The Modern Language Journal* 94, 103–115.

García, O. (2009) *Bilingual Education in the 21st Century: A Global Perspective.* Oxford: Wiley-Blackwell.

García, O. and Li, W. (2014) *Translanguaging: Language, Bilingualism and Education.* New York: Palgrave Macmillan.

Hornberger, N.H. and Skilton-Sylvester, E. (2000) Revisiting the continua of biliteracy: International and critical perspectives. *Language and Education* 14 (2), 96–122.

Mazak, C. (2006) Negotiating *el difícil:* Uses of English text in a rural Puerto Rican community (Doctoral dissertation). Critical Studies in the Teaching of English, Michigan State University.

Mazak, C. (2007) Appropriation and resistance in the (English) literacy practices of Puerto Rican farmers. In V. Purcell-Gates (ed.) *Cultural Practices of Literacy* (pp. 25–40). Mahwah, NJ: Laurence Erlbaum Associates.

Mazak, C. (2008) Negotiating *el difícil*: Uses of English text in a rural Puerto Rican community. *CENTRO: The Journal of the Center for Puerto Rican Studies* 20 (1), 51–71.

Mazak, C. and Herbas-Donoso, C. (2014) Translanguaging practices and language ideologies in Puerto Rican university science education. *Critical Inquiry in Language Studies,* 11 (1), 27–49.

Moore, E., Borras, E. and Nussbaum, L. (2013) Plurilingual resources in Lingua Franca Talk: An interactionalist perspective. In H. Haberland, D. Lonsmann and B. Preisler (eds) *Language Alternation, Language Choice and Language Encounter in International Tertiary Education* (pp. 53–83). New York, NY: Springer.

Morales, B. and Blau, E.K. (2009) Identity issues in building an ESL community: The Puerto Rican experience. *New Directions for Adult and Continuing Education* 121, 45–53.

Phillipson, R. (2009) English in higher education: Panacea or pandemic? In P. Harder (ed.) *Angles on the English-Speaking World: English Language Policy, Internationalization, and University Teaching.* Copenhagen, Denmark: Museum Tusculanum Press.

Phillipson, R. (2011) Robert Phillipson responds to Humphrey Tonkin's language and the ingenuity gap in science: The empire of scientific English. *Critical Inquiry in Language Studies* 8 (1), 117–124.

Sue, D., Wing Sue, D., Sue, S. and Sue, D.M. (2015) *Understanding Abnormal Behavior* (11th edn). Cengage Learning.

Tonkin, H. (2011) Language and the ingenuity gap in science. *Critical Inquiry in Language Studies* 8 (1), 105–116.

5 Surfacing and Valuing Students' Linguistic Resources in an English-Dominant University

Ellen Hurst, Mbulungeni Madiba and Shannon Morreira

Introduction

English is currently used by all higher education institutions in South Africa as the sole or main medium of instruction.[1] The majority of primary and secondary schools have an English medium policy in place from grade 4 onwards. However, the actual language practice in schools may vary widely depending on the geographical location of the school (in a 'rural' area, a poorly-resourced peri-urban 'township', a well-resourced suburb or a city centre), the history of the school, the first language of teachers, and multiple other factors which are often structural legacies of the apartheid system and of its education system, which was differentiated along racial lines. For this reason, in many English-medium schools, other languages are used informally in speech between teachers and pupils to 'bridge' between English and the home languages of students. This can result in students struggling when they get to Higher Education institutions, where the medium of instruction is not only English, but academic English, requiring a proficiency which they have not been exposed to nor had opportunity to acquire.

This chapter takes a decolonial perspective on this problem. This perspective posits that the classification of knowledge during modernity is *monocentric*, and involves the 'oppressive and imperial bent of modern European ideals projected to, and enacted in, the non-European world' (Mignolo, 2009: 39).

Mignolo describes the result as 'coloniality' or the 'colonial matrix of power', and has argued that

> such a system of knowledge (the 'western code') serves not all humanity but a small portion of it that benefits from the belief that in terms of epistemology there is only one game in town. (Mignolo, 2011: xii)

The monolingual perspective found in South Africa's universities relates to this monocentric view of knowledge, and reflects a Eurocentric discourse which is inappropriate in multilingual South Africa. This chapter considers some pedagogical practices being developed in one of South Africa's English medium universities, which attempt to address this monocentrism by providing literacy interventions that value students' multilingual linguistic resources. The focus is on an 'Extended Degree' programme in the Humanities. We argue that the use of African languages in academic spaces can contest dominant discourses and Eurocentrism in the academy.

The paper does this in two ways: firstly we analyse a set of *language histories* which challenge preconceived notions of homogenous groups of monolingual speakers of linguistically marginalised African languages. Secondly, we look at the effects of *multilingual glossaries* on the mobilisation of students' identities and how this kind of literacy practice can advantage the usually disadvantaged in the predominantly monolingual university space.

Literature Review

South Africa is a highly multilingual country, with eleven official languages, and many more minor languages. This is in keeping with language trends in the continent more generally – Desai (1995: 20) described multilingualism as the African *lingua franca*. As a result, the monolingual orientation of many educational institutions in Africa has been heavily critiqued in recent years. A number of authors have argued that one of the impacts of colonialism was the categorization and naming of African languages; for example the distinction between Shona and Ndebele in Zimbabwe and the distinction between Xhosa and Zulu in South Africa were a result of particular geographical locations of missionaries, and not a result of any objective dialect boundaries (cf Makoni *et al.*, 2006; Gilmour, 2006). These categorisations followed the traditions of cataloguing and classifying which were developed during the European Enlightenment – practices which underpin western epistemologies. Authors such as Gilmour (2006) have described the evaluative and classificatory approaches of early documenters of South Africa's languages, in order to show how these languages were classified in 'linguistic (and, by implication, cultural and 'racial') hierarchies' (Gilmour, 2006: 38):

> the development of colonial linguistics was fundamental to strategies by which Westerners interpreted the world, categorized its peoples, and affirmed the superiority of their own position within it. (Gilmour, 2006: 2)

Makoni and Pennycook (2005) argue that the colonial project of language 'invention' in Africa therefore needs to be disinvented.

The 'monolingual orientation' is defined by Canagarajah (2013: 1) as the belief that 'for communication to be successful we should employ a common language with shared norms', and that 'languages have their own unique systems and should be kept free of mixing with other languages'. The monolingual orientation arises from the European nation-state model of 'one nation, one language', and forms the basis for language policy at the majority of South Africa's higher education institutions, which were epistemologically modelled on European institutions.

Decolonial thinking (Quijano, 2007; Mignolo, 2011) posits that modernity, capitalism and colonialism are all still entwined, even in the present (supposedly postcolonial) world order. Whilst the world may be 'post'colonial in terms of linear time, to decolonial thinkers the knowledge structures generated in colonialism are still very much present, and serve to create binaries rather than dialectics and to celebrate monocentrism rather than polycentrism. Coloniality persists in modernity, and privileges the history of European ideas, particularly the very ideas surrounding modernity and rationality, resulting in other knowledges being consigned to the 'border'. In terms of decolonial thinking, then, such a monocentric logic would underlie the presence within 'post'-apartheid South Africa of English monolingualism in higher education institutions. The aim of decolonial thinking is to think beyond these constructed hierarchies through 'border thinking' in order to practice 'epistemic disobedience' and overcome the logic of coloniality (Mignolo, 2005, 2010).

It is our argument that the logic of coloniality and monocentricism can be countered in English-predominant universities by adopting a translanguaging pedagogy. The term *translanguaging* (originally *trawsieithu* in Welsh) was first used in Welsh schools in the 1980s by Cen Williams to refer to the use of

> one language to reinforce the other in order to increase understanding and in order to augment the pupil's ability in both languages. (Williams, 2002: 40, cited in Lewis *et al.*, 2012)

Thus, translanguaging pedagogy takes as its starting point the language practices of bilingual people who use their linguistic resources flexibly to make meaning of their lives and their complex worlds (García, 2011). Translanguaging pedagogy is based on the view that bi-/multilingual students have *one communicative repertoire* drawing on multiple languages from which they select features *strategically* to communicate effectively (García, 2011: 1). These students have the ability to use language fluidly, to translanguage in order to make meaning beyond one or two languages (Creese & Blackledge, 2010: 7–9; García, 2011: 2). It is also important to note that translanguaging

> takes the position that language is *action* and *practice,* and not a simple system of structures and discrete sets of skills, hence the use of an -ing form, emphasizing the action and practice of languaging bilingually. (García, 2011: 1)

Canagarajah (2013) emphasises that 'translingual practice' – the processes and orientations adopted in order to communicate using all available codes from speakers' repertoires – consists of an integrated proficiency, that 'can be creative, enabling, and offer possibilities for voice' (p. 6).

Madiba (2014) proposes translanguaging pedagogy as an effective method to develop African languages and include them in classroom contexts. The advantage with translanguaging pedagogy in multilingual classrooms is that it allows students to draw from their linguistic repertoire, going not only 'between different linguistic structures and systems, including different modalities, [... but also] beyond them' (Li, 2011: 1223). In this way bi-/multilinguals' learning is maximized as they are allowed and enabled to draw from the range of their linguistic resources, rather than being limited in doing so by monolingual instructional assumptions and practices (Hornberger, 2005). A further advantage of a translanguaging pedagogy is that it promotes *languaging*:

> the process of using language to gain knowledge, to make sense, to articulate one's thought and to communicate about using language. (Li, 2011: 1223)

Although languaging plays a key role in learning for both monolingual and multilingual learners, bi-/multilingual learners are able to draw on a more complex range of linguistic/conceptual resources in an ongoing process of inter- and intrapersonal meaning making (García & Li, 2014) in the learning space. In so doing they engage in processes of creativity and criticality. García and Li (2014) define *creativity* as

> the ability to choose between obeying and breaking the rules and norms of behavior, including the use of language. (p. 67)

This choice can occur at linguistic, cognitive, interactional and strategic levels. Linguistic creativity entails students challenging boundaries between languages or language structures, giving rise to new phonological, morphological, lexical and syntactic varieties. Creativity at this level often results in students constructing emergent academic registers which belong to neither their so-called first language nor the language of instruction; as will be shown later in this chapter, students use various creative strategies to develop terms and registers in their home languages. At a cognitive level, translanguaging promotes creativity by broadening access to concepts through different linguistic resources, and has the potential to stimulate alternative ways of organizing thought, negotiating, arguing, reaching decisions and solving problems. Furthermore, translanguaging can help multilingual students to develop academic literacy skills such as perspective taking and problem solving. At an interactional level, translanguaging provides multilingual students with the opportunity to learn new forms of turn-taking and other aspects of classroom interaction. At a strategic level, multilingual students learn strategies to deploy their linguistic resources to their advantage in learning and teaching contexts.

Criticality is defined by García and Li (2014) as

> the ability to use available evidence to inform considered views of cultural, social, political and linguistic phenomena, to question and problematize received wisdom and to express views adequately through reasoned responses to situations. (p. 67)

García and Li regard creativity and criticality as linked, since creativity is in many cases an expression of criticality. Translanguaging pedagogy aims to empower multilingual students to develop creativity and criticality in literacy events using all their available linguistic resources.

As translanguaging enables multilingual students to reflect on and construct or modify their sociocultural identities and values, it has the potential to transform historical institutional identities of South African universities which are premised on a monoglossic ideology. In this sense, translanguaging has the potential to counter the epistemological monocentrism and monolingualism of the European project of modernity.

Methodology

The data presented in this chapter was drawn from a cohort of approximately 150 students on the 'extended degree' programmes in Humanities at the University of Cape Town (UCT) in 2013. We consider the Humanities to be under-researched in terms of translanguaging pedagogies, despite the potential for Humanities fields to be highly responsive to calls for multilingual spaces in the academy. The extended degree programmes in the Humanities faculty at UCT enable students to undertake the standard BA and BSoc Sci degrees in four years instead of the three years typical of South African higher education institutions. The students on the programme come from groups designated by the government as previously disadvantaged, which map onto historical apartheid categorisations of people into 'racialized' groups.[2] This is intended for redress purposes – those groups which were historically disadvantaged are offered various types of support in order to increase the numbers of graduates from these groups and thus address the inequalities of the past. Many students from redress categories are multilingual and may speak English as a second or additional language.

The extended degree programmes at UCT offer a number of courses to students in their first year of entering the degree, to provide them with an orientation towards Higher Education, and to fill any gaps that might arise from different backgrounds and levels of provision in the education system.

Two sets of data from the foundation courses are considered here:

- Language histories – an assignment set in the first week of the foundation course 'Texts in the Humanities' that asks students to reflect on their language background.
- Multilingual glossaries in the course 'Concepts in the Social Sciences'.

Analysis

Language histories

The first set of data to be presented are from the 'Language History' assignment that students wrote during their first semester of the extended degree as part of the foundation course 'Texts in the Humanities'. The language histories were intended to surface the many linguistic resources of students. Reading through the histories presents a challenge to notions of homogenous groups of monolingual speakers: the students are often highly multilingual; in fact, not one student in the 2013 intake was entirely monolingual.

African language[3] speaking students, particularly those who had lived in Johannesburg, were especially multilingual. As the following three students describe, the residential areas surrounding Johannesburg are incredibly linguistically diverse[4]:

(1) … moving to Johannesburg I began to hear a lot of different languages because of the diversity of the population. On a daily basis I'd hear English, Zulu, Tswana, Sotho and even on the odd occasion Venda or Shangan.

(2) I was born in Joburg, South Africa, lived in Alexander 7 a section where you will find Xhosa's, Zulu's, Sotho's, Tshwane's and Shangan's living together. The most dominant language is Zulu mixed with Sotho and a little bit of English. My relatives in Joburg are multi-lingual, some

are Xhosa's by origin, some are Shona's from Zimbabwe, but when they are together they speak Zulu because Zulu is the main language that people from Alexander 7 use for communication.

(3) The time came when my mother had to leave the village and look for a job in the city; she had to bring me along with her. My mother moved to Johannesburg and settled into the Alexandra Township. The township had a huge number of different people from different backgrounds. As a new kid on the block I had to adapt to the new environment and my Xhosa language was no longer quite valid. People here were speaking many different languages which include amongst them Sotho, Pedi, Tswana and others. These three languages influenced me a lot.

Many students, as in the third example above, have stories about multilingualism stemming from migration, when their families have relocated to other parts of the country for work or education and there has been an impact on language use. Consider the following history (presented in full):

(4) Well, I was born and raised in Limpopo (One of the nine provinces in South Africa) in a small village called [X], where almost everyone spoke Sepedi, moreover, my family is Pedi, and so growing up all I could hear was this Pedi language. My two older sisters would play with me using this language and some of the family members as well. I learnt how to speak Sepedi, my home language, at the age of two. When I was five, my father decided that we move to Pretoria where he'd already been offered a job.

We then dislocated from [X] to Mamelodi (A well renowned township in Pretoria). Mamelodi contains a several dissimilar official languages namely, Afrikaans, Zulu, Xhosa, Ndebele, Northern Sotho, Tsonga, Tswana and the most preponderant one which is Southern Sotho, that is heavily used in Tsotsitaal (a variety of mixed up languages mainly spoken in townships). At the age of six, I was then taken to a primary school that only had Afrikaans as their Medium of instruction.

Being in that school for three years, I had to learn how to write and speak Afrikaans. Although I obtained good marks at it, I have to say Afrikaans was like a nightmare for me and I detested it. In my third Grade, My father lost his job and that, consequently, meant I had to go to a public school. A non-fee pay school. I was then taken to a local school that taught English and Tswana. That's where I learned I started learning both of these languages. My friends were Zulu, so I'd learn Zulu everytime I'm with them.

Moving over to high school, my father had gotten another job in Silverton-Pretoria-one that's more appropriate than the last one. As a result of that, we had to vacate to a place that's a bit closer to where he'll be working, for his convenience. We moved to a place called Nellmapius, about two kilometres to his workplace, furthermore, I went to high school in Nellmapius. That's where I learnt how to write and speak Southern Sotho, from grade eight up until ten. In grade eleven I then changed from studying Southern Sotho as my home language to studying Sepedi as my home language.

Living in Nellmapius I had to also learn Tsonga, being that two of my friends were Tsonga and they weren't hesitant about teaching me their language, because they didn't really know how to speak my language, so we had to speak Tsonga, moreover, our neighbours were also Tsonga. After my matric in Nellmapius secondary school, my aunt who lives in Johannesburg (Gauteng), asked me to come live with her for just a year, and so I went. During my gap year in Johannesburg, I got a job at a Company (...) (an electrical wholesaler). Almost all its employees were Xhosa and because of that I had to learn Xhosa. Four months later before I could learn more Xhosa, It was already too late because I had to come to the University of Cape Town.

This student mentions a number of different literacies – s/he is evidently literate in English; in addition s/he describes writing in Afrikaans, Southern Sotho and then Sepedi (as home language). Multilingualism is therefore accompanied by multiliteracy as the expansion of the spoken language repertoire is accompanied by an expansion of their written repertoire.

The category of 'home language' is the language chosen by parents or children as the child's language for the purposes of the medium of education in the early years at school, and later as one of their subjects. South African children all take at least two languages in school: their 'home language', and a 'first additional language'. Sometimes the home language in school is not the same as the actual language spoken in the home, as the child's language may not be available for study. In the above example, the student at one stage studies Southern Sotho rather than Sepedi as their home language (Southern Sotho and Sepedi are related, and to some extent mutually intelligible).

Many of the students were involved in complex multilingual practices. One student reports the following of their day-to-day language practice:

(5) At home Sepedi remained the main language spoken even though I always responded in a mixture of Setswana and Sepedi, beyond school and home I used Afrikaans, Setswana and English with friends.

These multilingual repertoires were commonly reported in the histories, and not just amongst students who spoke African languages. Many students whose family language was Afrikaans described a bilingual situation growing up. However, English was often privileged over Afrikaans by parents, reportedly to prepare the children for education, and to avoid the 'colloquial' forms of Afrikaans used by many of South Africa's township communities. The variety known as 'kombuis' Afrikaans (Kitchen Afrikaans), a working class variety, was particularly maligned, and referred to as 'broken' Afrikaans.

Even those students who were born in monolingual contexts were still required to become multilingual over time:

> (6) The language I heard first was my mother tongue language which was IsiZulu. I heard it first from my grandmother. As the years went past I slowly picked up a second language, English, but I was still fluent in isiZulu. By the time I went to school I could speak two languages English and IsiZulu with practically anyone.

> (7) I found it easy for me to learn my home language, because isiXhosa was our daily bread. There came a time when I had to go to pre-school and some things started to change a little bit because I had to learn on how to write and read in English.

The influence of the medium of instruction at school on students' repertoires is clear – many students begin to pick up extra languages only when they begin formal education, simultaneously expanding their repertoire into the written medium. In this context, some students have more of an advantage than others. While schools in South Africa typically claim to use English as a medium of instruction after grade 3, many students reported that their teachers continued to use their home languages. This obviously can put them at a disadvantage when they enter an English-medium Higher Education institution such as UCT. There were two clear settings where these disadvantages emerged: in 'township' schools (Example 8) and in 'rural' schools (Example 9):

> (8) The school I went to since I was child it was a Township school. With blacks only, no other races, a disadvantageous school with poor infrastructures, poor facilities, no internet access etc. The pre-school I went it was at the Township, with blacks only, same as my middle school and my high school. However the language that I learn and write at is Xhosa and English, but Xhosa did not differ [was not a new experience] only one language had differ [was new] it was English, because I had never had it during my pre-school. The language that my teacher used especially English teacher it was English, but other teacher they used Xhosa cause it was my home language, and that had affect my own use of language, cause I am not the best to Internationally recognised language and that limit my opportunities. I do not feel well by writing English in school cause it is not my home language and I am not the best in and it shows my weaknesses. The only language I feel the best when I am writing and reading is Xhosa. About my home language I feel very, very proud, it shows my dignity, my identity, it determines who I am, where I come from.

(9) Born in a small village, full of farms and green lands, in Umtata which is part of the Eastern Cape in South Africa. [Y] is the name of the village it had few people on that time, and most of them were unemployed, that lead to starvation in the village. Selling goods like crops and livestock was the option they had to go with so they can survive. The main language that was used on the village was isiXhosa. The old ones believed that we had some sort of connection with the dead, so in order for us to connect with them we had to use no other language than isiXhosa.

People on the village only knew isiXhosa, including my parents. When I grew up I was also introduced to the language, isiXhosa. Sadly for me I was never exposed to other African or South African languages when I grew up, since there was no television or radio at home or around the village, and we knew nothing about the outside world.

In 2001 my parents and I, moved to Cape Town which is part of the Western Cape, in South Africa. To get a job for my parents and to get better education for me. I started with school in one of the local schools in Khayelitsha. The school only specialised on two languages, English as a first additional language, and isiXhosa as home language. I was now being introduced to a new kind of language. It was very hard for me to learn the language, I was all alone because even my parents could not read or write English so they were no help to me. My friends and I at school we were using isiXhosa on our daily conversations, it was again another disadvantage for me because I only spoke English in the class room for about 40 minute a day.

In Example 8 above, the student describes difficulties particularly in terms of reading and writing in English, despite its early introduction after pre-school. On the other hand, they felt no difficulties reading and writing in their home language, isiXhosa: 'The only language I feel the best when I am writing and reading is Xhosa'. Example 9 highlights how little support this student could get from their home environment in terms of English literacy because their parents, growing up in a rural area, had not received English literacy education under the apartheid education system. It is clear in these cases that the effects of apartheid segregation and differentiated schooling for different 'racial' classifications are still felt today.

From the language histories data we can see that multilingualism, including multilingual literacy, is both required and valued elsewhere in the students' lives and by the students themselves – as one student describes:

(10) I can now read and write in 3 of South Africa's official languages. This became an advantage to me especially at work because I was working at a tourist venue. Firstly my managers loved me because I was multilingual, secondly I could communicate with all kinds of clients even if they were

foreign, most of them could still understand English because it's a universal language, I would speak to Afrikaners in Afrikaans, Xhosa people in Xhosa. I found that people loved it when I communicated to them in their home language because it made them feel more comfortable.

However, multilingualism is currently not valued by the academy, an institution of coloniality which has a Eurocentric monolingual perspective and expects students to be able to speak, listen to and write a very particular, exclusive form of English. This situation perpetuates what Mignolo (2010: 161) calls the 'colonial wound' – 'the fact that regions and people around the world have been classified as underdeveloped economically and mentally' – by excluding, devaluing and failing students who have incredible multilingual resources.

Language histories like these allow lecturers to surface and appreciate the value of students' resources in their lives; but how do we challenge the hegemony of English in South African Higher Education practice? The following section will consider literacy events which attempt this challenge.

Multilingual concept literacy glossaries

Although translanguaging pedagogy offers good prospects and possibilities for surfacing and valuing students' linguistic resources in English-predominant universities, its implementation in the tertiary classroom is still underdeveloped in general. However, some recent work at the UCT is applying this approach in order to promote *concept literacy*. This term is fairly new in South African educational literature and is used here to refer to students'

> ability to read, understand and use the learning area-specific words, terms and related language forms which are part of knowledge formation in the different disciplines or content areas. (Young *et al.*, 2009: 8)

The focus in concept literacy is on deeper understanding of concepts rather than simple definition. In South African universities, students' limited proficiency in the language of instruction can present a further barrier to developing deeper understanding of concepts.

Accordingly, the UCT multilingual glossaries project was launched in 2007 to support students for whom English is not the first language in learning concepts in various disciplines, with the aid of their first languages. The glossaries were designed from the start to be used face-to-face with students and online. The Vula Online Environment was developed by the university's Centre for Education Technology (now known as the Centre for Innovation in Learning and Teaching, CILT) and powered by Sakai. This networked Online Learning Environment provides students with easy access to the glossaries and other resources in different languages. The use of technology has made it possible to accommodate many languages and to provide a wide range of digital tools to enhance conceptual understanding, word meaning, contextual information, and comprehension scaffolds to guide students' learning of the concepts (see Madiba, 2014 for a detailed discussion of the multilingual online database).

The pedagogic use of multilingual glossaries for concept literacy at university level requires a good understanding of students' conceptual difficulties and theories of intervention to address them. Without a good theory of conceptual difficulty, it is easy for lecturers to apportion blame to students for being underprepared and lacking academic English proficiency (Madiba, 2010). Thus, Perkins (2007, 2009) argues that any intervention to address concept learning should be based on a good theory of conceptual difficulties and that such a theory should provide an explanation of what makes the learning of concepts hard for students (Perkins, 2007, 2009). Perkins' theory of conceptual difficulty identifies four factors as the main cause of students' conceptual difficulties. As Madiba (2010) discusses these factors in detail, they will only be briefly outlined in this chapter to show their implications for concept literacy. The first factor has to do with students' level of academic development versus the cognitive demands of the discipline. This factor is informed by educational developmental theories of scholars such as Piaget (1959, 1977) and Vygotsky (1986), who viewed learning to be developmental and constructive. Piaget's learning theories trace learners' conceptual difficulties to the lack of well-developed mental structures or certain logical schemata that allow encoding of aspects of content and their learning at a deep level (cf. Piaget, 1959, 1977). Thus, according to Piaget (1959, 1977), unless learners have reached a certain stage of internal development, instruction from outside may not be effective. In contrast to Piaget, Vygotsky (1986) argued that the learning of scientific concepts precedes the development of an established logical structure, and that such a development can be optimized through direct instruction.

The second factor has to do with the nature of the discipline knowledge or epistemological knowledge. According to Perkins (2007), concepts are by their very nature difficult to master as they are

> more abstract rather than concrete, continuous rather than discrete, dynamic rather than static, simultaneous rather than sequential, or organicism rather than mechanism, interactiveness rather than reparability, conditionality rather than universality and nonlinearity rather than linearity. (pp. 98–99)

The third factor has to do with *threshold concepts* (Meyer & Land, 2006). Each discipline has concepts that are key to its mastery and students often find these concepts difficult and also epistemologically 'troublesome', as they conflict with other kinds of knowledge previously constructed by students, such as ritual knowledge, inert knowledge, foreign knowledge or tacit knowledge (Madiba, 2010; Perkins, 2007, 2009).

The last factor has to do with conceptual difficulties related to language. The role of language in concept literacy is widely recognised (cf. Cummins,

1979, 2000; Vygotsky, 1986). Vygotsky, for example, maintains that there is a direct relationship between thought and language. According to him word meaning is an instance of the unity of thought and word, and as such one cannot be separate from the other (Vygotsky, 1986). This relationship question between language and conceptualization is important for a better understanding of the conceptual difficulties experienced by multilingual students in learning new concepts through an additional language. Whereas all students may experience difficulty in learning disciplinary concepts in higher education, students who learn concepts in an additional language have to relate new terms and concepts not only to their developing understanding of a specialist field and to their everyday knowledge (which is likely to be intimately linked with their first language), but also to their developing command of meanings and forms in the language of instruction.

Students who learn concepts in an additional language have to relate new terms and concepts not only to their developing understanding of a specialist field and to their everyday knowledge (which is likely to be intimately linked with their first language), but also to their developing command of meanings and forms in the language of instruction (Madiba, 2010; Nkomo & Madiba, 2011). As Cummins's (1979, 2000) studies show, students who have low proficiency in a language which is used as the medium of instruction may struggle to understand concepts and their relationship through that language which may then result in poor academic achievement. Cummins (1979, 2000) maintains that concepts are learned better in a language in which one has a high proficiency. This fact is also supported by neurolinguistic studies (cf. De Groot, 1992, 2002; Kroll & Stewart, 1994; Kroll & Tokowicz, 2005; Pavlenko, 2009) which show that students with low proficiency in a foreign language which is used as the medium of instruction tend to access concepts in this language through their first language (L1). As Madiba (2014) pointed out, students use different translanguaging strategies to understand discipline concepts and represent them in their first languages. For example, where equivalents are not found in their first languages, students borrow the foreign terms and adapt them to the linguistic structure of their languages. The next section presents examples of students translanguaging pedagogical and practical strategies as they attempt to define concepts selected for the Working with Concepts in the Social Sciences course.

Using multilingual glossaries in the social sciences

The second set of data to be analysed are drawn from the 'multilingual glossaries' assignment set for students in the foundation course *Working with Concepts in the Social Sciences.* This assignment required that students work over the course of the semester on definitions for a set of key concepts in the course, such as *socialization, identity* and *power.* Students then came together in groups in class and had conversations in which they translated the concepts into Afrikaans and the African languages which they spoke in the group. Students were grouped by language background so that each group had a minimum of two speakers of the same languages in it so that conversations within and across languages could be had. As can be seen in the Language Histories above, most students were multilingual, so that translations across numerous languages within groups were possible. After this interactive session, students were required to write up individual definitions in both English and a second language of their choice. We will comment here on some interesting effects of using multiple languages, although assessment of the final product focused on the English definitions (since tutors and the lecturer marking the task did not have enough proficiency across the multiple languages to spot errors in other languages).

Classroom observations during the group work phase of the assignment showed the effects of introducing African languages into the classroom. The normally silent student space, in which the lecturer's or tutors' voices were heard far more frequently than students, even where student participation was encouraged, became loud. Students argued, laughed and gesticulated forcefully in order to put their point across to other participants in the group. The multilingual nature of the task created an environment in which learning became active. Concept literacy could thus be seen to develop through the practice of languaging (specifically translanguaging) with the use of multiple languages, as well as paralinguistic and non-verbal modes such as gesture, allowing for greater meaning making between and within students. In one session the administrator of the lab we were in entered meekly and asked for the door to be shut because of noise. Students who did not normally speak in class were suddenly doing so, and debates broke out within groups as to the best ways in which to translate concepts, and the best sorts of idioms to use to relay social science meanings in another language. Translanguaging opened up spaces for creativity and criticality (García & Li, 2014) as the students debated meaning, creatively developing terms in their home languages and thinking critically about what such definitions might entail. Authority over the content was removed from the lecturer: in such a space, students had the knowledge and students were the experts.

The final phase in the assignment required that students take their notes from the classroom conversations and write up glossary definitions of their own. The following excerpts from students' work provide examples of the value of disrupting monolingualism:

(11) SOCIALISATION

English definition:

Young children grow up following from what the others (peers and adults) are doing. Socialisation can be explained in a way that a boy is supposed to play toys from toddler years until round about the age of nine, then go play soccer in the field with other boys until when he decides that he is an adult, during that process he knows that he should not be around or play with girls much. A person cannot be socialised in isolation, there has to be other people around to socialise him.

isiXhosa definition:

NgesiXhosa singayicacisa sithi 'intaka ikha ngoboya benye' okanye sithi 'umntu ngumntu ngabantu' ngoba umntu udinga ab anye abantu ukuze azoba ngumntu naye.

Example 11 makes use of isiXhosa idioms in explaining the term 'socialization'. The phrase *'intaka ikha ngoboya benye'* translates into English as 'a bird builds its nest with another's feathers', while *'umntu ngumntu ngabantu'* translates as 'a person is a person because of other people'. It can thus be seen that the English definition and the isiXhosa definition that the student provides are not direct translations of one another: rather, the isiXhosa definition is couched in culturally and linguistically relevant idioms that bring the concept closer to home for the student than is possible through the abstract language of academia. Translanguaging here also provides a space for the student to critically expand upon the idiom and bring it within the realm of social science, an act which shows the ways in which creativity and criticality are entwined (García & Li, 2014). The idioms the student has used are excellent ones through which to illustrate the concept of socialization; and suggest a more accurate understanding of socialization than is apparent from his English-medium definition. For instance, in the English-medium definition, the student's focus is on socialisation in childhood, with less indication that socialization is a lifelong process; the student's English-medium definition is also gendered in a particular way. In the isiXhosa idioms, however, there are no ageist or gendered connotations, but a better sense of socialization as applying to all people throughout life.

Example 12 shows particularly clearly the ways in which translations into other languages can be more succinct than the definitions students are able to provide in English, whilst still carrying complex meaning:

(12) POWER

English definition:

Power is the ability to control what happens. Power gives people to achieve things that normally would not be possible

IsiZulu definition:

Amandla.

The brevity of the isiZulu definition, compared with the lengthy English definition, shows that using a language other than English allows students to collapse weighty concepts into terms with which they are familiar. The simultaneous use of English is also important, however, as this allows a space for the students to expand upon the concept in the language which they are expected to use in the academic space. The cross-translation thus allows for a learning opportunity both in terms of learning the concept itself, and in terms of learning academic English.

Example (12) shows a direct translation from English into isiZulu/isiXhosa between the single words 'power' and *'amandla'*, but it also allows for a locally relevant history to be attached to the translation in a way which does not occur in the student's English elaboration on the word 'power'. In South Africa, the word *amandla* carries a particular history: it was a powerful term in the resistance against apartheid, used as part of crowd call and response during rallies in which the speaker at an event would shout, *'Amandla'* ('power'), to which the crowd would respond *'awethu'* or *'ngawethu'* ('to us'). It is thus a term which carries an historical and emotional valence within the South African context which allows it both to translate the socio-political concept of power, as required in the foundation course, and to exemplify the ways in which power can be enacted. This localized meaning can be read into the English definition only once the isiXhosa/isiZulu definition is taken into account: 'Power gives people to achieve things that normally would not be possible' becomes more meaningful when read in the light of Apartheid history and a translation of power as *amandla*. Again, we see the creative effects of translanguaging. Later in the semester the same student used *amandla* again as part of her definition of the sociological concept of agency, which refers to the free will individuals are able to exhibit in light of the social structures which constrain social life:

(13) AGENCY

The exercise of power in daily life. *Amandla.*

The above examples show a nuanced understanding of social science concepts, and show that the historicised identities of students were better able to be present when they wrote in languages other than English. The use of a bilingual/multilingual glossary thus has a double effect: it allows students to understand and illustrate concepts in more meaningful ways than would be possible in English alone, and also allows lecturers and tutors with a basic knowledge of the language and context to gain more insight into the student's work as evidence of learning.

The fact that both 'power' and 'agency' were defined by one student using the same term – *amandla* – while her English definitions differed significantly (Examples 12, 13), shows a potential weakness of the technique, as 'agency' and 'power', in the academy, refer to two different (though linked) concepts. Academic writing requires students to be very precise in their definitions, and to go beyond common-sense meanings of words. It is for this reason that the task was a multi-, or at least bi-, lingual one: the use of learner's mother tongues allowed for students to identify more closely with the material, while they were also able to expand upon the definitions where necessary in English, which is the language they are expected to use in academic work within the rest of the university.

That students appreciated this was apparent in course evaluations. The following examples serve to illustrate:

(14) It was insightful because we were able to define these concepts in our own words which is a good way of learning.

(15) To learn new concept in own language make it easier to get English quicker.

(16) It is hard to forget something once you hear it in your own language, and you turn to understand it better.

These responses show that students found it a useful literacy event in terms of scaffolding conceptual development and in getting a grasp on the kind of English expected in the academy. Students also found it valuable as a means of gaining a deeper, more personally relevant understanding of the concepts:

(17) It broadens my idea of the concepts and what they mean in different languages and the social meaning attached and associated with it.

(18) It gives us different interpretations.

(19) Some other words when translated to other languages they turn to be sentences not just one word so I understand more.

(20) They give me more insight about these concepts and I am able to apply them in real life.

Finally, evaluations showed that the exercise had a symbolic effect as well, validating the student's presence within the university:

(21) I liked the fact that this was an engagement which took place in African languages which does not happen frequently on the setting which we in.

(22) It was nice to use a different language to English.

The task set for students was unusual in that it validated multilingualism. In the usual university context, English monolingualism is celebrated, and those students who have multiple language resources are disadvantaged rather than advantaged. The task thus allowed students who usually have less cultural capital in the classroom setting to have more: in this assignment, to be bi- or multilingual was a distinct advantage. It can thus be read as a decolonial literacy event, which aimed to unsettle the usual norms of the university. It was for such a reason that the classroom was able to come alive in ways that it did not under monolingual English conditions.

Conclusions

The kinds of literacy events described in this chapter attempt to respond to the challenge of 'border thinking' – consciously rejecting the monocentric judgements of coloniality regarding our students' linguistic resources, and attempting to value multilingualism/translingual practice as valid linguistic practice in the South African context.

The language histories highlight how our students do not fit within a monolingual orientation, and how difficult it is for them, through their social and educational histories, to prepare for such an orientation. This innovative literacy event, in which the students shared their language histories, enabled them to surface their rich language resources, and it enabled us as teachers to acknowledge and value them.

The multilingual glossary takes this process of surfacing one step further by utilizing students' translingual practices to develop their understanding of key concepts in the social sciences. Alongside allowing students to frame concepts within their own historical-social contexts, this literacy event also overturned the typical dynamics regarding which language resources are valued in the classroom. Furthermore, it provided an entry-point into the academic norms of defining and explaining terms in academic writing.

Both these events in different ways gave voice to students who occupy a liminal space and are often disregarded and devalued by the centre/the university. Pedagogies which validate and surface students' linguistic capital are empowering for multilingual students, yet at the same time they are challenging for lecturers who often work with monolingual assumptions, and for the academy itself, which too often reproduces a Eurocentric viewpoint.

Notes

(1) Some South African institutions are dual medium.
(2) Apartheid racial categories were 'native' (black African), 'coloured' (mixed race), 'white' (European descent), and Asian/Indian. During 'high apartheid' (1948 to 1976), residential zoning within townships was furthermore segregated by language/ethnic groups.

(3) African languages here refers to the nine official African languages of South Africa: Ndebele, Northern Sotho, Sotho, Swazi, Tsonga, Tswana, Venda, Xhosa and Zulu. The other two official languages of South Africa are English, and Afrikaans (which developed from Dutch).

(4) Some names of people and places have been removed to protect participants' identities. The written English has not been changed except in the case of typographical errors for clarity.

References

Canagarajah, S. (2013) *Translingual Practice: Global Englishes and Cosmopolitan Relations.* New York: Routledge.

Creese, A. and Blackledge, A. (2010) Ideologies and interactions in multilingual education: What can an ecological approach tell us about bilingual pedagogy: In C. Helot and M. Ó Laoire (eds) *Language Policy for the Multilingual Classrrom: Pedagogy of the Possible* (pp. 3–21). Bristol: Multilingual Matters.

Cummins, J. (1979) Linguistic interdependence and the educational development of bilingual children. *Review of Educational Research* 49 (2), 222–251.

Cummins, J. (2000) *Language, Power and Pedagogy: Bilingual Children in the Crossfire.* Clevedon: Multilingual Matters.

De Groot, A. (1992) Bilingual lexical representation: A closer look at conceptual representations. In R. Frost and L. Katz (eds) *Orthography, Phonololgy, Morphology and Meaning* (pp. 389–412). Amsterdam: Elsevier.

De Groot, A. (2002) Lexical Representation and Lexical Processing in the L2 User. In V. Cook (ed.) *Portraits of the L2 User* (pp. 32–63). Clevedon: Multilingual Matters.

Desai, Z. (1995) The evolution of a post-apartheid language policy in South Africa: An on-going site of struggle. *European Journal of Intercultural Studies* 5 (3), 18–25.

García, O. (2011) From language garden to sustainable languaging: Bilingual education in a global world. *Perspectives* 34 (1), 5–9.

García, O. and Li, W. (2014) *Translanguaging: Language, Bilingualism and Education.* Basingstoke: Palgrave Macmillan.

Gilmour, R. (2006) *Grammars of Colonialism: Representing Languages in Colonial South Africa.* Basingstoke: Palgrave Macmillan.

Hornberger, N. (2005) Opening and filling up implementational and ideological spaces in heritage language education. *Modern Language Journal* 89, 605–609.

Kroll, J. and Stewart, E. (1994) Category interference in translation and picture naming: Evidence for asymmetric connection between bilingual memory representations. *Journal of Memory and Language* 33 (2), 149–174.

Kroll, J. and Tokowicz, N. (2005) Models of bilingual representation and processing: Looking back and to the future. In J. Kroll and A. de Groot (eds) *Handbook of Bilingualism: Psycholinguistic Approaches* (pp. 531–553). Oxford: Oxford University Press.

Lewis, G., Jones, B. and Baker, C. (2012) Translanguaging: Developing its conceptualisation and contextualisation. *Educational Research and Evaluation: An International Journal on Theory and Practice* 18 (7), 655–670.

Li, W. (2011) Moment analysis and translanguaging space: Discursive construction of identities by multilingual Chinese youth in Britain. *Journal of Pragmatics* 43, 1222–1235.

Madiba, M. (2010) Fast-tracking concept learning to English as an additional language (EAL) students through corpus-based multilingual glossaries. *Alternation* 17 (1), 225–248.

Madiba, M. (2014) Promoting concept literacy through multilingual glossaries: A translanguaging approach. In L. Hibbert and C. van der Walt (eds) *Multilingual Universities in South Africa: Reflecting Society in HIgher Education* (pp. 68–87). Bristol: Multilingual Matters.

Makoni, S. and Pennycook, A. (2005) Disinventing and (re)constituting languages. *Critical Inquiry in Language Studies* 2 (3), 137–156.

Makoni, S., Dube, B. and Mshiri, P. (2006) Zimbabwe colonial and post-colonial language policy and planning practices. *Current Issues in Language Planning* 7 (4), 377–414.

Meyer, J.H.F. and Land, R. (eds) (2006) *Overcoming Barriers to Student Understanding: Threshold Concepts and Troublesome Knowledge*. London: Routledge.

Mignolo, W. (2005) *The Idea of Latin America*. Malden: Blackwell.

Mignolo, W. (2009) Coloniality: The darker side of modernity. In S. Breitwisser (ed.) *Modernologies. Contemporary Artists Researching Modernity and Modernism* (pp. 39–49). Barcelona: Catalog of the Exhibit at the Museum of Modern Art.

Mignolo, W. (2010) Epistemic disobedience, independent thought and decolonial freedom. *Theory, Culture & Society* 26 (7–8), 159–181.

Mignolo, W. (2011) Epistemic disobedience and the decolonial option: A Manifesto. *TRANSMODERNITY: Journal of Peripheral Cultural Production of the Luso-Hispanic World* 1 (2).

Nkomo, D. and Madiba, M. (2011) The compilation of multilingual concept literacy glossaries at the University of Cape Town: A Lexicographical Function Theoretical Approach. *Lexikos* 21, 144–168.

Pavlenko, A. (2009) Conceptual representation in the bilingual lexicon and second language vocabulary learning. In A. Pavlenko (ed.) *The Bilingual Mental Lexicon: Interdisciplinary Approaches* (pp. 125–160). Bristol: Multilingual Matters.

Perkins, D. (2007) Theories of difficulty. In N. Entwistle and P. Tomlinson (eds) *Student Learning and University Teaching*. Leicester: The British Psychological Society.

Perkins, D. (2009) *Making Learning Whole. How Seven Principles of Teaching can Transform Education*. San Francisco: Jossey-Bass.

Piaget, J. (1959) *The Language and Thought of a Child*. London: Routledge and Kegan Paul.

Piaget, J. (1977) *The Development of Thought: Equilibration of Cognitve Structures*. New York: Viking.

Quijano, A. (2007) Coloniality and modernity/rationality. *Cultural studies* 21 (2–3), 168–178.

Vygotsky, L. (1986) *Thought and Language*. Massachusetts: Massachusetts Institute of Technology.

Williams, C. (2002) Ennill iaith: Astudiaeth o sefyllfa drochi yn 11–16 oed [A language gained: A study of language immersion at 11–16 years of age]. See http://www.bangor.ac.uk/addysg/publications/Ennill_Iaith.pdf (accessed February 2015).

Young, D., van der Vlugt, J., Qanya, S., Abel, L., Brombacher, A., Clark, J., Donaldson, D., Johnston, P., Johnson, Y., Rijsdijk, C. *et al.* (2009) *Understanding Concepts in Mathematics and Science. A Multilingual Learning and Teaching Resource Book in English, Xhosa, Afrikaans and Zulu, Vol 2*. Cape Town: Maskew Miller.

6 Translation Narratives: Engaging Multilingual Learners in Translingual Writing Practices

Julia E. Kiernan

Narrative in the Writing Classroom

The primary purpose of this chapter is to broaden our understanding of narrative – specifically, personal narrative via literacy narratives, which are regular components in American writing classrooms. These assignments are often one of the first to be assigned, and require students to tell an autobiographical story about their experiences with reading and/or writing: to pick an event and connect it to their feelings about reading and/or writing; and to connect this narrative to the current class discussions of reading and/or writing. This genre aims to position students in a role of authority, allowing them to choose what elements of their literate lives to include and exclude in the creation of their personal literacy narrative. This chapter posits that assignments such as the literacy narrative need to be reassessed, reimagined, and redesigned if they are to engage the growing number of students with multilingual backgrounds and capabilities who enrol in writing courses.

In order to reimagine the genre of narrative, however, it is important to first assess its usefulness in a writer's development. Narrative writing helps students to organize and make sense of their own experiences, which are significant steps in the formation of academic identity and critical thinking skills. The personal narrative has traditionally been categorized as a genre that is expressive in scope and nature, and, therefore, an uncomplicated genre for freshman students to engage with. Danielewicz (2008) argues that because these narratives are tied to ideologies of personal voice, and thereby expressive, they are useful starting points in the writing classroom. Gere (2001) also acknowledges the expressive nature of this genre, explaining:

> there is general agreement that personal writing is prose that gives significant attention to the writer's experiences and feelings. (p. 204)

Central in the work of many composition scholars is the contention that personal narrative, as an act of expression, is a straightforward writing task – students are familiar and comfortable engaging with writing that expresses personal emotions and feelings. In this narrative assignment students are typically asked to tell a story about a learning moment in their lives, and then step away from this moment and consider it through new eyes. This narrative, then, becomes an example of academic writing in its engagement with critical reflection. However, what is problematic is that the majority of personal narrative research (Danielewicz, 2008; Gere, 2001; Hindman, 2003; Lu & Horner, 2009; Mahala & Swilky, 1996; Robillard, 2003; Sullivan, 2003) is based within American paradigms that are often unfamiliar to international multilingual students. Due to their unfamiliarity with writing that embraces expressive personal reflection, international student reactions to this assignment range from confusion to frustration to despair, which often leads to poor assessment outcomes. This is especially troubling given that literacy narratives are usually assigned early in the academic semester, setting the bar for both teacher and student expectations of academic ability.

Ergo, the personal narrative can be a problematic genre for multilingual students to engage with due to its emphasis upon Westernized learning outcomes and its enforcement of American, monolingual, middle-class subjectivities. Sullivan (2003: 43), an American scholar, offers a commonplace justification for the continued implementation of this assignment:

> Those of us who teach personal writing, who begin our composition courses by asking students to write from and about a significant experience in their lives, do so because we believe the personal essay locates students in a topic and form that is familiar to them, that they have a decided interest and stake in, that they can write about with a sense of authority. We believe that writing about a significant experience provides students with an opportunity to engage in reflection, to consider important matters of purpose and audience, to practice and refine elements of craft.

However, this research project considers both the benefits of personal narrative in its move to engage students in critical processes of 'reflection', 'purpose and audience' and 'practice', and the drawbacks of this assignment in its failure to provide multilingual students with a 'sense of authority'. Thus, this chapter explores the gap in our understanding of personal narrative and its ability to locate 'students in a topic and form that is familiar to them'. This chapter will show that pausing to reimagine the genre of narrative provides spaces for multilingual students to create a sense of authority within their academic writing practices.

Reimagining Personal Narrative via a Translingual Approach

It has been argued that genre analysts need to focus on the action of a genre and the social situation it is part of (Gentil, 2011), which is a central component of rethinking the narrative within composition and other writing classrooms. A shift towards a translingual framework reflects population shifts evident within these writing environments and, perhaps, the ineffectuality of historically valuable genres. The new form of narrative proposed herein – the translation narrative – is an important site of inquiry because translation narratives work to position multilingual writers as experts within English-medium institutions (an intent of the literacy narrative). The notable difference, however, is that this sub-genre of narrative asks multilingual students to draw upon their multilingual resources, requiring them to narrate their translation processes and choices, which serves to illustrate the cognitive benefits of linguistic interaction. Essentially, this assignment is grounded in the claim that the ability to move between and within languages is a benefit to multilingual students enrolled in English-medium programs (Canagarajah, 2002; Lu, 2006; Mokhtari & Reichard, 2004), and that if we can combine the benefits of literacy narratives – such as reflection, self-awareness and critical thinking – within a new genre of narrative, namely, the translation narrative, then the skill of language negotiation is positioned as a usable asset and multilingual students are better prepared to master the same skill sets anticipated in earlier versions of personal narrative.

The translation narrative is a three-part assignment that moves in stages, each part scaffolding towards the final draft. The assignment incorporates library work, peer review and response, and personal reflection, as well as attention to formatting and structure; however, outside research is strongly discouraged – this assignment, while developing out of a researched topic, is written from the reflective position of personal narrative. It is worth approximately 20% of the overall grade, takes place early in the semester (usually the second out of five writing projects), and is allotted up to four weeks (of a 16 week semester) for completion. The three stages – a group translation, translation reflection, and the translation narrative – will be outlined in the following paragraphs.

Stage one of the assignment is a collaborative, research-based academic translation. Students are placed in groups of three to four students based on home language (e.g. all members of a group would speak a common language such as Mandarin or Arabic, etc.). The group then works together under the guidance of an information literacy librarian to find an academic text written in their home language – the topic of this text is decided upon by the group. Once students have chosen an academic text, they choose a short excerpt (~250 words), distribute a copy to each member, and are then given up to four days to translate the text into classroom English[1]. During the act of translation, group members work individually and do not collaborate with other members of their group. Three class periods later all group members bring their English-language translations to class and compare outcomes. An entire class period is allotted for students to look at each other's work; specific questions are provided to help students brainstorm the next step of this assignment (the translation reflection). For example, students are asked to consider:

- What is the same and different between your translation and the other translations in the group?
- Why do you think there **are** differences? Spend some time considering why there are similarities and differences between the texts. Look at specific places that are different.
- Do any of the meanings change? Where? Why? Does a change in meaning create a different **purpose** for the sentence? How do you think changes in meaning affect **purpose**?
- What are your overall impressions of this exercise? Do you have any new thoughts on translation and the **gain** or **loss** of meaning?

The purpose of this brainstorming activity is to encourage students to begin thinking about translation as a personal – rather than impersonal – process. Students are encouraged to discuss their answers to the above questions with each other and the teacher, and to use their responses to the above prompts to begin composing a one-page rough draft of their translation reflection, which would be due the following class period.

Stage two of this assignment, the translation reflection, begins on day 4 and is completed on day 7. It is a personal reflection on the translation process; students write a two to three page reflection on their experiences and feelings towards translation. They are encouraged to talk about what types of choices they made when translating as well as to explain why they made these choices. During this stage students also meet with the teacher for individual 10-minute conversations about the difficulties they may be encountering at this point in the assignment. The ultimate purpose of the translation reflection is encouragement of critical thinking and reflective practice; in this way, the moves of the translation reflection are similar to expectations of a traditional literacy narrative in its discussion of personal choices, feelings and outcomes. However, the major difference between genres is that in the translation reflection students are discussing recent actions, while in the literacy narrative students are more often looking backward and reflecting upon moments in their past. Still, the purpose of this section remains narrative in scope: students compose a text based in personal experience, which considers why literacies differ between individuals.

The third and final stage of this assignment is the translation narrative, which begins on day 9 and is submitted on day 13; it incorporates all previous steps and takes the format of an academic research paper. This final version is a combination of elements from the translation and the translation reflection; in essence, students create an essay that brings together the most useful parts of earlier drafts. The assignment is peer reviewed twice (on day 9 and day 12) and submitted for assessment on day 13. This final essay positions the students' translations as data, or research. They use this data as examples to support their personal reflections from stage two. The end result is an essay that brings together students' personal research, interpretations on the translation process, and practices of language negotiation. In this way, the final text produced is translingual because it works across, between, and within languages rather than simply English.

This redesign of the traditional personal narrative assignment responds to the common assertion within the field of multilingual education, particularly bilingual and translingual inquiry, that there are few initiatives at work to develop and implement multilingual frameworks within English-medium education systems (Hornberger & Link, 2012). Gentil (2011) explains:

> Research on the interrelationship between writing expertise and language proficiency, or more specifically, the cognitive and the linguistic dimensions of […] composing, has not paid much attention to such complicating factors as the breadth and depth of genre repertoires and cultural variations in the genre expectations against which writing expertise is evaluated. Nor has this line of research examined the modular nature of genre knowledge directly, taking genre as a context rather than an object of study. (p. 10)

The translation narrative, as a reimagined personal narrative genre, considers a number of the connections that Gentil describes as missing from current discussions; namely, the 'cognitive and linguistic dimensions' at play within the exploration of personal translation processes, as well as the 'cultural variations' associated with composing specific genres of narrative. As such, the translation narrative offers genre as an object, rather than only a context. This is because the narrative act of this assignment requires engagement with the process of translating and the negotiation of individual literacies; the assignment is shaped by the choices and realities of the student's language use, rather than outside genre expectations. Through approaching narrative as both personal and impersonal – which differs from mainstream assertions that 'when we stick to impersonal topics, students have a hard time making this cognitive connection' (Danielwicz, 2008: 421) – the translation narrative allows students to begin with the impersonal (e.g. the act of translation), and then move to personal reflection, self-awareness, and critical thinking. Ultimately, the translation narrative strives to develop the same skills as the literacy narrative, but does so through an academic rather than expressive tone, which is not only more familiar, but expected by many multilingual students. In doing this, the translation narrative aims to avoid outcomes where

> those new to the academy and inexperienced as writers can fall into an inarticulate silence because they feel that their life experiences have not given them access to narratives that will please their teacher readers. (Gere, 2001: 207)

Whereas consideration of genre and genre (re)design are certainly central to this research, the implementation of useable translingual strategies that encourage students to move between, across, and within languages in their writing remains a primary objective. These translingual strategies are associated with cognitive benefits for students (Alsheikh, 2011; Canagarajah, 2006; Creese & Blackledge, 2010; Gentil, 2011; Lu, 2006; Mokhtari & Sheorey, 2008); additionally, Hornberger and Link (2012: 240) contend that

> as school populations become increasingly linguistically diverse, refusing to acknowledge the language resources of students [...] limits the possibilities for their educational achievement. (p. 240)

In other words, there is a gap in our pedagogical understanding of how to engage multilingual students in work that considers the strengths and usefulness of language negotiation. Moreover, moving towards a reimagining of genre, such as personal narrative, positions teachers to engage with theories, such as translingualism. This interplay between the practical and the theoretical is a worthwhile move if we are to 'acknowledge the language resources of students' as pedagogically beneficial.

Translingual inquiry has also been recognized by a number of scholars, including those outside the discipline of composition and writing studies in terms of biliteracy. Hornberger and Link (2012) describe biliteracy as 'communication in two (or more) languages in or around writing' (p. 243); Gentil (2011) describes the consideration of biliteracy in the theory and pedagogy of genre as an attempt to

> combine insights from research in literacy and bilingualism in order to shed light on how multilingual writers develop and use genre expertise in more than one language. (p. 7)

In composition studies, translingual theory and research positions writing – principally English-medium writing – in constant relation to other languages, where a primary aim of translingual inquiry remains a recognition of the fluidity of language, and movement away from dominant ideologies of Standardized English (Canagarajah, 2012; Horner *et al.*, 2011a). Canagarajah (2013) further argues that the act of translanguaging in writing is the ability to produce texts that demonstrate successful language negotiation across diverse discourse communities, echoing earlier Living-English theories of Lu (2006) which argue that the most useful language is that which works to communicate, rather than that which abides by expected standardized conventions. Essentially, the act of translanguaging within writing is an act of linguistic interpretation, definition, and understanding that illustrates how translingual writing positions the individual on a continuum of self-inquiry (Tardy, 2011). This concept of a continuum is also central to the biliteracy work of Hornberger and Link (2012: 243), where

> the continua of biliteracy lens reminds educators that the more students' contexts of language and literacy use allow them to draw from across the whole of each and every continuum, the greater are the chances for their full language and literacy development and expression.

Thus, this research sees the idea of continuity and connection as central to translingualism and language negotiation within writing; the translation assignment is designed to illustrate the interrelationships of language to students, requiring them to engage in multiple languages and literacies in order to better understand the usefulness of all languages throughout their composing process. Consequently, the practice of translanguaging within the translation narrative is a pedagogical design that offers a

> possibility for teachers and learners to access academic content through the communicative repertoires they bring to the classroom while simultaneously acquiring new ones. (Hornberger & Link, 2012: 245)

Ultimately, this research is one practiced example of the

> changes being made at the organizational level to rethink the ways in which English is represented in U.S. composition teaching, the design of composition and writing program curricula, and the preparations of (future) teachers of postsecondary writing. (Horner *et al.*, 2011a: 271)

Through documenting students' choices and considering how ideologies of choice function within translation-based writing processes, this chapter considers the importance of translingual pedagogies in writing classrooms populated by multilingual students. In particular, this paper provides excerpts from a selection of translation narratives in order to analyze the rhetorical and contextual implications of translingual writing processes. This analysis of student translanguaging communicates textual evidence of the benefits of language negotiation, and illustrates how the encouragement of language negotiation develops critical thinking – students who translanguage must make a variety of rhetorical choices and are pushed to be critically reflective. Ultimately, the examples of student writing and consequent analysis attest that layered processes of cognitive negotiation take place when students are asked to compose translation narratives and move between languages in their writing. These narratives do more than provide rich personal stories (a primary outcome of literacy narratives); students who engage in these projects create texts that utilize critical thinking strategies to decipher linguistic difference. For these students, the mobilization of their multiple languages and literacies works to enhance the quality of their intellectual inquiry, as well as the quality and quantity of meanings and ideas they produce within translation narratives. Thus, important to this research is an understanding of the benefits of language negotiation, specifically how languages can be deployed in new ways so that multiple languages come together in a singular textual production.

A further goal of this research is to further the development of practical pedagogies positioned within translingual theory. Attention to ideologies of linguistic choice has been part of the culture of composition theory and practice for the last two decades; however, this culture has primarily explored teacher response in terms of student language negotiation, particularly in relation to deviations from standardized English expectations (Lu, 1994). And, while contemporary scholarship holds strong in this call to action (Canagarajah, 2013; Horner *et al.*, 2011a; Horner *et al.*, 2011b; Tardy, 2011), the majority of work remains seated in theory and teacher response rather than pedagogical strategy. Although the development of theoretical inquiry should remain central in our engagement with multilingual student writing processes, researchers must also shift their attention to practical strategies for engaging diverse student populations. As such, this research offers one pedagogical response, working not only to broaden our understanding of the genre of narrative – specifically, personal narrative – assignments in the writing classrooms, but also to consider ways in which traditionally monolingual genres can be redesigned via a multilingual lens.

Institutional Background and Student Populations

This research took place within a large research institution in the midwestern United States. The university enrolls approximately 50,000 students annually; in the fall of 2014 nearly 15% of these students, or 7500, were international (coming from over 130 countries globally). Of these international students, the majority enroll in a preparatory, or bridge, writing course in their freshman year; it is this course that serves as the basis for this research. As with many composition and writing programs in the United States, the department this study is housed in has devoted increasing attention to the academic success of diverse student populations. Consequently, a variety of changes have been made to the curricular and instructional practices of this specific preparatory writing course; of note to this project is the move to implement a content-based translingual theme. This shift towards linguistic engagement via negotiation is a response to the population changes of students who have enrolled in this writing course over the last decade. Historically, students in this course have been domestic American – from economically disadvantaged school systems, and members of racial, ethnic, linguistic minority, and migrant communities. However, this predominance of domestic American students has shifted drastically in the last decade: in 2008, 131 out of the total 344 students enrolled in this course were domestic; six years later, in 2013, the number of domestic students fell to 14 out of a total of 411 students. The change in population dynamics within these classes also reflects the larger changes at work within this institution. A decade ago, in 2004, 14 out of 8922 freshmen were from China (0.16% of the entering class); today, Chinese students account for nearly 17% of freshmen. While Chinese students remain the most common nationality of international students enrolled at this institution, there are growing numbers of Arabic, Spanish and Korean speakers, as well as students of other language backgrounds.

In response to enrollment shifts – today, this course annually serves an estimated 900 first generation, heritage language and English language learners – a team of teacher-researchers is working together to investigate and design writing pedagogies to better serve diverse learners. Faculty involved in the redevelopment of this course meet regularly to develop translingual writing assignments, exercises, and discussion points. Additionally, faculty workshops and cross-departmental dialogue are central in the redesign of this course. Thus far, a primary outcome of the translingual restructuring is the demonstration of

> near-term impacts such a […] translingual, asset based curriculum might provide first generation and international student writers. (Trowbridge, 2014)

This agenda aligns with the 2011 Modern Languages Association (MLA) report 'Foreign Languages and Higher Education', as well as scholars who maintain that 'the welcoming of translanguaging in classrooms is not only necessary, but desirable educational practice' (Hornberger & Link, 2012: 239). Thus, this programmatic shift is an important site of inquiry due to its valuing of translingual competences, which reflects a national shift toward asset-based, culturally sustaining pedagogical practices.

Student Iterations of the Translation Narrative

Example 1

There are a number of elements that must be included in this final stage of the assignment; namely, work from earlier drafts. Students are required to bring together excerpts of the original home language text, excerpts from their groupmates' English-language translation, excerpts from their own English-language translation, and narrative from their translation reflection. Although all these texts could come together to reach the word count for this assignment, peer review work considers how a close reading of earlier writing provides room for further analysis in terms of their chosen thesis. For instance, the first quote below comes from the translation reflection and uses only English, while the second quote comes from the translation narrative and provides a closer, more nuanced reading of ideas presented in the translation reflection, drawing upon both English and Mandarin to provide specific and detailed examples and personal interpretation:

> When I discussed about transition in my group, I find that I have a lot of difference between my translation and others such as sentence, organization, and etc. One of biggest difference is that we often use different vocabularies to express same meanings. For example, my group member likes to use 'pass' to describe process of total lunar eclipse. However, I prefer to use 'enter' or 'travel' in my translation. Why do people have difference in translation? The reason is that people will try their best to find exact vocabularies from their mind to translate words in other language.

In this excerpt we see the writer attempting to work through their own understanding of the translation process; the writing is both personal (e.g. the repeated use of 'I') and somewhat messy – the struggle inherent in the move to create a personal narrative is evident. However, in the later translation narrative, we see the development of clearer analysis that looks back to the author's earlier reflections, drawing on the personal 'I', but also looking outward to include other perspectives (e.g. 'many factors cause people', and the repetition of 'we').

> Many factors cause people have a different understanding on same-content article such as different language level, different experience, and etc. One of most essential factors is how familiar people are on both languages. In other words, language level decides how exact vocabulary is used by people and what type sentence people use. When we translate words '掠过' in English, '掠过' is a verbal vocabulary in Chinese and it means that one things fly through other things. To my surprise, three

different English verbs are used in three translations. Ping uses 'skim over' to explain '掠过' and Jialin like to use 'pass through' for these words. For me, I choose words 'travels into' to explain '掠过'. Why do we use three different words? I suggest that we gain different English education in China. Before this translation, I hardly see words 'skim over' or 'pass through' in my English education. So I believe that I might use 'skim over' or 'pass through' in my translation if I know both words.

Of note in this later version is that the writer is not simply reflecting back on their choices, but offering a critical reflection of the very process of translation and linguistic negotiation as a practice. Specifically we see the original:

> Why do people have difference in translation? The reason is that people will try their best to find exact vocabularies from their mind to translate words in other language.

developed into a much more nuanced argument in terms of both language negotiation and the writer's thesis, which is concerned with vocabulary in terms of meaning and purpose:

> Why do we use three different words? I suggest that we gain different English education in China. Before this translation, I hardly see words 'skim over' or 'pass through' in my English education. So I believe that I might use 'skim over' or 'pass through' in my translation if I know both words.

This latter example provides a more structured and detailed argument that borrows from the work of the reflection, but moves forward to make statements and claims about the process of linguistic negotiation. In addition, we see the genre of narrative being employed to make definitive statements about the translation process (e.g. 'Why do we use three different words? I suggest that we gain different English education in China. Before this translation, I hardly see …'), the writer is therefore positioning literacy as a social practice, embedded within socially constructed epistemological principles; in other words, this student's text offers one example of how

> [t]he ways in which people address reading and writing are themselves rooted in conceptions of knowledge, identity and being. (Street, 2011: 61)

Example 2

Ideologies of literacy are very important to narrative; this is perhaps one reason why the literacy narrative, as a genre, has been a popular assignment choice in American writing classrooms. Yet, the primary drawback of this conditioning is that it is based within Western notions of autonomy that expect a level of ease with this genre. As a result, it has been considered pedagogically sound to engage students with assignments that simply consider past, personal literacy experiences. However, Hornberger and Link (2012) suggest:

> pedagogical practices where students hear or read a lesson, a passage in a book, or a section of text in one language and develop their work in another [... are examples of] translanguaging [that] can be seen not only as a language practice of multilinguals, but a pedagogical strategy to foster language and literacy development.

In other words, what the assignment of the literacy narrative fails to do is consider its inability to engage students in social literacy practices. When we move to the translation narrative, we see that it begins in social practice (in a group setting) and then moves into personal literacy and language based transactions. Both assignments – the literacy narrative and translation narrative – work towards the same goal of personal reflection and exploration; however, the latter assignment sequence is more useful to multilingual students in its focus on the sociality of language and language practices among and between individuals. For instance, a Spanish student explains her perspectives on language negotiation through drawing upon both her original Spanish text and her groupmate's translations.

> When translating, my goal is to convey all the information that is given to me [...]. In this case, since the object of the translation is a scholarly article, it was important for me to keep the order of the words the same as well as using the closest translation of the word. I have noticed that sometimes it is relatively easy to this, but sometimes it can't be avoided. I noticed that how I understood the reading affected my goal to keep my English translation to the Spanish version. I don't know if Maria's [...] goal was the same as mine, but I can tell their translations differ to a word-by-word translation [...]. The differences in our understandings are shown when looking at a sentence of the original article:
>
> Bajo presiones enormes, los pueblos indígenas del continente parecen no poder detener la fuerte erosión cultural que esta acabando con una columna central de la identidad humana.

and then looking at mine:

> Under enormous pressure, the indigenous towns of the continent seem not to be able to stop the strong cultural erosion that is killing with a central column of the human identity.

And then at Maria's:

> Under huge pressures, the indigenous towns of the continent don't seem
> to be able to stop the big cultural erosion that's destroying the central
> column of the human identity.

This student writing illustrates the sociality of language and language negotiation, particularly in terms of individualized 'conceptions of knowledge,
identity and being' that are exemplified in her identification of personal goals
tied to the process of translating. The writer goes on to offer a close reading
of one of these goals – word order – where she not only integrates Spanish
into her English-medium essay, but also offers another social dimension to
the process of translation.

> The differences are reflected on our word choices. For example: the trans-
> lation of the word 'acabando'. 'Acabando' can be translated to 'ending',
> yet I used 'killing' instead. I think that what is being talked about; the
> disappearances of languages, is an important matter, and that is why I
> decided to use 'killing'. It can be inferred that Maria also felt strongly
> about the subject because she used 'destroying' when she could have used
> 'finishing' or 'terminating'.

This interpretation of the above textual comparisons also offers a further
consideration of the social implications of language in terms of the personal
choices surrounding the translation of 'acabando'. Moreover, this text is
inherently translingual in its movement between, across, and within
languages.

While there remains no clear definition of what a translingual text
embodies structurally, theorists and scholars do argue that movement across
boundaries and standardizations is central. In composition studies the primary benefit of translingual writing is seen as its nullification of borders,
be these social or linguistic. Moreover, while this example does move
between and across languages; it is not a definitive illustration of the structure of a translingual text, it is simply one illustration of the choices a multilingual student made when reflecting upon the personal moves during the
act of translation.

Example 3

An inherent benefit of the translation narrative is the ability for students
to narrate the usefulness of the choices they make within this process.
Again, this attention to the benefits of student choice is similarly implicit to
the literacy narrative in that students are provided with the opportunity to
pick any literacy moment they wish to convey, which is seen as an empowering move. For multilingual international students, however, there is a strong

need to reassess how we position choice within writing activities as choice can both advantage and disadvantage the writer, depending on the genre at play. In the translation narrative, choice is used to develop critical thinking skills. In this way, we see how when

> people use a language, they realize some of its meaning potential by making linguistic choices among possible options in specific contexts. (Gentil, 2011: 13)

In fact, the narrative that surrounds choice in this assignment is an important step in the development of a writer's critical thinking skills. Here, an Arab student critically reflects upon this ability to choose:

> Of course I also had a hard time translating Arabic words, because some Arabic words need more than one English word to replace, and the other way around of course. Another difficulty I found was that it was slightly hard for me to translate the text and make it have the same meaning and purpose. When I first started translating then I realized that this is an Academic text and I cannot interpret it into regular English text. You can interpret a sentence into several rephrased sentences but making sure it remains within the same style was challenging mostly because I had to keep it academic. For example the phrase
>
> وقد تم تحليل قياسات الجسم البشري، والنشاط البدني، لعادات الأكل ومدة النوم التي كتبها العربي الاستبيان نمط الحياة في سن المراهقة.
>
> was especially hard for me to translate, mainly because I knew some words in English, but not in Arabic. This was the first time I encountered anything like this [...]. One thing I learned from this assignment was the awareness of my cross-cultural shifting. I go back and forth from Arabic to English all day and it was only in this essay I realized different languages have different ways of thinking, meaning I actually have a different mindset or attitude when I speak Arabic. I never actually analyzed two different languages like that before, usually it's just word choice and sentence structure, but there's more to it.

When this author discusses 'replace'(ment), and its relationship to 'meaning and purpose' as well as 'interpretation' (all in the introduction to the Arabic phrase) the writer is essentially discussing and reflecting upon the role of personal choice within the process of translation. Consequently this narrative of personal choice offers one way to consider Gentil's (2011) call to investigate the 'cognitive and linguistic dimensions', (p. 10) or choices, at play within multilingual constructions of narrative. In this way, the narrative action surrounding the process of translation not only requires engagement with the process of translation, but also a discussion of the choices fundamental to the negotiation of individual literacies. In the follow-up interpretation the writer describes his own ability to choose the direction of a translated text in his discussion of 'cross-cultural shifting' and the 'mindset[s]' and 'attitude[s]' at work in the negotiation of his choices. This concept of shifting is important to a translingual approach as it positions writing and language as fluid rather than a static standardization, illustrating a benefit of language negotiation – 'I realized different languages have different ways of thinking' – specifically, this points to how the encouragement of language negotiation develops critical thinking skills.

Looking Forward

What these three examples of student writing show us is that the act of translation, while seemingly impersonal, is entangled with the personal through close reading, social practice and linguistic choice. Students almost always consider each of these elements within this assignment; however what is striking is the differentiation of critical reflection and analysis in each completed assignment. The only consistency is that each narrative develops out of the common act of translation. In writing about the process of translation student goals become individualized, which results in texts that not only move between, across, and within languages, but also are deeply personal. In this way, the translation narrative ends up being quite similar to the personal narrative; in both genres of narrative, students tell a story about their experiences with reading and/or writing and connect this story to their experiences as an academic writer – it is simply the way this story is sought out that is different.

And, while these examples of student translanguaging describe instances of the relationship between language negotiation and the development of critical thinking within the genre of narrative, they are just a glimpse into the work that can be achieved in this field. Through exploring a gap in our understanding of narrative, particularly the personal literacy narrative, this research has worked to position the translation narrative as a practical and effective genre, which is accessible to multilingual international students who attend American institutions of higher learning. The provided examples of student writing illustrate the layered processes of cognitive negotiation and rhetorical choice that take place when multilingual students are asked to translanguage. As such, this line of pedagogy provides a useable response to current practice, such as the reality that

> while L2 writing studies aim to address L2 writers' needs specifically, they still leave out the needs of writers who must write alternatively in two languages or more, often reading (or speaking) in one language and writing in another. (Gentil, 2001: 6–7)

In terms of American composition and writing programs – where the majority of personal narrative writing in university settings is situated – the translation narrative allows multilingual students to compose writing that exists beyond standardized English-medium norms, and moves the genre of narrative beyond a singular American experience.

Still, this is just one approach; there are many other translingual pedagogies being developed in America and other regions of the world. At this point in the history of composition and writing studies the discussion of translanguaging within student writing has been primarily theoretical in scope; it is important to foster conversations about reassessing, reimagining, and redesigning genre – particularly in terms of diverse learners – and to learn and borrow from each other so that our approaches to student writing are able to engage every member of our growing classroom community.

Note

(1) When there are members of the class that do not have a shared home language, they often choose to work in English. These students choose a text written in high-academic English, and translate this scholarly text, which is often full of jargon and other technical, discipline specific language, into a form of classroom English that is more conversational in style.

References

Alsheikh, N. (2011) Three readers, three languages, three texts: The strategic reading of multilingual and multiliterate readers. *The Reading Matrix* 11 (1), 34–53.

Canagarajah, S. (2002) Multilingual writers and the academic community: Towards a critical relationship. *Journal of English for Academic Purposes* 1 (1), 29–44.

Canagarajah, S. (2006) Toward a writing pedagogy of shuttling between languages: Learning from multilingual writers. *College English* 68 (6), 589–604.

Canagarajah, S. (2012) Toward a rhetoric of translingual writing. The working papers series on negotiating differences in language and literacy. University of Louisville.

Canagarajah, S. (2013) *Translingual Practice: Global Englishes and Cosmopolitan Relations.* New York, NY: Routledge.

Creese, A. and Blackledge, A. (2010) Translanguaging in the bilingual classroom: A pedagogy for learning and teaching? *The Modern Language Journal* 94 (1), 103–115.

Danielewicz, J. (2008) Personal genres, public voices. *College Composition and Communication* 59 (3), 420–451.

Gentil, G. (2011) A biliteracy agenda for genre research. *Journal of Second Language Writing* 20, 6–23.

Gere, A.R. (2001) Revealing silence: Rethinking personal writing. *College Composition and Communication* 53 (2), 203–223.

Hindman, J.E. (2003) Thoughts on reading 'the personal': Toward a discursive ethics of professional critical literacy. *College English* 66 (1), 9–20.

Hornberger, N.H. and Link, H. (2012) Translanguaging in today's classrooms: A biliteracy lens. *Theory into Practice* 51 (4), 239–247.

Horner, B., NeCamp, S. and Donahue, C. (2011a) Toward a multilingual composition scholarship: From English only to a translingual norm. *College Composition and Communication* 63 (2), 269–300.

Horner, B., Lu, M.-Z., Royster, J.J. and Trimbur, J. (2011b) OPINION: Language difference in writing: Toward a translingual approach. *College English* 73 (3), 303.

Lu, M.Z. (1994) Professing multiculturalism: The politics of style in the contact zone. *College Composition and Communication* 45 (4), 442–458.

Lu, M.-Z. (2006) Living-English work. *College English* 68 (6), 605–619.

Lu, M.Z. and Horner, B. (2009) Composing in a global-local context: Careers, mobility, skills. *College English* 72 (2), 113–133.

Mahala, D. and Swilky, J. (1996) Telling stories, speaking personally: Reconsidering the place of lived experience in composition. *Journal of Advanced Composition* 16 (3), 363–388.

Mokhtari, K. and Sheorey, R. (2008) *Reading Strategies of First- and Second-Language Learners: See How They Read.* Norwood: Christopher-Gordon Publishers, Inc.

Mokhtari, K. and Reichard, C. (2004) Investigating the strategic reading processes of first and second language readers in two different cultural contexts. *System* 32, 379–394.

Robillard, A.E. (2003) It's time for class: Toward a more complex pedagogy of narrative. *College English* 66 (1), 74–92.

Street, B.V. (2011) New literacy studies and the continua of biliteracy. In F. Hult and K. King (eds) *Educational Linguistics in Practice: Applying the Local Globally and the Global Locally.* Bristol: Multilingual Matters.

Sullivan, P.A. (2003) Composing culture: A place for the personal. *College English* 66 (1), 41–54.

Tardy, C.M. (2011) Enacting and transforming local language policies. *College Composition and Communication* 62 (4), 634–661.

Trowbridge, K. (2014) *Research.* Teaching Diverse Learners. See http://wrac.msu.edu/research/

7 Affirming the Biliteracy of University Students: Provision of Multilingual Lecture Resources at the University of the Western Cape, South Africa

Bassey E. Antia and Charlyn Dyers

Introduction

With lecture halls in South Africa and elsewhere becoming increasingly multilingual and multicultural, there is greater recognition of the challenges posed to teaching and learning by the linguistic diversity and literacy heterogeneity of students. Although the scholarship on reading and/or writing in multiple languages (severally referred to as biliteracy/biliteracies, multilingual literacies, pluriliteracies) has yielded useful insights, questions of strategy for responding to this challenge continue to exercise the minds of scholars. This chapter reports on an initiative at the University of the Western Cape, South Africa, intended to affirm the academic biliteracy (i.e. multilingual literacies) of students. In the initiative, multilingual and multimodal learning resources were made available to students on an undergraduate course, and students' reflections on the experience of using the resources were elicited. Hornberger's continua of biliteracy model provided the design principles for the learning resources, and served as framework for discussing students' responses.

In the first part of the chapter, we provide a background of the linguistic diversity and literacy heterogeneity of students at the University of the Western Cape. Secondly, we formulate the research problem as well as our objectives. Thirdly, Hornberger's continua of biliteracy model is described, and we show

how the model was applied to the creation of a set of multilingual and multi-modal lecture resources. Fourthly, the procedure for eliciting students' reflections is sketched, and fifthly the students' reactions are presented. In the conclusion, a literacy practices framework is employed to interpret the findings and to draw out further implications of the model for the development of multilingual lecture resources in South African higher education.

The University of the Western Cape: Background to a Space of Diversity

As described in its official website, the University of the Western Cape (UWC) in Cape Town, South Africa, was established by a 1959 Act of the South African Parliament as a university college for people classified as 'Coloured' (that is, people of mixed African, European and Asian descent). Under the *apartheid* regime in South Africa (1948 to 1994), every effort was made by the ruling Afrikaner Nationalists to keep people of different ethnic origins separated through various strictly enforced policies and laws. Apart from the Coloured people, other major ethnic groupings recognized at the time were as follows:

- White (consisting of Afrikaners who were descendants of Dutch settlers, as well as English-speaking people who were mainly descendants of British and other European settlers);
- Black (which consisted of the various indigenous African groups, the largest of which were the Zulus and Xhosas); and
- Indian (people whose ancestors were brought to South Africa from the Indian sub-continent).

In higher education, one of the laws used to keep these groupings separate was known as the Extension of University Education Act of 1959, which led to the establishment of a number of 'non-white' universities. It was this Act that gave birth to the University of the Western Cape (UWC), which was formally opened as a bilingual English/Afrikaans medium university in 1960.

No sooner had UWC been established than it became a hotbed of opposition to the *apartheid* regime. Staff and students protested against the racial premises of the institution's founding, as well as against the dominant role of the Afrikaans language in the running of the institution. They also challenged other discriminatory policies of the regime in the educational and other sectors. Activism in the institution against *apartheid* policies eventually culminated in the doors of learning at UWC being thrown open in 1982 to persons of all races.

A defiant open admissions policy with clearly defined admission quotas for different groupings, and an ideologically motivated low tuition fee regime in spite of a (state-engineered and punitive) weak resource base – these two factors meant that the UWC, from relatively early on in its history, was committed to cultivating a diverse student body. The institution has also traditionally been an important destination of choice for the poorest of the poor in the national pool of applicants for university admission in South Africa (Letseka *et al.*, 2010; Stroud & Kerfoot, 2013; Antia, 2015). Now, given the legacy of education for Black people under apartheid (Heugh, 2003), it is not surprising that one of the challenges the institution had to grapple with after its doors had been flung open was how to respond to the perceived academic literacy development needs of its new student demographic. It is no surprise that UWC was the first university to establish a Writing Centre as part of a broader set of initiatives around students' academic literacy development (Antia, 2015).

Periods of major shift can be discerned in the ethnic composition of the student body at UWC. Until the late 1980s, Coloured students were a clear majority, accounting for 82% of the student population in 1988. However, in the 1990s, the Coloured student population dropped by half while the Black student population rose 4-fold to 58% (Tamminga, 2006: 36). In 2015, of the 20,097 registered students, about 6,818 (34%) ethnically identify with indigenous Black African groups in South Africa (Xhosa, Zulu, etc.), while 9,317 (42%) identify as Coloured. South African students classified as White and Indian constitute 1,112 (6%) and 957 (5%) respectively of the demographic. International students from countries in the southern African region, and from further afield in East, Central and West Africa as well as from Asia, Europe and the Americas, make up an estimated 10% of the student population at the institution (UWC Office for Quality Assurance and Management Information Systems – personal communication).

The linguistic diversity associated with the above student profile is reflected in language biographies which students produce as part of the requirements of a module taught by the authors of this chapter (see chapter by Hurst et al. for more detail). For the past several years, language portraits created by students on a third year linguistics module called 'Multilingualism' graphically capture the multiplicity of languages and varieties which UWC students associate with a host of literacy events, that is, situations in which writing is important to students' daily activities (Street, 2011a, 2011b). These could, for example, be reading or writing in contexts such as texting and other social media interactions, learning, soap opera subtitles, work, religious worship, and so on. Apart from English, standard and non-standard varieties of Afrikaans and isiXhosa are typically the most dominant codes mentioned by South African students in descriptions of their language portraits. Other codes mentioned include isiZulu and other indigenous African languages: siSwati, Setswana, Sesotho, and Venda. Adding codes mentioned by non-South African students drives up the figure to over 100 languages and varieties reported to be used each year by students taking the module.

The challenge which this linguistic diversity poses in the academic space of a university in the South African context is perhaps best gleaned from several of the arguments which Martin-Jones and Jones (2000) offer for putting forward the term *multilingual literacies*. Firstly, UWC students are truly multilingual and differently literate in each of the languages in their repertoire. This multilingualism is at variance with the continued hegemony of English in the University, in spite of an institutional language policy providing for three named languages (English, isiXhosa and Afrikaans). In respect of students being differently literate in each of their languages, it should be noted that only English and Afrikaans are maintained as formal languages of schooling in South Africa beyond the third year of primary school, while African languages continue to be taught only in the language classroom. Consequently, Xhosa students tend to be more academically literate in English than in isiXhosa. Coloured students (many of whom have the informal variety of Afrikaans as home language) would often have had some literacy exposure to formal Afrikaans in high school as a taught first language or as a medium of instruction, and would therefore presumably be more academically literate in this language than Xhosa students are in isiXhosa. However, after two or three years of English-only university education, it is typically the case that for some of these Coloured students the balance of their academic literacy tips more towards English.

Secondly, the communicative repertoire which these students bring to academia and which should be acknowledged is multiply complex in terms of the purposes assigned to different spoken and written varieties of specific languages. Furthermore, there may be strong views regarding which varieties or languages should be used for a range of purposes at university. These views may contest established knowledge about cognitive benefits associated with specific languages.

Thirdly, the students' communicative repertoires are shaped by issues of access and opportunity. As suggested earlier, skills of writing, reading and listening may differ according to language/variety, and they depend on levels or quality of previous academic exposure. Indeed school-level literacies have continued to be of concern in South Africa. The deeply worrying inefficiencies of the current school education system are highlighted in a report by Spaull (2013), who notes:

> South Africa has the worst education system of all middle-income countries that participate in cross-national assessments of educational achievement. What is more, we perform worse than many low-income African countries [...] the vast majority of South African pupils are significantly below where they should be in terms of the curriculum, and more generally, have not reached a host of normal numeracy and literacy milestones. (p. 3)

The reference in such descriptions is typically to literacy in English, but attempts at introducing indigenous African languages into teaching and learning in higher education have made it obvious that students' often excellent 'basic interpersonal communicative skills' (BICS) in these languages can lead to erroneous assumptions about their ability to cope with tasks that require 'cognitive/academic language proficiency', or CALP (Cummins, 1984). In other words, academic literacies (and the institutions which aim to foster them) require development not only in English, but also in other languages.

Fourth, these students do not always use their codes in compartmentalized fashion. More often than not, while they are engaged in many literacy events, students creatively draw on all of their codes in ways that are readily apparent (e.g. word borrowing) or less so (e.g. discourse organization patterns), leading to linguistic and stylistic syncretism of all sorts. Of course, for some students, the only language system they are familiar with is linguistic syncretism, which formal education largely rejects.

In sum, UWC students' repertoires of multiple languages/varieties and literacies pose a challenge for teaching and learning in a relatively monolingual environment of English medium instruction. Breier (2010) cites a study by the South African Human Sciences Research Council which found that

> UWC had the second highest proportion of respondents in the low socio-economic status (SES) category who had not completed their degrees (79%): of these, black African non-completer respondents made up 64%, and coloured, 33%. (p. 55)

It is therefore no surprise that UWC sets a premium on teaching and learning. Its Institutional Operating Plan (UWC, 2010–2014) contains a section titled 'The Development of Graduate Attributes at UWC', which commits it to

> improve opportunities for all students to succeed in their studies through a responsive teaching and learning process that is able to address the learning needs of all students. (p. 4)

Problem and Study Objectives

The UWC context as sketched above underscores the importance of a pedagogy of biliteracy or multilingual literacies; in other words, it calls attention to the need to teach in ways that give expression to, or recognize, the different language and literacy assets that students bring to the site of learning. Indeed, the modalities for teaching in this manner have continued to exercise the minds of researchers, irrespective of whether the goal is to evolve a pedagogy of linguistic and literacy accommodation and development, or to practice a pedagogy with a deeply political and transformative agenda. Although several pathways have been proposed (e.g. Hornberger, 2000;

Baker, 2006; García, 2009; Airey, 2009), the view is still being expressed (e.g. Hornberger & Link, 2012; García *et al.*, 2007) that there are no simple, readily available strategies for affirming the communicative repertoires which students bring to the classroom in particular contexts. García *et al.* specifically note that

> schools have ignored the complexity of Hornberger's continua, and pedagogical frameworks informed by the model have yet to be developed. (2007: 214)

Hornberger and Link enlist support from work by Canagarajah (2011) and pointedly ask how educators should engage with students' linguistic and literacy diversity in order

> to facilitate successful school experiences and greater academic achievement for students from culturally and linguistically different and often minoritized backgrounds [...]. (Hornberger & Link, 2012: 243)

This (continuing) concern is no doubt linked to the socio-cultural diversity of learning contexts, but also to the multiplicity of literacy events in learning contexts, from tutorials or discussion groups, to lecture materials (the focus of this chapter), textbooks and assessment tasks. Thus, given three considerations – namely, the potential negative impact which linguistic and literacy hegemonies can have on a diverse student body, UWC's commitment in its Operating Plan to evolve responsive teaching strategies to address students' learning needs, and the continuing search for strategies to operationalize a pedagogy of biliteracy or multilingual literacies – this chapter sets itself the following objectives:

- to reflect and report on how lecture resources can be developed in a way that gives expression to a relevant model of biliteracy;
- to assess students' reactions to the lecture resources in terms of the model's claims around scholastic attainment (in terms of subject content and biliteracy development) and empowerment; and
- to use a literacy practices framework to understand the students' reactions and the broader social factors that need to be considered in the production of such resources.

The authors provide more course-specific motivations while describing the design principles for the multilingual resources. Subsequent parts of this chapter successively present a model of biliteracy, outline the development of the multilingual lecture resources, describe data collection, examine students' experience of the resource, and offer some further implications of the experience for future work and similar initiatives.

Hornberger's Continua of Biliteracy

Teaching and research have traditionally taken a compartmentalized, non-context-sensitive and non-ecological view of variables relevant to the attainment of language and literacy objectives in education. Attention is typically paid to written language as though it operated in complete isolation from spoken language; production skills are ripped apart from reception skills; the effects and resources of the culture of orality which is dominant in the communities from which many students hail are often not acknowledged and leveraged in the educational process of fostering a culture of literacy; instruction around the acquisition or the use of a second language proceeds as though a first language were non-existent, irrelevant or a liability; or as though the discourse constituting different languages were meaningful to some students who seem to make no such distinction; and so on. An ecological model, in contrast, recognizes that development in any language or literacy dimension is influenced by the overall environment in which variables of context, content and media intersect. As Hornberger puts it,

> The very notion of bi (or multi-) literacy assumes that one language and literacy is developing in relation to one or more other languages and literacies ... (Hornberger, 2002: 37–8)

Given institutionalized or widespread contrary discourses and practices, this ecological claim is indeed very important. The continua of biliteracy model associated with Hornberger (e.g. Hornberger, 1989; Hornberger & Skilton-Sylvester, 2000; Hornberger, 2004; see introductory chapter of this volume) is a very useful framework for seeing the injustice meted out to generations of students by educational policy (thankfully violated on occasion by teachers and students sometimes even without their intending to do so). In terms of a broader political agenda, the model suggests that less powerful positions in educational policy and practice could be mainstreamed to subvert orthodoxies of hegemony. The model is a framework for thinking through the variables that need to be considered in evolving educational arrangements.

In this model, language and literacy as means and goals in education are seen as developing within a space constituted by four intersecting axes – context, development, content and media – each of which has three continua. Collectively, these axes invite reflection that cuts across three dimensions: learners' backgrounds and the broader social context (empirical questions), the goals for the curriculum (policy questions) and the substance of the course as well as modalities for mediating it (pedagogical questions).

Language and literacy learning arrangements that acknowledge each axis and the range of each continuum have brighter prospects of success than those that do not. Collectively, these axes and the constitutive continua are believed to create the space for valorizing the linguistic and literacy resources that students bring to the site of learning. But beyond acknowledging these resources, the space constituted by these continua allows for building on or extending these resources for the attainment of scholastic goals around language and literacy as well as subject matter.

Application of the Model to the Development of a Set of Lecture Resources

The authors teach (in English) a third year undergraduate linguistics module on multilingualism. The module examines changing conceptions of, and responses to, language and multilingualism in the literature, in society, in families and in education. The module encourages critique of received ideas, and it fosters in students new ways of thinking about the subject. Each year, the student cohort is typically diverse and numbers in excess of 200. Two major resources for mediating the module content are PowerPoint slides (on which lectures are based) and a course reader; this is in addition to prescribed reading.

In 2014, the authors embarked on a project to produce Afrikaans and isiXhosa PowerPoint versions of select topics in the module. There were several rationales. Firstly, there was a felt need to do something about students who appeared to be having difficulties understanding the course content, and were therefore obtaining low marks in assessment tasks. Secondly, it seemed only natural in a course on multilingualism that students (themselves multilingual) be given an opportunity to critically reflect on experiencing multilingualism in this course. Thirdly, the authors also felt the need to use the module to draw students' attention to those sections of the university's language policy that have largely not been implemented: the clauses encouraging learning materials to be made available in English, Afrikaans and isiXhosa – the three recognized official languages of the institution. Fourthly, critical reflections of students on tasks around multilingual learning resources would enable the authors to develop a UWC 'database' of experiences, which could in turn provide a basis for them to reflect on language diversification initiatives in South African higher education and to engage with relevant theoretical frameworks.

Hornberger's biliteracy model seemed an appropriate source from which to draw design principles for producing lecture resources, and on which to base critical discussion about experience with the resources. Consequently, in keeping with several of the continua in Hornberger's biliteracy model, lecture resources on two topics were produced in both written and audio/podcast forms, using formal varieties of Afrikaans and isiXhosa (for one topic) and informal varieties of both languages (for the second topic).

A lecture on globalization and multilingualism was produced (as PowerPoint slides and as podcast) in the formal varieties of Afrikaans and isiXhosa, while one on a typology of multilingualism was produced in informal varieties of both languages. The rationale was to try to determine which language variety (and which mode – written or spoken) would be reported as making it easier to understand the content. Formal Afrikaans has a more diffuse geographical base than formal isiXhosa; as such, the formal variety of isiXhosa was easily identifiable with the 'deep' variety employed in the Eastern Cape, the traditional heartland of the different Xhosa clans, while the informal variety followed a pattern associated with urbanized youth or students in the Cape Town area.

The materials were translated as follows: the formal language varieties were translated by competent home language speakers of the languages who lecture on the module or a comparable module in a different department. The informal varieties were produced by postgraduate students who had themselves previously taken the module. The translation brief was for the English PowerPoint slides on the two selected topics (globalization and multilingualism; a typology of multilingualism) to be translated in a particular variety (formal or informal) of Afrikaans and isiXhosa for third year linguistics students. For the audio material, one individual was recorded reading the Afrikaans varieties, and another the isiXhosa varieties. The informal written versions, and especially the recorded podcasts, were required to express as far as possible the manner in which isiXhosa and Afrikaans are employed in the Western Cape communities from which many UWC students hail. These are communities in which language use (Afrikaans or isiXhosa) is characterized by hybridity of elements from English, isiXhosa, Afrikaans, Arabic, and so on. Consequently, the translations into these varieties reflected this eclecticism. The resources targeted only receptive skills, but of two kinds – aural (the podcasts) and visual (the written versions).

Together with the English language slides (reflecting the institutional and societal language of power), materials were thus available in several language varieties, some of which were the first and others second languages of the students. Although not an explicit part of the translation or recording brief, content in the English slides and even the written translations was on occasion adapted to the lifeworlds of Afrikaans and isiXhosa-speaking students. Table 7.1 shows the resources generated from each of the two topics selected for the project.

The resources satisfy Hornberger's definition of biliteracy as 'any and all instances in which communication occurs in two (or more) languages in or around writing' (Hornberger, 1990: 213); the backgrounds of the students for whom these lecture resources were intended, and the decisions taken in the production of the resources, illustrate a number of points in Hornberger's model. In terms of the context of biliteracy, the students were bi- or multilingual, with varying histories of literacy experience in contexts sketched

Table 7.1 Overview of the translated lecture resources

Topic of English source materials	Formal Afrikaans		Informal Afrikaans		Formal isiXhosa		Informal isiXhosa	
	Written	Spoken	Written	Spoken	Written	Spoken	Written	Spoken
Globalisation and multilingualism	+	+			+	+		
Typology of multilingualism			+	+			+	+

earlier in this chapter. As a result of these different histories and different competences in academic English (and the consequent allure of academic content in non-English home languages), on the development of biliteracy axis the resources in principle afford students the opportunity of (academic) language learning, especially of the L1. In terms of the content of biliteracy, the material was sometimes adapted, for instance when local examples were provided. From the media of biliteracy perspective, the material was delivered in spoken and written modes, in languages (Afrikaans, isiXhosa) with varying degrees of structural differences to the English resources the students also had; and the material in principle allowed for simultaneous exposure to two languages.

Figure 7.1 presents an extract from the translation into formal isiXhosa, while Figure 7.2 presents an excerpt from the translation into informal Afrikaans.

Data Collection

In the 2014 third year class on multilingualism, there were 211 registered students. Two alternative tasks were proposed as major assignment towards the end of the course. Students without knowledge of either isiXhosa or Afrikaans were encouraged to critically comment on a language biography

---

I – Globalization neMultilingualism

Yintoni i-globalization? Ngokunxulumene *noxinzelelo* lwendawo kunye nexesha, ukuphuhliswa kobugcisa, ukutshintsha-tshintsha iindawo, iimeko zentlalo nezopolitiko, kunye nokulungelelaniswa kwezoqoqosho, njl njl. (nguAntia, 2000).

Ubugcisa bolwazi nonxibelelwano, kunye nokusetyenziswa kweelwimi ezininzi. Indlela **ekhawulezileyo** yokusebenzisana maxa onke, ngokusebenzisa iindlela ezahlukeneyo zonxibelelwano kunye nosasazo (u-Facebook, i-Blackberry Messenger, u-Gmail, u-Yahoo Instant Messenger, u-Skype, njl njl.), ezithi zisidibanise neentlobo ezikhoyo *zeelwimi ezahlukileyo.*

Figure 7.1 Translation into formal isiXhosa

Skyfie 7: Negotiated multilingualism

- Negotiated multilingualism het lewe gekry uit die contestation tussen Engels en plaaslike tale. Lande moet onderhandel wat die rolle van die plaaslike tale teenoor die rol van Engels is. Dus, lande moet language policies ontwikkel. Byvoorbeeld: die National Language Policy van Suid Afrika, die Western Cape Language Policy en die UWC language policy.
- Dink byvoorbeeld aan die language policies wat by jou skool was? Of die language policy by jou werksplek?
- Belangrik: nie alle language policies is geskryfde dokumente nie, sommige language policies onstaan spontaan uit daaglikse social practices wat as aanvaarbaar in die land of gemeenskap gesien word.

Figure 7.2 Translation into informal Afrikaans

that was provided to them from the standpoint of relevant concepts that had been encountered over the semester. The alternate task (the focus of this chapter) was addressed to the 147 students in the class who knew English and either Afrikaans or isiXhosa. Fifty-two of the 147 students identified with Afrikaans as home language, 48 identified with isiXhosa and 47 identified with English as home language (while knowing some Afrikaans or isiXhosa).

The students were required firstly to read/listen to materials in English and secondly in the relevant other language. After that, they wrote an essay in English according to a specific template of questions. Students were required, among others, to identify content in the English source material (course reader or PowerPoint slides) which they had found difficult to understand; state what translated version (language variety, mode – written or spoken), if any, had made the content easier to understand; indicate their general preference for a particular translated version in view of how it had helped them to understand the material better (if applicable); describe their more subjective impressions of the translated documents; relate their experiences to claims in the literature on bi/multilingual (resources in) education; and offer a critique of the resources provided. Subsequent parts of this chapter draw on data from these essays.

Students' Responses to the Translated Lectures: Linkages with Hornberger's Biliteracy Model

Consistent with what was described as the potentials of Hornberger's model as a political agenda, students' responses clearly articulate a need in UWC for educational practices to subvert powerful positions around the axes of context, media, development and content. In subsequent sections, students' responses are presented and discussed under each of these four axes.

Entanglements of epistemic access and power on the context axis

With respect to the bi/multilingual-monolingual continuum of the context axis, 57% of students self-identifying as Xhosa said they found it helpful to have material in isiXhosa (irrespective of variety), and therefore indicated a preference for lecture resources in their 'own' language as well, rather than in just English. A lower figure (38% of students) that self-identified with Afrikaans indicated that having material in Afrikaans aided their understanding of the content; and these students indicated a preference for lecture materials in Afrikaans as well as English.

In particular, the preference by 57% of the Xhosa students for lecture resources being made available in isiXhosa is, in a sense, a vote for the traditionally less powerful end of the bi/multilingual-monolingual continuum of the context axis. It challenges the higher education correlate of submersion education, which 'gates out' languages used by (typically minority) students in their homes because the goal is for them to be mainstreamed into the majority language as quickly as possible (Baker, 2006: 219).

What these figures clearly suggest is that current practices in respect of lecture materials may not be taking into account the preferred languages of epistemic access of between one-third to over half of the two groups who form a majority of the student demographic at UWC. Not surprisingly, the figures for students who wanted lecture resources only in English were low: 30% for Xhosa students, 21% for Afrikaans students and, paradoxically, only 40% for students who self-identify with English as home language. The latter group, while appreciating the advantages of facility in English which they enjoy, may also have found that their own learning is aided by materials in dual languages and varieties. The interpretation related to empathy would be consistent with Hornberger's (2004) claim, albeit in reference to the content continua, that the biliteracy model provides a framework for addressing

> cultural stereotyping, intercultural respect, and conflicting or overlapping cultural traditions and particularities. (p. 168)

The lecture resources would appear to have created cracks in the walls of imposed or assumed belief in the pre-eminence of monolingual English language instruction. Consider the following views from several respondents:

> (1) Having lecture notes (in isiXhosa) made me acknowledge firstly how languages are not different at all, just the colonialism has installed the idea that there are better languages than others. Having lecture slides in my language made me not feel helpless.

> (2) Having materials in Afrikaans made me feel very strange and nostalgic because I was not used to having lectures in my home language ... It was something quite different and quite refreshing ... It was rather satisfying to get lectures in my home language.

(3) The Afrikaans materials had a great effect on me as it had made me realize how important the concept of multilingualism is. Being able to read in another language, other than English has allowed me to understand the concepts easily in Afrikaans.

These views allow for at least two comments. It would be recalled that one objective in creating these lecture resources was for students to have an experience of multilingual epistemic access and to use this experience to reflect critically on what they were learning about multilingualism. Students' reflections were to be a means for us as lecturers to determine whether important *threshold concepts* around multilingualism (e.g. critique of assumed/imposed beliefs around essentialism of language hierarchies; benefits of multilingualism) had been grasped. Threshold concepts are

> fundamental understandings that sit at the heart of a body of knowledge. Students need to 'get' them in order for core disciplinary knowledge to make sense. They are like a portal, opening up a new and previously inaccessible way of thinking. (Centre for Teaching and Learning, Southern Cross University, 2015: paragraph 1)

These concepts are transformative, as they represent a major shift in thinking. They are also associated with 'troublesome' knowledge, because they disrupt previously held views (Meyer & Land, 2006).

In their different ways, the three student Excerpts above (1 to 3) all suggest the attainment of relevant threshold concepts. Excerpt (1) underscores the transformative ('made me acknowledge firstly how languages are not different at all') and disruptive ('colonialism has installed the idea that ...') aspects of 'troublesome knowledge'. In Excerpt (2) the disruptive perspective is highlighted ('strange', 'quite different'); and in Excerpt 3 the transformative dimension ('made me realize how important ...'). In sum, these excerpts reflect how a set of multilingual learning resources that were designed on the basis of Hornberger's biliteracy model appear to have contributed to students' achievement of key learning outcomes in the module. This is quite consistent with the claim of the model that the prospects of scholastic goals being attained are enhanced by a pedagogy that attends to both the more powerful and the less powerful endpoints of the various continua. It is also consistent with the model's attention to issues of power and critical reflection. The Xhosa student's view about colonialism and essentialized language hierarchies in Excerpt (1) resonates with the point made by Hornberger and Skilton-Sylvester (2003) that the critical reflection around language and power which the biliteracy model promotes

> can allow new speakers, readers, and writers of a language to see that the values placed on particular languages and varieties are not fixed, but socially and culturally constructed. (p. 40)

A second striking point in Excerpts (1) and (2) is the differential effect of the multilingual lecture resources on Xhosa and Coloured students. The Xhosa student in excerpt (1) says access to 'lecture slides in my language made me not feel helpless', whereas the Coloured student in Excerpt (2) speaks of nostalgia and of a refreshing experience. These two different characterizations are meaningful from the standpoint of the sociolinguistics of isiXhosa and Afrikaans, and from the perspective of the biliteracy model. As mentioned earlier, English and Afrikaans are the only languages of formal schooling in South Africa; and whereas Xhosa university students would have had hardly any substantial high school literacy exposure to their home language, students with Afrikaans as home language (whatever the variety) are more likely to have had such exposure, even if that experience ceased upon admission into UWC because of exposure to English-only tuition.

The Xhosa student's characterization of the experience is, therefore, profound as it conveys release or liberation from a feeling of disempowerment that has a long history. On the other hand, the characterization provided by the Coloured student in Excerpt (2) suggests an individual who has been less disempowered, whose previous privilege was disrupted and who is grateful for something akin to a restoration. Whereas for the Coloured student in Excerpt 2 the lecture resources symbolize a pedagogical luxury articulated around linguistic/literacy accommodation that is not indispensable, for the Xhosa student the resources are taken up as necessity – as a pedagogical tool with a deeply political and transformative agenda and that disturbs a prevailing, oppressive orthodoxy. Taken together with the previous point on threshold concepts, these interpretations make it clear that the biliteracy model has the potential to disrupt hegemonic practices: not for the sake of disruption, but because in such disrupted spaces interesting and important forms of learning can take place.

As is to be expected, there are contrary opinions. It is a reflection of people's complex relationships to language that a one size fits all approach is ill-advised, and underscores the need for diversity. One may ethnically identify (in registration or other forms) with language X but not wish to have X as a medium of learning for any range of reasons, from proficiency to received ideas through lack of awareness of its value as a resource. In the following extracts, students self-identifying as Afrikaans- or isiXhosa- speaking are opposed to the use of their home languages in learning on grounds that appear to be ideological (Excerpt 4), practical (Excerpt 5) or both (Excerpt 6).

(4) I definitely regard English as the language of learning and it was almost as if I unconsciously shut down any form of understanding when reading or listening to the Afrikaans translations. This then created a negative language attitude towards Afrikaans in a learning/educational context.

(5) Having materials in Xhosa made me realise that I am losing the language I call my mother tongue language, [...] I found it difficult to understand materials in my home language. [...] I would not like to have multilingual lecture materials in Xhosa because I am used to English as the medium of instruction and for me to understand Xhosa is going to take a while [...]. I would not recommend that the department of linguistics produce learning materials in other languages, they should stick strictly to English.

(6) My home language use of Afrikaans is not the standardised one and the Kaaps variety of Afrikaans is not suitable for academic use, for the variety is not that elaborate.

All three excerpts reflect clearly the point by Jones and Marilyn-Jones about the multiplicity of purposes students assign to the different languages or varieties in their repertoire, and their holding rather strong views about which language gets used for what purpose. Although the Kaaps variety of Afrikaans was being used in an academic context, precisely demonstrating that the problem of a so-called 'restricted code' (Bernstein, 1972) can be overcome, the student in Excerpt (6) nonetheless holds fast to the unsuitability argument for primarily ideological reasons. So far we have examined students' responses as they reflect issues on the context axis (especially the bi/multilingual-monolingual continuum); in the process we have underscored the entanglements of power and epistemic access, showing the involvement of issues of policy at macro context levels (e.g. languages used in schools within South Africa) and students' previous school literacy exposures. In the next section, we examine students' responses from the standpoint of the media of biliteracy.

Subverting hegemonic power: Epistemic access on the hinges of 'new media'

The manner in which students' preferences make a case for the subversion of hegemonic practices is perhaps more evident on the media of biliteracy axis (obviously in its intersection with other axes). There are two relevant continua here: structure (comprising languages) and mode of biliteracy. English, Afrikaans (in formal and informal varieties) and isiXhosa (in formal and informal varieties) are different in a number of aspects relevant to this discussion. In word morphology, Afrikaans tends to use more compounding than, say, English; and the informal varieties of Afrikaans and isiXhosa tend to be more overtly indebted to English vocabulary than are their formal varieties. In terms of structure, therefore, the uptake of the various varieties will be examined. In terms of modes, the uptake of the written versus the spoken (podcast) materials is revealing.

Of the number reacting to the formal/informal varieties, 53% of the Xhosa group and 65% of the Afrikaans group preferred the informal variety as a means of epistemic access, in contrast to the 40% (Xhosa) and 27% (Afrikaans) preferring the formal variety. Recalling the suggestion in an earlier section that the Afrikaans group would have been exposed to some formal Afrikaans in high school, it is rather surprising to see a relatively high figure (65%) of students in this group preferring the informal variety of Afrikaans as a means of epistemic access. Perhaps woven into objective issues of epistemic access (as in Excerpt 7 below) are issues of nostalgia to which reference was made earlier (see Excerpt 2). This point will be revisited momentarily. For now, though, consider the views in Excerpts (7) and (8) by a Coloured and a Xhosa student respectively, describing and justifying their preference for the informal varieties which had been used for the topic in question (typology of multilingualism):

(7) The typology translation was much easier to understand in Afrikaans than in English. I thought this to be odd as I always felt I understood academic work better in English than in Afrikaans, [...] I had difficulty with understanding what "truncated" meant [as in 'truncated multilingualism']. The Afrikaans translation called it 'afgekapte'. In my knowledge, "iets wat afgekap is, gewoonlik iets wat in stukkies is" [to my knowledge, something that is 'afgekapte' means that it is in pieces]. This makes sense as truncated [multilingualism] means the different levels of competency one might have in different languages. In other words, bits and pieces of a language.

(8) If I had to choose one of the materials as the most helpful, it would have to be the translated PowerPoint slides on the Typology of Multilingualism. The reason why I chose this form of material is because it is in a variety of isiXhosa which I speak and understand ... reading the lecture slides gave me a clearer sense of what is going on in Typology. It also gave me a means of being able to come up with my own examples without having to use examples directly from the slides or the course reader.

The Coloured student in Excerpt (7) illustrates how terminology encountered in the informal variety made it easier to understand a concept encountered in the English and formal Afrikaans materials. This is an important aspect of epistemic access. No less important, however, are ownership and re-creation of knowledge, which we find in the Xhosa student's view in Excerpt (8). The informal variety has enabled the student to appropriate the material to the extent that the student is confident of being able to come up with original examples.

Hornberger's biliteracy model, like much contemporary thinking on the subject of academic literacies, emphasizes the importance of acknowledging and leveraging non-school language/literacy assets in the process of educating. This really is the rationale for those points in the biliteracy model that are clustered around the less powerful positions. In this view, the usefulness of a language for epistemic access becomes a highly nuanced and multifaceted notion. It could relate to:

- the resource value of a language/variety in solving a specific learning need (as in Excerpt 7 on truncated multilingualism);
- the symbolic or nostalgic value of the language/variety (see Excerpts 8 above and 9 below), leading to motivation as described in Excerpts (10) and (11) below;
- a much more general cognitive processing issue that supports recall (Excerpts 12 to 14 below).

These various issues all potentially contribute to the achievement of academic goals. To illustrate, in Excerpt (9) a different Xhosa student, apparently brought up in a different part of the country, in the heartland of the Xhosa, reports a preference for the formal variety as a means of epistemic access. This is the variety to which this student is accustomed:

(9) [These materials] were in my home language, the language that I acquired from birth and the language that I grew up speaking which made it very easy for me to understand the concepts and terms. The most important thing with regards to my understanding of these isiXhosa podcasts and PowerPoint slides is that they use the standardised Xhosa variety which is the variety that is used in my region in the Eastern Cape. I understand this variety of isiXhosa much better than any other varieties.

Illustrating the idea of 'different strokes for different folks', the students in Excerpts 7 and 9 credit 'having a sense of what is going on', being able 'to come up with my own examples', and the ease of understanding 'the terms and concepts' to their different varieties of isiXhosa. The positive attitudes spawned by using languages/varieties to which students are accustomed can be seen in Excerpts (10) and (11) below:

(10) Having materials in Xhosa had really made me feel very positive towards completing this assignment ... since there was not only a written Xhosa but also an audio or podcast of Xhosa. So the experience of doing this assignment had much been easier and enjoyable more than others I ever done because they were never like this one: that is, they had not my mother tongue involved.

(11) Having this joy of having an Afrikaans lecture boosted me and motivated me to have this assignment completed long before due time.

It is not often the case that students express, or lecturers hear, such positive sentiments around assignments! Both students speak of joy/enjoyment, of feeling positive/motivated and 'boosted', and of completing the task (in record time); this illustrates in part the point made by Baker (2006) that where

> multilingual classes exist, then learning, motivation and self-esteem may be raised by celebrating multiliteracies. (p. 334)

The issue of general cognitive processing is seen in Excerpts 12 to 14 below:

> (12) Reading in isiXhosa also helped me in a sense that it is the language I 'think' in (I generate my thoughts in), hence I did not have to translate the English texts to isiXhosa in order for me to make a better and clearer meaning out of them (like I always do) ... I remember these topics clearer now because I have read them in isiXhosa. I have isiXhosa words that can help me remember meanings of concepts when writing a test, these words could also act as form of clues should I be presented with them in a test.

> (13) What also made me happy was the fact that I had more time to interpret things carefully because the fact that I naturally think in isiX-hosa was accompanied by isiXhosa notes. This made me understand concepts clearer without the hassle of translating my isiXhosa thoughts to English [...].

> (14) If I was given a test on typology and globalization I believe that I would definitely pass it and my performance would be better than the performance on other topics which have not been translated [...]. I believe so because now I understand both these concepts in my language and it would be impossible for me to forget their meanings and definitions and it would be easier for me to recall and remember them as I would first recall them in isiXhosa and translate them to English when I write the test.

All three excerpts present L1 isiXhosa as a central cognitive processor, the base on which understanding, interpreting and recall take place. When another language (L2) is involved (receptively or productively) in any given literacy event (see final section of this chapter), there is translation into and out of isiXhosa. As Excerpts (12) and (13) show, translation of input or output is dispensed with when no other language is involved; the time and cognitive effort thus saved, according to Excerpt 13, goes into 'interpret[ing] things carefully'.

It is interesting to note from the above Excerpts (12 to 14) how the media of biliteracy (the structures of the different languages/varieties) interact dynamically with the development continua of reception-production, L1-L2, and oral-written. Written L1 (isiXhosa) or L2 (English) material is received, and orally processed in L1 (isiXhosa) for optimal written production in L2 (English). Oral processing is of two types: (a) translation in private or self-directed speech, and (b) *xhosalization*, the morpho-phonological adaptation into isiXhosa of English terms as a mnemonic device (Paxton & Tyam, 2010: 255).

Xhosalization is a pervasive practice, and is probably what the student in Excerpt 12 is referring to in saying

> I have isiXhosa words that can help me remember meanings of concepts when writing a test, these words could also act as form of clues should I be presented with them in a test.

Some years back, on noticing a (then unexplained but relatively widespread) prefixing of 'i' to English terms occurring in students' test scripts, the first named author obtained some data (recorded student reflections) in a bid to understand this practice. It transpired from the focus groups that, for instance, the isiXhosa prefix 'i' was attached to 'marginalization' (however else other parts of the word were spelled) because this made the resulting form ('imarginalization') pronounceable 'the isiXhosa way', and this in turn ensured that this term was recalled while answering a question on the consequences of monolingual language polices in multilingual environments. This is reminiscent of the importance of hybridity in the pluriliteracies approach. García *et al.* (2007) illustrate this point with the way Latino adult migrants in the US develop 'their own hybrid writing system that used the Spanish alphabet to capture English speech sounds' (p. 216). In the xhosalization example, students strategically employ an isiXhosa prefix (and, in other cases, represent isiXhosa phonemes with English graphemes) in order to be able to recall English terms. Interestingly, in written work in English, the students do not return the word to the shape in which it was originally encountered, once the morpho-phonological adaptations have served their initial mnemonic function.

To round off this section, for the authors as lecturers, the multilingual/-dialectal lecture resources are becoming an effective means of challenging the hegemony of English, in order to reach diverse segments of the class more on their own terms, and to have more motivated students claiming to be able to work more efficiently, and expending fewer cognitive processing resources on subsidiary tasks. Let us turn to a second structural issue, which has to do with modes of language (listening versus reading), their various affordances and their requirements.

Students, as has been noted earlier, had also been presented with lecture resources in the form of podcasts in Afrikaans/isiXhosa, in addition to the translated PowerPoint slides. From the essays in which statements of preferences between written and spoken materials could be discerned, 38% of respondents in the Xhosa group and 46% of the Afrikaans group preferred the written materials (in other words, reading), while 31% of respondents in each group preferred listening (to the recorded podcasts). The simultaneous use of both modalities (spoken and written) was chosen by 15% of the Xhosa students and 21% of the Afrikaans students. Although for isiXhosa the authors had been led (by the assumption of students' more oral use of this language) to expect a higher figure for listening only, the 31% recorded is not too distant from the figure (38%) recorded for Xhosa students who preferred reading. (It should be pointed out that our percentages do not amount to 100% for each group as not all students responded to all the questions we asked in our assignment.)

Many Xhosa students have uneven skills in reading and listening. It should not be seen as a problem that written material in isiXhosa often only becomes truly meaningful when it is heard; that is, when read aloud by someone else. Excerpts (15) and (16) reveal how material in written L1 is only understood when it is spoken in L1:

> (15) the voice of the speaker in the podcast was clear and loud and the pronunciation was more understandable than when I read ... In typology and globalisation slides I was unable to read and pronounce some words until I had to listen the podcast.

> (16) I found that both the recordings and the slides were helpful ... It helped with reading the difficult isiXhosa words because I heard how it is read in the recording. I discovered that I knew the meaning of those isiXhosa words even though I did not know how to read them at first [i.e. when they were first encountered in the slides]

This theme of understanding written material being contingent on ability to pronounce words or hearing words pronounced is a different one from xhosalization but equally quite pervasive. Whereas xhosalization was said to be a mnemonic device, this one seems to be about understanding. If it were therefore argued that the effect of sustained exposure to literacy is the compartmentalization of visual processing (of graphemes, words, sentences and of whole written texts) from phonological processing (vocalization involving pronouncing phonemes and words, and applying intonation contours to make sense), then these students have been spared such compartmentalization, or they have simply resisted it. We see them combining both forms of processing to make meaning. So, in the light of Hornberger's model, injunctions by school teachers requiring students not to vocalize while they are engaged in the so-called silent reading (even of texts written in tonal languages) may simply deprive students of useful meaning-making resources. In the next section, issues from the essays are framed in terms of the development of biliteracy axis.

Deepening learning of L1 as self-rehabilitation and as response to L2: Readiness for action on the development axis

At some points in their essays, students' accounts of their experiences with the multilingual resources read like voyages of self-discovery. Sometimes these voyages culminate in a feeling of despondency over the loss of a part of self, at other times in a readiness to act to reclaim what is perceived to have been lost. At yet other times, the journey culminates in an attitude that could pass for defiance, and unapologetically seeks to fashion a different sense of self. Consider the following comments:

(17) I read through standard Afrikaans lecture slides and was shocked to find that it was overwhelming and a bit confusing. [...] I was naïve in thinking that because Afrikaans is my primary language I would understand academic Afrikaans as well as I do English.

(18) Having the material in Xhosa and having to understand it was challenging, as much as isiXhosa is my mother tongue. [...] I have to argue against what Baker (2010) [says. What Baker] forgets to acknowledge is the fact that you have to be competent both in reading and writing your mother tongue in order to be comfortable.

The student in Excerpt (17) discovers (or finds the multilingual lecture materials reiterating) the difference between Cummins' basic interpersonal communication skills and cognitive/academic language proficiency, a theme that can be read into the comment in Excerpt (18) where this particular student is presumably referring to a Baker (2006: 334) quote: 'Where multilingual classes exist, then learning, motivation and self-esteem may be raised by celebrating multiliteracies'. The feeling of the student in Excerpt (17) may well be described as despondency, as s/he appears to accept the situation. But as if to reiterate the point that the term 'mother tongue' can be a polysemous misnomer (used in senses dealing with self-identification, L1, language most frequently used and proficiency, cf. Phillipson 1992), the student in Excerpt (18) realizes that the credentials of isiXhosa as mother tongue are of little help as far as academic literacy is concerned.

The students in Excerpts (17) and (18) are representative of many others who merely observe how the space of academic discourse disables them linguistically, and have no action or response plan. In contrast, the students in Excerpts (19) (comment repeated from Excerpt (5)) and (20) below respond to this disability in two very different ways: the former, with a plea that multilingual resources be discontinued; the latter, with a readiness to act to remedy this disability or to 'self-rehabilitate'.

(19) Having materials in Xhosa made me realise that I am losing the language I call my mother tongue language, [...] I found it difficult to understand materials in my home language. [...] I would not like to have multilingual lecture materials in Xhosa because I am used to English as the medium of instruction and for me to understand Xhosa is going to take a while [...]. I would not recommend that the department of

linguistics produce learning materials in other languages, they should stick strictly to English.

(20) Having had access to the materials made me feel appreciative and motivated to learn more isiXhosa even though it did not develop me nor improve my understanding.

Beyond the mere excitement of seeing isiXhosa being used for academic purposes, it would appear the trigger for readiness to act in Excerpt (20) had to do with what may have been perceived, on the one hand, as the resource or potential value of especially written isiXhosa for academic purposes and, on the other hand, its relative inaccessibility (as many are unable to read it, not having been exposed to much literacy in it). It is not clear in Excerpt (19) whether the student intends to attribute the zero benefit of isiXhosa materials for his/her understanding to issues of cognitive academic language proficiency. There is, however, an important point to be made here about bilingual learning arrangements and motivation for language and literacy development. In submersion education, students are unable to discover the educational significance of any language and literacy other than the ones foisted on them. There is, therefore, no impetus for developing the competence to communicate in or about writing in more than one classroom language.

In contrast, many multilingual learning arrangements, like translanguaging in the classroom or, in our case, the provision of multilingual lecture resources, lead to students' improving knowledge of their weaker classroom language(s) (Lewis *et al.*, 2012; Hornberger & Link, 2012). Where the weaker language is the L1, the motivation can come from any number of sources which, ultimately, underscore the dynamic interaction of the elements in Hornberger's biliteracy model. The reasons could include: difficulty in processing academic content in the L2; a feeling that, with some effort in developing literacy in the L1, the same or adapted L2 content presented in L1 could be easier to understand; the need for a stereoscopic perspective facilitated by the more or less different structures of two languages/varieties; and so on.

Firing salvos and returning fire: From the trenches of the content axis

On the content axis, the continuum of vernacular/non-professional to literary/professional genres and styles appears, in our particular case, to be very closely related to the continuum on structure (formal and informal varieties) on the media axis. As a result, in this section the focus will be especially on the mix of texts that are decontextualized (abstract, detached from the lifeworlds of students) and contextualized (adapted and made meaningful in, or relevant to, the students' lifeworlds). As mentioned earlier, on occasion the translators 'localized' or expanded on the source content while producing the multilingual Afrikaans and isiXhosa resources, so that the resulting content would suit contexts the students could more easily relate to. The students were very appreciative when they felt such content localization had taken place (Excerpt (21)), but they formulated lethal criticisms when they felt it had not taken place (Excerpts (22 to 25)). The fire returned by the authors has to do with their contestation of certain expectations of the students.

Consider Excerpt (21):

(21) the examples presented within the Afrikaans slides and podcasts made the concepts much easier to comprehend and grasp as opposed to the English slides which had not used as many examples which were as concise, that is, the example used to describe truncated multilingualism made it much easier for me to comprehend…whereas the English had not used many examples to explain this concept.

In the informal Afrikaans discussion on the concept 'truncated multilingualism' the translator used an example of a greeting typical of Kaaps Afrikaans, with which most of these students were familiar: 'Awe ma se kind, what's up?' ('Hi there. How are you?'). This was used as further clarification for the different interactional regimes operating in different dialogic spaces according to definitions of truncated multilingualism (see Dyers, 2008: 114–5).

Indeed, in many essays, the perceived usefulness of the Afrikaans and isiXhosa resources was judged by the extent to which content in the English lectures had been broken down, exemplified or clarified. As the following excerpts from four different students show, these translated resources were seen as being of limited value if they had the same content status as the English originals:

(22) Had the translated PowerPoint slides and the podcasts been more descriptive and offered actual definitions, or even examples as to how to apply the terms, then it would have been helpful.

(23) The podcast on globalization and typology of multilingualism were both not useful because they were actually repeating what the PowerPoint slides were saying rather than explaining and giving more clear examples so that we could understand better.

(24) I would recommend that the translations of the lectures from English to the other languages (isiXhosa in my case) try to find terms within these languages that are […] explanatory to the concepts.

(25) In my opinion, having multilingual lecture materials would be beneficial to students but only if the material is not a direct translation as this does not clarify any difficulties experienced. At first glance the podcasts seems to help to a certain extent, however when analyzing the

difference between how many of the English concepts and explanations were simplified or made easier to grasp and understand, it becomes evident that many of the difficulties were in fact not clarified in the Afrikaans podcasts.

If these excerpts are interpreted as criticism of the translations, it needs to be clear how this is so. In terms of functional translation theory, this is a question of the adequacy of these translations (at the level of content) for this specific audience. What was desired by the students who formulated the most lethal criticisms – too outspoken to appear in print – were exegetical and substantially localized translations. Explanations had to be built in, further examples provided, terms very transparent or descriptive, local perspectives mainstreamed, connections between ideas made more explicit, and so on. In order to be worthwhile, materials in Afrikaans and isiXhosa need to help students overcome difficulties with the English originals.

Indeed, on inspection of the English and translated materials, it became evident that the students were largely right about several of these difficulties. But neither the difficulties nor the associated hopes for the translated materials are all of the same kind. While addressing some issues (e.g. consistently providing local examples, explicit definitions, cohesion marking) seems more feasible and easily defensible within an accommodation framework, other presuppositions, for instance that material in the L1 (in the sense of high level of proficiency) must somehow be readily understandable *simply by virtue of being in L1*, are somewhat more problematic. This would be the case with, for example, the demand for transparent terminology. It would be difficult to point to examples where, in the specialized texts of, say, physics written in a language X, the relevant terminology is readily understood by all who are very proficient in X irrespective of whether or not they have prior knowledge of physics and previous academic literacy credentials in physics in X.

All the expectations, not just those related to transparent terminology, raise several questions: where does one draw the boundary lines between reasonable linguistic/literacy accommodation and compromising the discipline of discovery study (e.g. formulating own definition from a set of ideas, making sense of metaphorical terminology, among other forms of constructivist reading)? Is everything in the English text readily comprehended by English home language users only on account of their linguistic competence; and, if not, is it realistic to expect such comprehension in relation to material in Afrikaans or isiXhosa?

From literacy events to literacy practices: Implications

Reading and listening to the multilingual lecture materials, either as part of a student's normal process of learning or for purposes of writing an assignment, may be viewed as a series of literacy activities or events (e.g. study sessions possibly with note-taking, completing a written assignment). Aspects of these materials are interpreted differently on the basis of different discourses around 'what should be' or ideological frames. To understand these discourses in relation to students' views as documented in the excerpts, concepts from the literacy practices framework can be drawn upon. Barton (1994) distinguishes between *literacy events* and *literacy practices* as follows:

> Literacy events are the particular activities where reading and writing have a role; literacy practices are the general cultural ways of using reading and writing which people draw upon in a literacy event. (p. viii)

Street (2011a, 2011b) similarly views literacy practices as those uses, values or meanings that underpin specific literacy events and that embed them within socially determined structures or ideological spaces. As an instance of values, consider the discourse of empathy and accommodation which students who did not think they needed materials in languages other than English drew on to validate (or construct the purpose) of the multilingual lecture materials. One student who did not want the isiXhosa materials conceded that these multilingual lecture materials 'would be beneficial for those coming from less privileged backgrounds to not be left in the dark'. Students expressing similar views seem to draw on a discourse of tolerance and appreciation of co-learner vulnerabilities in the community of practice which the class (to an extent) represents, in order to authenticate others' – if not their own – participation in literacy events.

The analysis in the previous sections indicates that students expect non-English lecture resources to be explanatory and more like exegetical commentaries on the English originals. They accept that English will inevitably be there and that, in order to be worthwhile, materials in additional languages need to help them overcome difficulties with the English originals. There are expectations related to definitions being provided, examples from the local environment which students can relate to and other elaborations, terms being descriptive, connections between ideas being more explicit, and so on.

Another consideration informing students' interaction (or lack thereof) with the lecture resources has to do with ideologies of language (Weber & Horner, 2013: 16–22). Let us illustrate with one such ideology, the ideology of language hierarchy. The language hierarchy ideology views certain languages (e.g. English or specific varieties of it) as more naturally dominant than others (e.g. Afrikaans, isiXhosa or other varieties of English) in certain domains (e.g. higher education). The discussion around threshold concepts earlier in this chapter shows cases of changed and unchanged ideologies and attitudes around language and literacy. With what has been regarded as the Englishization of the world today, opportunities abound for upward mobility that is linked to the learning or use of any of several Englishes – authorized or spontaneously cobbled together. English-only education has become an aspiration for many parents and for many prospective university students in

South Africa. For an ever-enlarging segment of the national population in South Africa, literacy events in contexts that are seen as helping to climb the social ladder of opportunity need to be in English if they are to be worthwhile. The students' views therefore mediate a certain conception of literacy activities and underscore the usefulness of Street's ideological model of literacy, according to which literacy effects or shapes cannot be pre-determined, vary contextually and are underpinned by meanings deriving from broader questions of interest and power (Street, 1984).

There are three important take-home messages here. Firstly, the social forces that produce language hierarchies have had the effect of changing people's relations to languages. The idea of several definitions for mother or native tongue (based variously on origin, identification, frequency of use, competence, cf. Phillipson, 1992) is clearly well founded. A language associated with one's origin is not necessarily one in which a high level of competence is attested; neither is it necessarily valued for certain functions, as Excerpt (19) points out. These views, as well as some students' preference for the English materials, may contest established knowledge about cognitive benefits associated with specific languages, and this is an aspect that will certainly engage the attention of the authors in future.

A second take-home message flowing from the first, then, is that in developing multilingual resources, there need to be some opportunities for multilingual academic literacy development. In the same way as many universities in, say, the English-speaking world have academic literacy or development programs to help various categories of students cope with academic Englishes, it would certainly be (ideologically) desirable to have similar initiatives for Afrikaans and especially isiXhosa at UWC, given the students' acknowledgement of the loss of such literacies owing to the hegemony of English at school. Although academic literacies acquired in one language or discipline are certainly transferable, the limits to transferability become evident when it is that recalled literacy events and the underlying practices are actually contextual and non-autonomous.

Finally, on a more practical but no less important note linked to Hornberger's media continua, great care needs to be taken with the quality of translations in order to ensure that these languages (irrespective of the varieties used) are shown to be treated with the same care and respect as English and truly add value to students' engagement with these materials. Although not described in this chapter, there were occasional criticisms of the linguistic quality of the isiXhosa translations.

Conclusion

The authors' rationale for offering their students translated PowerPoint lectures as well as podcasts in both formal and informal Afrikaans and isiXhosa is firstly to give expression to UWC's official language policy of 2003, and secondly to begin a process of determining how to draw away from mediating lecture content in English only. They want to develop resources that diversify language and literacy modalities in learning and also to unlock attitudes which the module is influencing or needs to influence. In these ways, they see their ongoing research in the Linguistics Department at UWC as making a contribution to the diversification of languages of instruction in South African Higher Education.

The study has thus far shown that the majority of the students studying the module are positively disposed to the type of learning support offered by the translated materials. Those who self-identify as speakers of Afrikaans in particular have responded positively to especially the informal variety used, as many of them speak this variety at home. Xhosa-speaking students were, for largely ideological reasons, more divided in terms of their attitudes towards the formal and informal isiXhosa texts offered. This was in spite of the acknowledgement by many of these participants that they struggled with the formal isiXhosa, particularly the PowerPoint text. Clearly, a major issue here is whether such students possess the necessary academic literacy in formal isiXhosa that would enable them to cope with texts of this nature, especially as they are the products of a schooling system that requires them to write most of their final examinations in English.

On the basis of on-going analysis of data and application of insights yielded, the authors plan to continue producing all their lectures as well as assessment tasks in both formal and informal Afrikaans and isiXhosa (in both written and audio format as required) and to encourage lecturers in other modules to do the same, particularly at first year level. In this way they hope to counter dominant academic literacies by continuing their research within a collaborative network of postgraduate students, lecturers and translators as part of their attempt, in the words of Hornberger (2000):

> to contest the imbalanced (asymmetrical) power weighting of the continua of biliteracy in educational research, policy, and practice, through initiatives which explicitly pay attention to and grant agency and voice to actors and practices at what have traditionally been the less powerful ends of the continua. (p. 365)

References

Airey, J. (2009) Estimating undergraduate Bilingual Scientific Literacy in Sweden. *International CLIL Research Journal* 1 (2), 26–35.

Antia, B. (2015) University multilingualism: A critical narrative from the University of the Western Cape, South Africa. *Journal of Multilingual and Multicultural Development* 36 (6), 571–586.

Baker, C. (2006) *Foundations of Bilingualism and Bilingual Education* (4th edn) Clevedon: Multilingual Matters.

Barton, D. (1994) *Literacy: An Introduction to the Ecology of Written Language*. Oxford: Blackwell.

Bernstein, B. (1972) Social class, language and socialization. In P. Giglioli (ed.) *Language and Social Context: Selected Readings*. Harmondsworth: Penguin.

Breier, M. (2010) Drop out or stop out at the University of the Western Cape? In M. Letseka, M. Cosser, M. Breier and M. Visser (2010) *Student Retention and Graduation Destination: Higher Education and Labour Market access and Success* (pp. 53–65). Cape Town: HSRC Press.

Canagarajah, A. (2011) Codemeshing in academic writing: Identifying teachable strategies of translanguaging. *The Modern Language Journal* 95 (3), 401–417.

Centre for Teaching and Learning, Southern Cross University (2015) Threshold Concepts. See http://scu.edu.au/teachinglearning/index.php/91 (accessed May 2015).

Cummins, J. (1984) *Bilingualism and Special Education: Issues in Assessment and Pedagogy*. Clevedon: Multilingual Matters.

Dyers, C. (2008) Truncated multilingualism or language shift? An examination of language use in intimate domains in a new non-racial working class township in South Africa. *Journal of Multilingual and Multicultural Development* 29 (2), 110–126.

García, O., Bartlett, L. and Kleifgen, J. (2007) From biliteracy to pluriliteracies. In P. Auer and W. Li (eds) *Handbook of Applied Linguistics* (Vol. 5, pp. 207–208). Berlin: Mouton de Gruyter.

García, O. (2009) *Bilingual Education in the 21st Century: A Global Perspective*. Malden, MA: Wiley/Blackwell.

Heugh, K. (2003) A re-take on bilingual education in and for South Africa. In K. Fraurud and K. Hytenstam (eds) *Multilingualism in Global and Local Perspectives. Papers from the 8th Nordic Conference on Bilingualism, November 1–3, 2001, Stockholm Rinkeby* (pp. 47–62). Stockholm: Centre for Research on Bilingualism, Stockholm University, and Rinkeby Institute of Multilingual Research.

Hornberger, N. (1989) Continua of biliteracy. *Review of Educational Research* 59 (3), 271–296.

Hornberger, N.H. (1990) Creating successful learning contexts for bilingual literacy. *Teachers College Record* 92 (2), 212–229.

Hornberger, N. (2000) Multilingual literacies, literacy practices, and the continua of biliteracy. In M. Martin-Jones and K. Jones (eds) *Multilingual Literacies: Reading and Writing Different Worlds* (pp. 353–367). Amsterdam: John Benjamins.

Hornberger, N. and Skilton-Sylvester, E. (2000) Revisiting the continua of biliteracy: International and critical perspectives. *Language and Education* 14 (2), 96–122.

Hornberger, N. (2002) Multilingual language policies and the continua of biliteracy: An ecological approach. *Language Policy* 1, 27–51.

Hornberger, N. and Skilton-Sylvester, E. (2003) Revisiting the continua of biliteracy: International and critical perspectives. In N.H. Hornberger (ed.) *Continua of Biliteracy: An Ecological Framework for Educational Policy, Research and Practice in Multilingual Settings* (pp. 35–67). Clevedon: Multilingual Matters.

Hornberger, N. (2004) The continua of biliteracy and the bilingual educator: Educational Linguistics in Practice. *Bilingual Education and Bilingualism* 7 (2–3), 155–171.

Hornberger, N. and Link, H. (2012) Translanguaging and transnational literacies in multilingual classrooms: A biliteracy lens. *International Journal of Bilingual Education and Bilingualism* 15 (3), 261–278.

Letseka, M., Cosser, M., Breier, M. and Visser, M. (2010) *Student Retention and Graduation Destination: Higher Education and Labour market Access and Success*. Cape Town: HSRC Press.

Lewis, G., Jones, B. and Baker, C. (2012) Translanguaging: Developing its conceptualisation and contextualisation. *Educational Research and Evaluation* 18 (7), 655–670.

Martin-Jones, M. and Jones, K. (2000) (eds) *Multilingual Literacies: Reading and Writing Different Worlds*. Amsterdam: John Benjamins.

Meyer, J. and Land, R. (2006) *Overcoming Barriers to Student Understanding: Threshold Concepts and Troublesome Knowledge*. London: Routledge.

Paxton, M. and Tyam, N. (2010) Xhosalising English? Negotiating meaning and identity in Economics. *South African Linguistics and Applied Language Studies* 28 (3), 247–257.

Phillipson, R. (1992) *Linguistic Imperialism*. Oxford: Oxford University Press.

Spaull, N. (2013) *South Africa's Education Crisis: The Quality of Education in South Africa 1994–2011*. Johannesburg: Report Commissioned by the Centre for Development and Enterprise.

Street, B. (2011a) Literacy inequalities in theory and practice: The power to name and define. *International Journal of Educational Development* 31, 580–586.

Street, B. (2011b) New literacy studies and the continua of biliteracy. In F. Hult and K. King (eds) *Educational Linguistics in Practice: Applying the Local Globally and the Global Locally* (pp. 59–67). Bristol: Multilingual Matters.

Street, B. (1984) *Literacy in Theory and Practice*. Cambridge: Cambridge University Press.

Stroud, C. and Kerfoot, C. (2013) Towards rethinking multilingualism and language policy for academic literacies. *Linguistics and Education* 24 (4), 396–405.

Tamminga, W. (2006) The doors of learning shall be opened. In W. Spierenburg and H. Wels (eds) *Culture, Organization and Management in South Africa* (pp. 19–46). New York: Nova.

University of the Western Cape (2010) Institutional Operating Plan 2010-2014: The Development of Graduate Attributes at the University of the Western Cape. Bellville: UWC.

University of the Western Cape (2015) *History*. See http://www.uwc.ac.za/Pages/History/aspx (accessed May 2015).

Weber, J.-J. and Horner, K. (2012) *Introducing Multilingualism: A Social Approach*. London: Routledge.

8 Creative Collaboration in Higher Education: A *Coleg Cymraeg Cenedlaethol* Case Study

Gwawr Ifan and Rhian Hodges

Introduction

Firstly, this chapter sets out to explain the context of bilingual higher education in Wales, detailing the development of the *Coleg Cymraeg Cenedlaethol*, and will focus on the pedagogical practices used in bilingual secondary and higher education. It will discuss the incentive behind the development of an interdisciplinary module, bringing together two different academic schools in a higher education institution. Though delivered through the medium of a minority language, the advantages of actively engaging in the use of two languages in terms of resources and assessment methods will be considered. Focusing on this module as a case study, the chapter aims to evaluate its effectiveness, and will consider the pedagogical merits of studying a module of its kind in terms of (a) interdisciplinary teaching in a minority language and (b) enhancing opportunities for translanguaging and biliteracy practices. It will also suggest recommendations for the further development of similar models in the future.

Background

Wales is a devolved nation forming a distinct part of the United Kingdom. It is a country with its own unique language, which is among the oldest Celtic languages in Europe. Of a population of 3.1 million people, 562,000 people in Wales are able to speak Welsh (Office for National Statistics, 2011). However, according to the Welsh Language Use in Wales 2013–2015 survey, only 67% of Welsh speakers perceive their written Welsh language skills to be 'good' or 'very good' (Welsh Government and Welsh Language Commissioner, 2015). Whilst still considered a minority language, it is a main tool of communication for a high percentage of the population. As a result, Welsh-medium education for all ages is at the forefront of policy for the Welsh Government (2013), whose vision is:

> an education and training system that responds in a planned way to the growing demand for Welsh-medium education, reaches out to and reflects our diverse communities and enables an increase in the number of people of all ages and backgrounds who are fluent in Welsh and able to use the language with their families, in their communities and in the workplace. (Welsh Government, 2010: 4)

In 2011, 30% of Welsh speakers were aged between 3 and 15 years old (Office for National Statistics, 2011), and this young demographic is largely due to the success of firmly established Welsh-medium education (Hodges, 2012; Thomas & Williams, 2013). While Welsh-medium schools offer education primarily through the medium of Welsh, they could also be considered to be bilingual schools, as both English and Welsh languages are naturally used in order to 'develop every individual to be confidently bilingual' (Lewis, 2011: 67).

Despite the success of bilingual secondary education, higher education continues to be a constant battleground for competing language choices (G.R. Jones, 2010; Davies & Trystan, 2012). In order to satisfy the need for linguistic provision and linguistic progression from secondary schools to higher education, a steering group for Welsh Medium Provision in Higher Education was developed by the Higher Education Funding Council for Wales [HEFCW] in 2004, aiming to 'set out actions to create a sustainable system for Welsh medium higher education in the future' (HEFCW, 2004). In time, this prompted the development of the Centre for Welsh Medium Higher Education to implement HEFCW's strategy, which ultimately led to the establishment of the *Coleg Cymraeg Cenedlaethol* [Welsh-medium National College] as a formally incorporated company in 2011.

The *Coleg Cymraeg Cenedlaethol* is a virtual learning college that works with Universities across Wales to train new Welsh-medium researchers and lecturers and provides funding to develop cross-institutional Welsh medium opportunities for students. It is currently possible for Welsh-speaking students to study over 500 courses entirely or partly through the medium of Welsh, with scholarships of up to £5000 awarded to students who study courses in Welsh (*Coleg Cymraeg Cenedlaethol*, 2014a).

Of all Welsh Universities, Bangor University, a traditional university established in 1884, offers the highest number of Welsh-medium modules, and more students choose to study their subjects in Welsh than at any other higher education institution (*Coleg Cymraeg Cenededlaethol*, 2014b). As the University is situated in an area where, on average, 69% of the population speak Welsh, 'Playing a leading role in Welsh language and culture, both locally and nationally' is one of the institution's key priorities (Bangor University, 2013: 2). In 2010/11, the University had 9200 full-time students and 1980 part-time students. Of those, 1795 noted that they could speak Welsh fluently and another 743 noted that they could speak some Welsh or were learning Welsh (Bangor University, 2013). The University therefore considers developing and enhancing Welsh-medium modular provision to be of the utmost importance in order to fully meet the needs of these students.

Although the development of the *Coleg Cymraeg Cenedlaethol* is of great significance and value for the future provision of Welsh-medium higher education, the authors of this article, who are *Coleg Cymraeg Cenedlaethol* lecturers at Bangor University, were faced with linguistic challenges which led to the case study discussed in this chapter.

B. Jones (2010) observes that there is a 'kaleidoscopic variety' (Baker, 1993: 15) of bilingual pedagogical practices used in education in Wales. In higher education in Wales, following the development of the *Coleg Cymraeg Cenedlaethol* and the increase in Welsh-medium education, a constant challenge faced by lecturers and practitioners is to encourage the simultaneous use of two languages – Welsh and English – within students' studies. Biliteracy can therefore be used to enrich pedagogical practice and educational experience, through

> the ongoing, dynamic development of concepts and expertise for thinking, listening, speaking, reading, and writing in two languages. (Reyes, 2006: 269)

Huang (1995: 276) highlights the complex influences that shape biliteracy practices, such as

> the value of skills, sentiments attached to the languages, judgments of significant others, and experience of formal schooling. (Huang, 1995: 276)

By sensitively constructing biliteracy practices – both written and oral components in higher education (Hornberger, 2007: 3, see also introductory chapter), students are given the opportunity to engage and strengthen their own cultural identity and self-esteem (Huang, 1995) while, at the same time, embracing the wider linguistic and social context that is available to them as bilinguals.

Code-switching is a specific example of a strategy used regularly in oral biliteracy development which has been scrutinised by educational researchers in Wales (e.g. Robert, 2009; Clapham, 2012). Code-switching as a technique to introduce and normalise the use of a given language in schooling is a key aspect of emergent biliteracy (Reyes, 2006). As students become more confident users of two academic languages, they may move beyond code-switching to read in one language and discuss in another, or listen to one language and make notes in another: the type of behaviour described as 'translanguaging' by Williams (1994). While code-switching may be more prevalent in younger children as they develop initial biliteracy skills, 'translanguaging' (Williams, 1994) may be a more suitable pedagogical tool that occurs naturally in Welsh-medium higher education:

> The notion of translanguaging refers broadly to how bilingual students communicate and make meaning by drawing on and intermingling linguistic features from different languages. (Hornberger & Link, 2012: 240)

A common concern amongst students studying any subject through the medium of Welsh is the need to depend regularly on English-medium sources; therefore, translanguaging may be considered not only 'necessary, but desirable educational practice' (Hornberger & Link, 2012: 239) in bilingual communities.

However, it could be argued that Welsh-medium higher-education teaching has traditionally offered what García (2009) refers to as 'double monolingualism'. Previously, in an attempt to fill the gap in Welsh-language provision, academic schools have often developed translated versions of modules previously only available in English, sometimes gaining funding to translate core texts from English into Welsh (e.g. Grout & Palisca, 1997). It could be argued that such practices can undermine the unique context of the Welsh language, and therefore do not embrace the benefits of biliteracy, where important skills for bilingual students are developed. According to García's theory, rather than creating another 'monolingual' module, it may be considered better practice to embrace the natural bilingual culture in which Welsh students live, communicate and work. Rather than restricting students to the limited resources available in Welsh, it may be more beneficial to broaden their horizons, and to educate them in the widest cultural and linguistic context possibly available to them. Thus their bilingualism may be seen as an academic skill, contributing towards their academic progression, rather than limiting their resources.

As students who choose to study in Welsh are in a minority within Welsh universities, they will usually have to study in relatively small sized classes. This escalates difficulties for the lecturer to use more innovative teaching methods that are readily available with larger classes, e.g. group work, peer-learning etc. As breaking traditional institutional boundaries is encouraged by the *Coleg Cymraeg Cenedlaethol*, one option that occurred to the authors when developing new programme offerings was the development of an interdisciplinary module, building on class sizes by combining student groups from different Schools and Colleges. In contrast to the concept of the 'subject approach', this model:

> incorporates and connects key concepts and skills from many disciplines into the presentation of a single unit. (Adeyemni, 2010: 11–12)

Interdisciplinary teaching is becoming an increasingly customary practice in higher education, and is a progressively important aspect for university graduates considering 'the complexity and multi-dimensionality' (King, 2010) of graduates' careers. It is considered to enrich student understanding; allow students to gain and apply knowledge, develop skills and strategies and construct a more integrated web of knowledge and information (Adeyemni, 2010). It has also been found, for example, that medical students following an interdisciplinary module 'felt strongly that interacting with residents from other disciplines increased the value of the course' (Julian *et al.*, 2007). Because of the increase in class sizes, such provision may be more appropriate for language-minority students as it is less isolated (Malarz, 1998). By allowing academic socialization (Lea & Street, 2006) to take place in interdisciplinary modules, it is possible to bring minority language speakers together to create a stronger sense of community, in contrast with what would previously have been a limited community of minority language students in individual academic schools.

Case Study

After receiving a grant from the *Coleg Cymraeg Cenedlaethol* to develop an interdisciplinary module through the medium of Welsh, the '*Cymdeithaseg Cerddoriaeth yng Nghymru*' [Sociology of Music in Wales] module was created by two coordinators from the School of Music and the School of Social Sciences, Bangor University. The module combined key themes from sociology and music and drew upon cultural, musical and social factors often unique to the Welsh language and Wales. In the process of validation, it was argued that the establishment of this module would combine rare specialist knowledge in Music and Social Science through the medium of Welsh, and create larger teaching groups enabling the use of a variety of teaching methods.

Although a plethora of research focusing on aspects central to Welsh music in relation to culture, society and politics are written in Welsh (e.g. Wyn, 2006), the main language of international research and publication in the academic fields of both music and sociology is English. Consequently, both schools have limited resources available to fulfil the requirements of higher education teaching through the medium of Welsh. As a result, the module coordinators created a bibliography which included both Welsh and English sources within the field. In order to ensure that students fully understood the content of English-medium works when provided with Welsh-medium lectures, it became evident that students should be given the opportunity to develop confidence in three required translanguaging skills noted by B. Jones (2010: 19): reading, understanding and summarizing. As a result, seminars were included in the weekly contact hours, and students were afforded an opportunity to fully explore biliteracy practices. English-medium texts (with rare exceptions) were set in lectures, and key questions were provided as a base for thorough discussions (through the medium of Welsh) in the seminars. This opportunity would allow students to enhance their knowledge and develop a more thorough understanding of the text. This also allowed students to practice moving easily from one language to another, while also varying their use of academic literacies, i.e. switching

> writing styles and genres between one setting and other, to deploy a repertoire of literacy practices appropriate to each setting, and to handle the social meanings and identities that each evokes. (Lea & Street, 2006: 368)

During the early stages of developing the module, it was foreseen that the variety of Welsh and English resources and references as well as the use of biliteracy skills developed whilst reading, discussing and preparing written and oral assessment would give students a 'culturally sensitive view of literacy practices' (Street, 2011: 61), especially as the module was directly relevant to the culture, heritage and community of Welsh-speaking students, rather than being a literal translation of a module already offered through the medium of English.

Evaluation of Module

The module was developed during spring and summer 2012 and was offered for the first time to Welsh-speaking students in the School of Music and School of Social Sciences, Bangor University in autumn 2012. The module was developed and validated in both schools. The module followed the usual credit weighting and teaching patterns followed by the individual schools.

As shown in Table 8.1, for music students this was a 10 credit module, and a 20 credit module for sociology students. As a result, sociology students were issued with an extra assessment component for seminar contributions, in which students were asked to submit a portfolio of prepared notes as evidence of general preparation, and were also marked for oral contribution. Reading lists for seminars with preparatory questions were provided at the beginning of the semester.

Methodology

The module was team-taught, with a total of 6 members of staff (including module coordinators) from both schools offering individual lectures

Table 8.1 Module details

	Music	Sociology
Level	5 & 6	5 & 6
Credits	10 credits	20 credits
Weekly contact hours	1 (& 1 optional)	2
Assessment	• 7 minute oral presentation (30%) • Written assignment, 2500 words (70%) (*note*: seminars not assessed for music students, though students are welcome to attend voluntarily)	• 10 minute oral presentation (30%) • Written assignment 2000 words (50%) • Seminar contributions and portfolio (20%)
Number of students on module (2012/2013)	6	8
Number of students on module (2013/2014)	6	4

during the semester. These were asked to provide general feedback on their teaching experiences on the module at the end of the semester. Excluding module coordinators, four members of staff were asked to provide feedback, of which two responses were received. The main source of data comes from in-depth semi-structured interviews with a combination of music and sociology students who studied the module in different years. This qualitative research strategy was chosen as it is considered that 'through language people can often best articulate and explain their thoughts, opinions, emotions and experiences' (Carey, 2009: 111).

All students who participated in the module were invited to participate in the evaluation. The research methods deemed most appropriate for this evaluation were a focus group facilitated by an independent moderator and in-depth semi structured interviews with individual students. Of the cohort invited to take part in this research, six students participated in primary data collection. Three students contributed to the focus group and three students participated in in-depth interviews. All were carried out through the medium of Welsh, the usual communication language used between Welsh-speaking students and staff. Predetermined starter questions were set, focusing on linguistic background of students, their biliteracy processes in higher education in general, positive and negative feedback of the module and ideas for further development. The benefits of using in-depth interviews and a focus group were that they resulted in the collection of deep, rich social data relating to the experiences, feelings and unique viewpoints of individuals (Kitzinger, 1995; Bryman, 2008) as epitomised by Prior *et al.* (2003):

> focus groups are especially appropriate for studying public attitudes [...T]hey foster the use of participants' (rather than researcher) priorities, language and concepts. (p. 193)

The research gained ethical approval from the College of Arts and Humanities Ethics Committee and the College of Business, Law, Social Sciences and Education Ethics Committee; and the students gave their permission and informed consent to participate in the research. Ethical guidelines and protocols were adhered to and key principles such as confidentially and anonymity were upheld following the Data Protection Act 1998 and ESRC Social Research Guidelines.

Results

Overarching research themes are collated within the table below (see Table 8.2) highlighting relevant quotations from the research data. Following the table, the research themes are discussed individually. General themes regarding biliteracy are discussed at the beginning of this section, and are followed by an analysis of case study benefits and challenges.

Linguistic background

Participants were from a wide variety of geographical areas across Wales, and as a result of this their linguistic backgrounds were of a diverse nature (Table 8.3). The one common characteristic was that all participants had followed Welsh-medium secondary education.

Students noted that reading English sources in Welsh-medium education is something that they are accustomed to since secondary education, and that they are by now 'used to it ... it isn't a problem anymore'. (Participant no. 6, Music student, interview). There was a clear difference in biliteracy practices and processes of students according to their linguistic background. Whilst the students from Welsh-speaking households preferred to find Welsh-medium resources first before going on to read English-medium resources, 'to ensure understanding' (Participant no. 4, Music & Welsh student, focus group), the students from English-speaking households said they preferred to read English texts first, practicing translanguaging by writing notes for their assignments in Welsh. Interestingly, therefore, reading practices for these students were influenced by the language of the home more than by that of secondary education.

Table 8.2 Primary research data quotations

Research	Selected quotations from primary research data (translated from Welsh)
Linguistic background	English was the main social language [in school], as so many pupils come from English-medium backgrounds. They were more comfortable speaking English. I spoke exactly the same amount of Welsh and English growing up. Since coming to University, I only speak Welsh. I'm a part of the Welsh speaking student community. (Participant no. 6, Music student, interview)
	Welsh is my first language. I speak Welsh at home, and we are a bit of a mixture really, because mam and dad speak English together (although they're both fluent in Welsh) but they speak Welsh with my brother and I. My dad's mother is English, so maybe that's why he's more comfortable speaking English. But I have been raised in a Welsh-speaking household. (Participant no. 5, Music student, interview)
	Everyone in our family speaks Welsh. Mam, Dad and my extended family. Everybody from this area speaks Welsh. You hear the Welsh language everywhere. (Participant no. 2, Sociology student, interview)
	English is the language of my home (my grandparents speak English too). I received Welsh-medium primary and secondary education. (Participant no. 3, Music student, focus group)
Creative thinking and learning	It makes you think more creatively to try to word something in Welsh. You have to think one step in Welsh – how am I going to explain this in Welsh and make sense of it in Welsh. (Participant no. 5, Music student, interview)
	There's more English-medium resources than Welsh-medium resources and this is true of other modules, and when I was in school. I think I'm used to this by now! It's not a problem by now, it makes you think more I think. (Participant no. 2, Sociology student, interview)
	I think it's beneficial [to be biliterate] because if the articles are available, we can read Welsh and English material, and it gives us a wealth of information. Also, reading English material and writing in Welsh you can express yourself in your own words. (Participant no. 1, Sociology student, focus group)
Confidence	I'm more comfortable speaking Welsh, but I'm more confident writing in English. (Participant no. 5, Music student, interview)
	I'd say I was pretty confident in Welsh. I think in Welsh every time [...] I'm very comfortable in English as well, but I don't have as much confidence compared to Welsh if I'm honest. I would choose to do everything in Welsh [...] I hardly ever write in English ... If I had to write an essay in English, I wouldn't know how to put it together [...] I'd be all over the place! (Participant no. 2, Sociology student, interview)
	I think my Welsh and English speaking abilities are equal. I might have a little less confidence speaking Welsh, and then I'll turn to English. But in terms of my written skills, my Welsh is better than my English. (Participant no. 1, Sociology student, focus group)

Interpretation v translation	When translating English resources to Welsh, there is less chance to be guilty of plagiarism. That was beneficial. It was also good to read sources from different places, so you were aware of other places, and not just Wales. I tend to be quite lazy – I read and make notes in Welsh, aside from quotations, and then I translate it, but in a different way. (Participant no. 6, Music student, interview)
	There's a tendency to translate – not that I do this! But there's a tendency to translate word for word, as it's not available in Welsh, but it's so much easier to plagiarise without referencing. (Participant no. 5, Music student, interview)
	I try to word things differently in Welsh, and then compare back with the English. It's important for me to word things in Welsh. Welsh is my language! (Participant no. 2, Sociology student, interview)
	The majority of the books were in English, so it was hard to analyse what the authors were saying. (Participant no. 4, Music student, focus group)
Simultaneous use of two languages	Last semester I had to do a module completely through the medium of English and I had to write the assignments in English too. But that was my choice, because it was easier! But in one module, because the lecturer was Welsh speaking, I wrote the assignment in Welsh, even though the lectures were in English. (Participant no. 6, Music student, interview)
	The lectures were more or less 90% in Welsh […] throughout the 3 years of University; I rarely read any reading material in Welsh. On the whole the majority of the material was in English. (Participant no. 5, Music student, interview)
	I think it's OK for both languages to work together, but there should be a line drawn between them, in order to separate them, which makes learning simpler and clearer. (Participant no. 2, Sociology student, interview)
Terminology	Yes, a terminology handbook would be a good idea. I know one exists in the sciences, and it should be available for this. (Participant no. 6, Music student, interview)
	A bilingual handbook would have been very useful. (Participant no. 5, Music student, interview)
	A bilingual handbook would be handy especially as this is a new module, but I'm not one to use English material anyway, i.e. bilingual PowerPoint slides wouldn't be very useful – I would probably ignore the English material on them! The terms are important in a module like this which is new for everybody. This helps us to find English terms, and it also helps us to write English and Welsh terms too. (Participant no. 2, Sociology student, interview)
	There were terms that I wouldn't know what they were in English. (Participant no. 6, Music student, interview)
	Understanding terms […] during the lecture, we hear the terms in Welsh. If I'd have to write the essay on a musical topic, then I wouldn't have known the terms. (Participant no. 1, Sociology student, focus group)

Table 8.3 Linguistic background of participants in interviews/focus groups

Participant	Main subject	Main language spoken at home	Main community language	Secondary education
1	Sociology	English (Welsh with Grandparents)	Welsh	Welsh
2	Sociology	Welsh	Welsh	Welsh
3	Music	English	English	Welsh
4	Music & Welsh	Welsh	Welsh	Welsh
5	Music	Welsh (parents speak English with each other, Welsh with children)	Welsh	Welsh
6	Music	Welsh	English	Welsh

Creative thinking and learning

In general, students considered it beneficial to actively engage biliteracy in higher education (see quotations in Table 8.2). When working in English they can 'enhance the way they learn', (Participant no. 5, Music student, interview) and add to the depth of their knowledge by reading a broader selection of texts, which will in turn 'enrich the information they produce' (Participant no. 5, Music student, interview). They also felt encouraged by their biliteracy practices to be 'more creative' when having to 'make sense of it and explain in your own words' (Participant no. 6, Music student, interview). As suggested by Hibbert and Van der Walt (2014), 'students will use the strategies and literacies they have developed up to that point to further their education'. Although reading mainly English-medium sources, students felt that writing in Welsh (the language they are most accustomed to and are most comfortable using since secondary education) allows them to 'convey it better in [their] own words'. (Participant no. 4, Music student, focus group). This finding contradicts the view mentioned by Knapp (2014) that bilingual students, 'do not fully exploit their multilingual resources and that their preferred language choices tend to lead to a mere reproduction of knowledge' (p. 165). Our findings suggest that through translanguaging students follow a process that requires interpretation and a deeper understanding of the subject area rather than merely surface level learning.

Confidence

It became evident however that there was a tendency even amongst students from Welsh-speaking households to suffer from a lack of confidence in their written and formal Welsh (e.g. see quotation given by Participant no. 5, Music students, interview, in Table 8.2). It was a common theme for students to feel as if their choice of language influences their ability to structure and formulate assignments:

> If I had to write an essay in English, I wouldn't know how to put it together ... I'd be all over the place! (Participant no. 2, Sociology student, interview)

This research highlights that a close relationship exists between a lack of language use and its impact on the confidence of a speaker. It could be argued, therefore, that a circle of dependence exists between use, confidence and perception which could possibly impact upon assessments in a wider context.

Interpretation vs. translation

Some students noted that biliteracy, especially the practice of translanguaging, adds to the amount of time it takes to prepare for assignments, and that it was more difficult to ensure they fully understand the information at hand. One student from a Welsh-speaking household noted that it was 'difficult to analyse what the author was trying to say' (Participant no. 2, Sociology student, interview) when reading English sources. Some participants even revealed the tendency to use online translating services such as Google Translate to 'get it to make sense first' (Participant no. 5, Music student, interview). However, such practice was also recognised by others as plagiarism if directly copied into their assignments, and noted that they try to avoid 'translating word for word' (Participant no. 5, Music student, interview. See further quotations regarding plagiarism in Table 8.2).

Simultaneous use of two languages

Perhaps one of the difficulties which led to the tendency to translate was the difficulty to create a smooth flow from one language to the next in one text. Though the use of two languages in various situations was found to be beneficial at times, e.g. 'having the lectures in Welsh and the seminar texts in English' (Participant no. 6, Music student, interview), it seemed to be more difficult to combine two languages. One student commented on the fact that she doesn't like to use an English quote in a Welsh essay, as 'it doesn't flow well using both languages. It's better to choose one language and stick to it'. (Participant no. 5, Music student, interview. See also quotation given by participant no.2, Sociology student, interview, in Table 8.2). As a result, students didn't always feel comfortable to use both languages freely. In particular, one student from a Welsh-speaking household felt that too many English texts were set as required readings for the seminars, and that coordinators should develop more Welsh-language sources. However, this particular student also failed to attend seminars (which were voluntary for music students) due to timetable clashes, and noted that she would probably have benefited from discussing work in Welsh (Participant no. 4, Music & Welsh student, focus group).

Terminology

An added difficulty with biliteracy in this module was that students were introduced to a new terminology unfamiliar to them and beyond their own discipline. It was therefore more difficult for them to code-switch and translanguage from one language to the other, as they were only familiar with the terminology in Welsh, the language used in lectures. This led to some students choosing an essay question that was more closely related to their own discipline:

> Because in the lecture we would hear the terms in Welsh, if I would have chosen to write the essay on a musical topic, I wouldn't understand the terms. (Participant no. 1, Sociology student, focus group)

A key research theme to emerge from the primary data was the need to develop a terminology handbook (see Table 8.2; cf. Hurst *et al.*'s chapter in this book), especially as this was a new, interdisciplinary module. This need was felt by music and sociology students alike, as such a resource would equip students with the introductory knowledge and key concepts required to further develop biliteracy practices.

Discussion

For pedagogical, cultural and linguistic reasons, it seemed that students and staff alike welcomed the opportunity to have a new and different chance to work and learn in higher education. However, suggestions were made by students regarding future development of this module and bilingual provision in general. Despite a consensus among students that they would not welcome bilingual PowerPoint slides, care should be taken when considering resources that are available in both languages, ensuring that basic terminology is introduced to students in both languages, to allow them the freedom and ability to translanguage independently and confidently, and also to build biliteracy capacity in their new subject area. Assessment methods should also be carefully constructed to ensure confidence building. Introducing different assessment methods can offer a more varied and interesting way of educating and assessing students' understanding, allowing them the freedom to use both languages as they wish. As various students noted their lack of confidence in both written Welsh and English assignments, initial oral formative assessment may be an effective means of developing the confidence of students in working and exchanging between languages expressing their ideas and findings in a language and register that is less formal and more comfortable for them. Indeed, it could be argued that oral seminar work could aid to develop the skills of students working in their second language in particular, as research focusing on Welsh learners in north Wales found that the main issues of concern for respondents was a lack of confidence, and a lack of vocabulary and pronunciation (Andrews, 2011: 52).

Whilst this module was praised by students for the use of oral assessments in seminars, it would be beneficial for all students to attend and participate in this aspect of the assessment. Though they were well-attended by some willing music students, not all students took advantage of this opportunity. Making seminars an integral part of the module for all students would make them feel as if they were treated equally, and would avoid emphasising the divide between the two disciplines. If this was successfully developed, more thought should be given to enhancing the academic socialization (Lea & Street, 2006) of students from different disciplinary backgrounds. Even if minority-language interdisciplinary modules could serve as a means of bringing small and isolated student groups together, one could argue that the concept of academic socialization is at odds with that of interdisciplinary modules. Students may have already formed their own community within their discipline, thus it could be difficult for them to be re-socialized. Thus it is the seminar facilitator's responsibility to ensure that the seminar is led in a student-centred manner according to individual needs, while allowing for cross-fertilization of ideas and interdisciplinary themes.

Despite students considering seminar work interesting and effective on the whole, it seems that more work needs to be done to focus on the development of confidence for those engaging in biliteracy practices such as translanguaging when preparing for written work. Biliterate students need to be encouraged to be confident when interpreting resources in both languages, rather than the tendency of merely translating work from one language into another. Such tendencies are considered common with students working in their second language due to 'difficulties associated with L2 academic writing'. (Pecorari & Petrić, 2014: 270), and a lack of confidence in finding their own style, leading to the 'borrow[ing of] language that has been used ... by someone else' (Flowerdew & Li, 2007: 162).

Even when working within a single discipline, it was felt that more help should be given to students studying bilingually in general, which could aid student understanding and successful assignment preparation. This, in turn, would ensure that studying bilingually strengthens their future prospects, rather than limiting their confidence and ability to use their weaker language. Instead of focusing only on course content, more emphasis could also be put on how to use two languages to develop new pedagogical strategies in higher education. These strategies could include new modes of technological communication which offer 'new ways to interact and connect with other people' (Guarda, 2012: 23). Such help could be offered within each module, for example more contact time, one to one discussions and small formative assessments, offering examples of scholarly writing in both languages. An example of this is currently being developed by the School of Music and will be introduced during the next academic year for Music students who are following Level 4 *'Astudio Cerddoriaeth'* [The Study of Music] core module.[1] Moreover, a Level 4 School of Social Sciences core module, *'Sgiliau Ymchwil'* [Research Skills] currently includes a biliteracy skills package as a part of the module where students are assessed on translation and translanguaging practices in order to develop these essential biliteracy skills.[2] This aspect of the module is facilitated by Canolfan Bedwyr, Bangor University's Centre for Welsh Language Services, Research and Technology.[3] However, it would also be beneficial to consider developing a generic, multidisciplinary Welsh study skills module at College or University level, offering a wide array of skills relating to academic language use in higher education. Though such modules are currently offered to individual schools as and when required, making them available to students from different schools could give students the opportunity of being a part of a larger student group, to develop and enhance their academic community, and give tutors a wider variety of pedagogical methods for introducing information in a creative way.

Conclusion

This module introduced many different ideas to students, including assessment methods, linguistic resources and interdisciplinary themes. The evaluation of the module serves as a useful practice to consider the development of similar interdisciplinary modules for minority-language students in the future. The interdisciplinary aspect contributed to students' enjoyment, and allowed them to get involved with a larger group of people. The teaching and assessment methods allowed for new and different approaches to biliteracy, and results show that the use of new strategies is a welcome development for students in higher education. Though a substantial amount of time and effort needs to be invested firstly to create interdisciplinary modules, and then to evaluate and adapt the modules accordingly, positive student responses suggest that such investment is worthwhile.

Further investigation should be made into the general support that students on all Welsh-medium modules are given when working in two (or more) languages. More focused research is also needed within single subject disciplines as biliteracy is increasingly becoming integral to the development of teaching and assessment methods and is a crucial component of pedagogical philosophy.

Notes

(1) For further details, see www.bangor.ac.uk/music/undergraduate-modules/WXC-1001
(2) For further details, see http://www.bangor.ac.uk/so/undergraduate-modules/SCU-1001
(3) For further details see http://www.bangor.ac.uk/canolfanbedwyr/index.php.en

References

Adeyemni, D. (2010) Justification of a multidisciplinary approach to teaching language in Botswana junior secondary schools. *The Journal of Language, Technology & Entrepreneurship in Africa* 2 (1), 8–20.

Andrews, H. (2011) Llais y dysgwr: Profiadau oedolion sydd yn dysgu Cymraeg yng ngogledd Cymru. *Gwerddon* 9, 37–58.

Baker, C. (1993) Bilingual education in Wales. In H. Baetens Beardsmore (ed.) *European Models of Bilingual Education* (pp. 7–29). Clevedon: Multilingual Matters.

Bangor University (2013) *Bangor University Welsh Language Scheme: Prepared in Accordance with the Welsh Language Act 1993.* See www.bangor.ac.uk/canolfanbedwyr/pdf/LS_Saesneg_2013.pdf (accessed March 2015).

Bryman, A. (2008) *Social Research Methods.* Oxford: Oxford University Press.

Carey, M. (2009) *The Social Work Dissertation: Using Small-Scale Qualitative Methodology.* Maidenhead: Open University Press.

Clapham, J. (2012) Dadansoddiad o ddefnydd athrawon dan hyfforddiant o gyfnewid cod mewn dosbarth uwchradd dwyieithog: Achos o Gymru. *Gwerddon* 10/11, 159–195.

Coleg Cymraeg Cenedlaethol (2014a) *What is the Coleg Cymraeg Cenedlaethol?* See www.colegcymraeg.ac.uk/en/media/main/pdfs/informationleaflets/CCC_GeneralLeaflet_2014_English_pdf (accessed March 2015).

Coleg Cymraeg Cenedlaethol (2014b) *Undergraduate Prospectus.* See www.colegcymraeg.ac.uk/en/media/main/pdfs/CCC_EnglishProspectus_2014.pdf (accessed March 2015).

Davies, A.J. and Trystan, D. (2012) 'Build it and they shall come?' an evaluation of qualitative evidence relating to student choice and Welsh-medium higher education. *International Journal of Bilingual Education and Bilingualism* 15 (2), 147–164.

Flowerdew, J. and Li, Y. (2007) Plagiarism and second language writing in an electronic age. *Annual Review of Applied Linguistics* 27, 161–183.

García, O. (2009) Education, multilingualism and translanguaging in the 21st century. In A. Mohanty, M. Panda, R. Phillipson and T. Skutnabb-Kangas (eds) *Multilingual Education for Social Justice: Globalising the Local* (pp. 140–158). New Delhi: Orient Blackswan.

Grout, D. and Palisca, C. (1997) *Hanes Cerddoriaeth y Gorllewin.* Cardiff: Gwasg Prifysgol Cymru.

Guarda, M. (2012) Computer-Mediated-Communication and Foreign Language Education, *Journal of E-Learning and Knowledge Society* 8 (3), 15–37.

Hibbert, L. and Van der Walt, C. (2014) Biliteracy and translanguaging pedagogy in South Africa: An Overview. In L. Hibbert and C. Van der Walt (eds) *Multilingual Universities in South Africa: Reflecting Society in Higher Education* (pp. 3–14). Bristol: Multilingual Matters.

Higher Education Funding Council for Wales (2004) *Steering Group for Welsh medium provision in higher education.* See www.hefcw.ac.uk/documents/policy_areas/welsh_medium/Strategy%20for%20Strat%20Fmwk%20page.pdf (accessed March 2015).

Hodges, Rh. (2012) Welsh-medium education and parental incentives: The case of the Rhymni Valley, Caerffili. *International Journal of Bilingual Education and Bilingualism* 15 (3), 355–373.

Hornberger, N. (2007) Biliteracy, transnationalism, multimodality, and identity: Trajectories across time and space. *Lingust Educ.* doi:10.1016/j.linged.2007.10.001.

Hornberger, N. and Link, H. (2012) Translanguaging in today's classrooms: A biliteracy lens. *Theory Into Practice* 51 (4), 239–247.

Huang, G.G. (1995) Self-reported biliteracy and self-esteem: A study of Mexican American 8th graders. *Applied Psycholinguistics* 16, 271–291.

Jones, B. (2010) Amrywiaeth Caleidosgopig: Addysg ddwyieithog yng Nghymru heddiw. *Gwerddon* 5, 9–26.

Jones, G.R. (2010) 'Factors influencing choice of higher education in Wales', *Contemporary Wales* 23 (1), 93–116.

Julian, K., O'Sullivan, P.S., Vener, H.H. and Wamsley, M.A. (2007) Teaching residents to teach: The impact of a multi-disciplinary longitudinal curriculum to improve teaching skills. *Med Educ Online* 12, 12.

King, C.J. (2010) *The Multidisciplinary Imperative in Higher Education.* Research & Occasional Paper Series: Centre for Studies in Higher Education. See http://cshe.berkeley.edu/sites/default/files/shared/publications/docs/ROPS.%20King.Multidisciplinary.9.13.10.pdf (accessed March 2015).

Kitzinger, J. (1995) Qualitative Research: Introducing focus groups. *British Medical Journal* 311, 299–302.

Knapp, A. (2014) Language choice and the construction of knowledge in higher education. *European Journal of Applied Linguistics* 2 (2), 165–203.

Lea, M.R. and Street, B.V. (2006) The 'Academic Literacies' model: Theory and applications. *Theory Into Practice* 45 (4), 368–377.

Lewis, G. (2011) Addysg Ddwyieithog yn yr unfed ganrif ar hugain: Adolygu'r cyd-destun rhyngwladol. *Gwerddon* 7, 66–88.

Malarz, L. (1998) *Bilingual Education: Effective Programming for Language-Minority Students* in Curriculum Handbook (Association for Supervision and Curriculum Development). See http://www.ascd.org/publications/curriculum_handbook/413/chapters/Bilingual_Education@_Effective_Programming_for_Language-Minority_Students.aspx (accessed March 2015).

Office for National Statistics (2011) *Census: Key Statistics for Wales.* See http://ons.gov.uk/ons/rel/census/2011-census/key-statistics-for-unitary-authorities-in-wales/stb-2011-census-key-statistics-for-wales.html (acessed March 2015).

Pecorari, D. and Petric, B. (2014) Plagiarism in second-language writing. *Language Teaching* 47 (3), 269–302.

Prior, L., Wood, F., Lewis, G. and Pill, R. (2003) Stigma revisited: Disclosure of emotional problems in primary care in Wales. *Social Science and Medicine* 56, 2191–2200.

Reyes, I. (2006) Exploring connections between emergent biliteracy and bilingualism. *Journal of Early Childhood Literacy* 6 (3), 267–292.

Robert, E. (2009) Accommodating new speakers? An attitudinal investigation of L2 speakers of Welsh in south-east Wales. *International Journal of the Sociology of Language* 195, 93–115.

Street, B. (2011) 'New Literacy Studies and the Continua of Biliteracy' In F. Hult and K. King (eds) *Educational Linguistics in Practice: Applying the Local Globally and the Global Locally.* Bristol: Multilingual Matters.

Thomas, H. and Williams, C.H. (eds) (2013) *Parent, Personalities and Power: Welsh-Medium Schools in South-East Wales.* Cardiff: University of Wales Press.

Welsh Government (2010) *Welsh-Medium Education Strategy.* See from gov.wales/docs/dcells/publications/100420welshmediumstrategyen.pdf (accessed March 2015).

Welsh Government (2013) *National Literacy and Numeracy Framework*. See learning.wales. gov.uk/docs/learningwales/publications/130415-Inf-guidance-en.pdf (accessed March 2015).

Welsh Government and Welsh Language Commissioner (2015) *Welsh Language Use in Wales 2013–2015*. Cardiff: Welsh Government and Welsh Language Commissioner.

Williams, C. (1994) Arfarniad o ddulliau dysgu ac addysgu yng nghyd-destun addysg uwchradd ddwyieithog. Unpublished PhD thesis. Bangor: University of Wales.

Wyn, H. (2006) *Ble wyt ti rhwng? Hanes canu poblogaidd Cymraeg 1980–2000*. Talybont: Y Lolfa.

9 Bilingual Academic Literacies for Chinese Language Teachers

Danping Wang

Introduction

Research on Chinese as a foreign language (CFL) education has prolifer-ated in academic journals in step with the rapid development of Chinese language education from kindergarten to university level in many parts of the world (Scrimgeour, 2014; Wang, 2007; Zhang & Li, 2010). In the most recent decade, Chinese scholars seeking academic positions and promotions in China have started to need a sound track record of publishing in both Chinese and English with reputable international publishers (Li, 2006; Shi, 2002). In recent years, a few new bilingual and peer-reviewed journals launched by Western publishers have aiming to attract research articles on CFL teaching and learning (e.g. *Chinese as a Second Language Research* by De Gruyter). This has created new opportunities for CFL teachers to publish in their native language at international level. CFL teachers find it an urgent challenge to develop sufficient bilingual literacy to allow them to read, write and publish scholarly work in both local and international journals. The challenge to them is multi-fold, as they need to develop and maintain special-ist literacy skills in both Chinese and English while demonstrating a good standard of research abilities in the two academic discourse communities. To understand their efforts and struggles, this study investigated bilingual scholars' understanding of academic literacies and the factors that influence their linguistic choices. Adopting a narrative approach, the study examined three native Chinese-speaking CFL teachers who returned to China after obtaining their research degrees in the West.

That the importance of English publishing is influencing scholars' aca-demic lives in the 'Expanding Circle' context is well documented (e.g. Canagarajah, 2002; Lillis & Curry, 2010). As members of an emerging profes-sion, CFL teachers have to deal with changes in academic norms, cultural values, and conflicting ideological, social and educational standards.

Globalization has brought new challenges in foreign language teaching and teachers' education in general (Kramsch, 2014). One of the most important aspects highlighted in recent literature is to integrate research into teachers' activity (Bates, 2008). As Malinen *et al.* (2012) point out, a research-based approach to teachers' education could help pre-service teachers internalise a research-oriented attitude towards their work. More importantly, teachers equipped with research skills are more prone to adopt 'an analytical and open-minded approach to the work, drawing conclusions based on observations and experiences, and develop teaching and learning environments in a systematic way' (Malinen *et al.*, 2012: 574). Nevertheless, research methodologies and academic writing are not necessarily an integral part of learning content for CFL teachers during their Master or PhD programmes in China. In a recent study, Wang *et al.* (2013) examined the Beijing curriculum for Chinese language teachers' education programmes at the postgraduate level, which focused primarily on introducing general language theories and Chinese linguistics. In order to accelerate their career development and mobility, many young native Chinese teachers educated in China are searching for alternative ways to improve their research skills (e.g. to collaborate with overseas scholars or to obtain another research degree, preferably in English-speaking countries). As a result, there is an increasing number of CFL teachers choosing to further their studies in research universities outside China where foreign language education research is more developed (Singh, 2013; Singh & Han, 2009), and educational theories and research methodologies are integrated (Singh & Cui, 2011).

Previous studies have indicated that the lack of both English language proficiency and knowledge of foreign language teaching and learning theories is one of the major challenges faced by CFL teachers. For instance, focusing on CFL teachers' language choices for classroom teaching, Wang and Kirkpatrick's study (2012) confirmed that teachers' English literacy played an important role in engaging international students in active classroom learning and improving their professional development. English was the only foreign language for the majority of CFL teachers, so many rely on English to get access to new theories and knowledge in language education research. However, their English proficiency varies, which prevents them from achieving excellent teaching performance and fulfilling personal career aspirations. For example, Ruan (2013) found that teachers' English posed challenges to this pedagogical initiative because they were not always able to frame activities for their students in English as part of an attempt to introduce a tasked-based teaching approach in beginners' Chinese classes in Denmark. Teachers used 'big English words' such as 'emperor', whereas Danish students only understood 'king'. Similarly, in Australia, Orton (2008) reported that over 90% of CFL teachers were ethnically Chinese and born and educated in Mainland China (Orton, 2011: 153), where English was taught for examination success at the cost of low intercultural understanding. Their insufficient English ability was identified as one of the major causes of a very high attrition rate among students in Australia. As

Orton (2008) noted, '94% of the Chinese learners drop out before Year 12, usually once the language is no longer mandated' (p. 5). Despite an increasing number of studies on CFL teaching and learning, there is little research specifically looking at the English literacy of CFL teachers, and even less attention has been given to their long-term bilingual literacy development.

In this study, I will firstly outline the research subjects' everyday language choices in their research activities, and secondly identify factors that have influenced their language choices. Moreover, I will briefly compare the writing samples offered by research participants to understand their perceived differences between Chinese and English writing conventions. At the end of the paper, I will give some suggestions for enhancing academic literacies for bilingual or multilingual scholars.

Bilingual Academic Literacies as Social Practices

Bilingual literacies refer to the conjunction of literacy and bilingualism, indicating that literacy-related knowledge – genre, linguistic, cognitive, socio-cultural understanding – can be an integral part of bilingual proficiency (Hornberger, 2003: 3). Bilingual academic literacies refer to 'the ability to use two languages for the purposes of generating, interpreting and/or analysing evidence' (Singh & Cui, 2011: 539). In brief, bilingual academic literacies are the ability to use two languages for academic purposes. According to sociocultural theory, academic literacies (like other literacies) are social practices, subject to the influence of a specific, local socio-political context (Street, 1984; Lillis & Curry, 2006). Many social factors contribute to shaping one's academic literacy, involving both visible and invisible settings. As Gentil (2005: 433) argues:

> The contexts of biliteracy include not only the physical, material, visible settings within which individuals engage in communication in particular languages in or around writing, but also the personal subjective, and intersubjective perspectives or orientations within which each individual evaluates and responds to the interactional, institutional, and societal contexts of biliteracy.

Bilingual academic literacies are constructed and developed over a long course of practices within a bilingual discourse world where people have to constantly balance and negotiate their literacy knowledge in the first language (L1) and the second language (L2). Ideally, a bilingual or multilingual society would provide better social conditions for children to develop a more balanced bilingual literacy. As academic writers assess and adjust strategies, focuses, interests and rewards depending on the communities for which they write, Curry and Lillis (2004) argue that it is important to take account of social situations, which influence every aspect of the participants' understanding of academic literacies. However, language choice for academic writing and publishing is never neutral. For bilingual scholars, it is English literacy that is often being added to, or eventually replacing, one's L1 literacy (Gentil, 2005, 2011), which sometimes can lead to confusion or tensions.

With the rise of China's soft power, the Chinese government has been seeking opportunities to earn the Chinese language a prominent status on a par with English. The most conspicuous attempt that China has made to promote the use of Chinese in academic areas is the rapid spread of Confucius Institutes across the world. Over the last decade, up to December 2015, 500 Confucius Institutes (each in collaboration with a local university) and 1002 Confucius Classrooms (each in collaboration with a local school) have been established in 134 countries and regions (Hanban, 2016). Meanwhile, the Chinese government has been very alert to the influence of English and possible 'infiltration of Western ideas' into Chinese society, particularly in higher education (The Wall Street Journal, 2015). The last ten years have witnessed several national campaigns on 'Saving Chinese from English' in order to bolster Chinese language pride and national cohesion (The Economist, 2010). Huang Youyi, the then director of the China International Publishing Group, proposed taking preventive measures to preserve the purity of Chinese at the 2010 Chinese People's Political Consultative Conference, as China Daily reported (2010):

> Huang Youyi: If we do not pay attention and don't take measures to stop the growth in the mingling of Chinese and English, Chinese won't be a pure language in a couple of years... In the long run, Chinese will lose its role as an independent linguistic system for passing on information and expressing human feelings.

Following this meeting, commonly used English acronyms such as *GDP*, *WTO* and *NBA* were banned from appearing in Chinese media, and English numbering systems such as a), b), c), d) were replaced by the Chinese Heavenly-Stems system – 甲乙丙丁. In academic writing, mixing codes of English in Chinese text has often been regarded as intolerably 'polluting' the purity of the Chinese language (Yan & Deng, 2009). In such studies, English was judged by politicians to be a threat to the Chinese language and even harmful to national cohesion. Ironically, English is taught throughout the educational system in China from grade one in primary school, and even in kindergarten, up to university level, and has been widely adopted as a medium of instruction in elite Chinese universities in order to gain international prestige (Kirkpatrick, 2011). In the context of CFL education and research in China, Wang and Kirkpatrick (2012) investigated the impact of the official policy of monolingualism on teachers' language choices in four leading universities in Beijing. Some participants supported monolingualism in teaching practice, while others expressed the urgent demand for using English to achieve promotion, career mobility and international recognition.

Bilingual Literacy as Professional Aspirations

Among many genres of academic writing, the peer-reviewed research journal article is the primary model for validating research achievements and legitimating new knowledge across fields. There is consensus among academics in the West that one's scholarly worth is evaluated according to the number of research journal articles one has managed to get published (Canagarajah, 2002). As the means of gatekeeping of knowledge in each discipline, research articles enable researchers to secure academic positions and promotions. Publishing research articles in recognized journals is the primary professional aspiration for many scholars within the academic culture.

The 'Center/Periphery' paradigm is frequently used in academic literacies research to demonstrate the differences of power and resources of academic discursive practices at local and global level. For individual CFL teachers, there is a tension in the power relations between knowledge construction in Chinese and in English. Today, English is the most important language in academic publication, accounting for about 75% of all articles abstracted (Canagarajah, 2002: 35). Research journal articles in other languages inevitably lose their visibility and accessibility to mainstream disciplinary communities. Although it is often taken for granted that Chinese scholars should primarily write to the Chinese academic community in Chinese, CFL involves a good deal of common areas with other foreign language teaching and learning, such as English as a Foreign Language education. As a new discipline, CFL scholars write to offer new perspectives on the basis of much existing literature on foreign language education or to theorise new concepts with distinctive observations. That is to say, despite the fact that Chinese language education research addresses questions of close concern to Chinese academic communities, Chinese scholars are still motivated to publish their work in English-medium journals in the hope of being recognised for their professional achievements by a larger readership in the 'Center'. For CFL scholars who attained research degrees from English-speaking countries, publishing in Chinese academic communities may position their work only at a local level and give it only peripheral status. Publishing in English, on the contrary, would help increase the perceived importance of CFL research, and make their works more likely to be read by scholars in English language academic communities.

Bilingual academic literacies are the norm in many universities around the world (Singh & Cui, 2011). Much discussion has taken place about the linguistic interdependence hypothesis, which strongly argues that academic skills developed in one language can be transferred to or coordinated with another (Cummins & Swain, 1986). As Bell (1995) stated,

> the development of initial literacy in any language inevitably stimulates such cognitive change as the ability to differentiate between text and meaning [and] such learning will be carried over to any subsequent literacies. (p. 687)

Nevertheless, research examining bilingual scholars' L1 and L2 writing practices is kept separate as two independent research domains, although many studies claim to have focused on bilingual or multilingual academic writing (e.g. Cho, 2010). As Gentil (2011) has pointed out, bilingual literacy is used to refer to academic writing ability acquired by L2 learners of English, assuming that one's L1 academic literacy is well established. Current studies on academic writing focus overwhelmingly on developing English academic writing, rather than addressing the needs of bilingual children and scholars who must write frequently and alternatively in two or even more languages.

Cho (2010) interviewed four Korean scholars in faculty positions in Korea and the United States, using narrative inquiry to examine their bilingual academic literacy identities. Participants in the study admitted that there has been very little instruction in academic writing in Korean. They tended to believe that Korean was not the language for academic writing and therefore they used Korean merely for email exchanges with friends and families. The study showed that bilingual literacy development requires tremendous individual agency in deciding when and which language to use for what writing purposes. Unlike these Korean participants, who were trained in a non-language related discipline, CFL professionals are language teachers whose research areas are directly connected to both the L1 and L2 of learners. In order to participate in both local and international academic communities, bilingual CFL teachers need to read and write regularly in two languages in order to maintain their bilingual literacy for teaching and research.

There appears to be very little literature up to now on how foreign language teachers respond to the global demands to become proficient in bilingual academic writing and publishing. Due to the internationalisation of China's higher education, there are many excellent, prolific Chinese scholars writing high quality academic articles in English on subjects related to science and technology in and outside China (Li, 2006). Similarly, Chinese language teachers have also seen the importance of writing for international readers in order to voice a Chinese perspective in language teaching research. It appears that Chinese language teachers need to develop bilingual research literacies in order to fulfill their immediate local commitments and long-term career pursuits. Therefore, it is important to know how such teachers develop bilingual research literacy in their everyday research activities. Specifically, the study sought to answer three research questions:

(1) What are bilingual teachers' language choices for academic activities?
(2) What are the factors influencing their bilingual academic literacies development?
(3) What are their perceptions about the differences in Chinese and English writing conventions?

Research Design

This study adopted an interpretive perspective to examine bilingual teachers/scholars' academic literacies practices. In order to obtain a holistic view of their bilingual research practice and experience, this study used a narrative approach to examine three native Chinese-speaking CFL teachers from three top universities in Mainland China. In applied linguistics research, narrative studies have emerged as a new method of data collection and analysis particularly with language learners and teachers (Barkhuizen *et al.*, 2013). It is argued that this is because narratives can retain the concreteness and complexity of knowledge, making this open to further interpretation and creative theorisation (Canagarajah, 1996). In teacher education and development, participating in narrative research also supports:

> opening up the meaningfulness of teachers' experiences to social influence; when teacher educators have access to a teachers' internal cognitive struggles as they are unfolding, this allows them to calibrate their mediation to address the teachers' immediate needs and/or concerns. (Johnson & Golombek, 2013: 87)

In this sense, narrative data from teachers participating in this study have not only enabled me to gain a fuller picture of their everyday language choices but also enriched my understanding of their struggles over multifaceted factors that influence their language practices.

The three participants were invited to share their stories and experiences of language use for research purposes, in particular reading and writing. The three participants were chosen because (1) they are able to read and write in both English and Chinese for academic purposes; (2) they have the goal of developing bilingual academic literacies; and (3) they have at least one degree from China and one from a Western education system. The age range of the three teacher participants was from 31 to 46, and they were all currently working as faculty members, after returning from overseas with a postgraduate degree. Among them, two were female and one was male. All participant names used here are pseudonyms. Their personal information can be seen in Table 9.1.

All participants chose to use Chinese in interviews because they believed it was 'more comfortable' for them to talk in the shared language to another native Chinese speaker (i.e. the interviewer). Each participant was interviewed for no less than 80 minutes. Interview recordings were firstly transcribed verbatim into Chinese and then translated into English for analysis. The data analysis adopted a structural coding method, which allowed the researcher to quickly access data that are more likely to be relevant to a particular analysis in order to generate frequently appearing themes (Saldaña, 2013: 84). A structural code was assigned to each particular question. This

Table 9.1 Personal information

Surname	Gender	Age	Qualifications	Experience of studying abroad	Position
ZHANG	M	46	PhD in Linguistics MA in English BA in English	Four years of PhD in the UK	Associate Professor
TAN	F	39	PhD in Linguistics MA in Linguistics BA in Chinese	Three years of PhD in the UK	Associate Professor
CHEN	F	31	MEd in Education BA in English	Two years of MEd in Canada	Lecturer

structural coding analysis was more suitable for the identification of large segments of texts from interview transcripts, and these segments formed the basis for an in-depth analysis within or across topics and were helpful for follow-up analysis.

Language Choice

Participants were firstly asked to describe their daily scholarly life and research activities in a number of aspects, including reading, writing, participating in workshops/seminars/conferences, email, telephone, online or face-to-face communication for research purposes. Following this, they were invited to explain why they would prefer to use the chosen language for particular activities. All participants admitted that they used a substantial amount of Chinese for daily research activities after returning to China. As native Chinese scholars who were educated in the Chinese education system long before they went abroad to study in English-speaking countries, they had developed solid literacy skills in reading and writing Chinese for general purposes. However, regarding academic literacy, none of them reported formally learning the genre in Chinese and there were some signs of low confidence in writing Chinese articles for publication. For instance, Chen, whose first degree in China was followed by a Master's degree in Canada, found herself feeling helpless when writing her first paper for CSSCI journals (Chinese Social Science Cited Index). She continued to use English for academic reading and writing, and Chinese mostly for communication with colleagues in her Department and for conference presentations in China. When asked about her Chinese academic writing experience, Chen expressed her worries that not having enough formal Chinese academic writing training would affect her professional identity as a Chinese language teacher:

I can't think of any formal instruction in academic writing in Chinese. I really hope there can be a workshop to teach us how to write academically for publishing articles in Chinese journals. [...] After I came back, I had a culture shock in my own country as I find I cannot write in Chinese for research purposes as comfortably as I do in English. (Chen)

Chen's stories bore some resemblance to academic writing studies with immigrant students in the UK or US who have acquired good academic literacy in English but suffered from L1 deficiency/attrition (Cho, 2010; Shi, 2002). She continued,

It was not a problem before, but I constantly feel it has become a professional deficiency for me as a Chinese language teacher in China. [...] I have studied the style and structure of Chinese academic writing by myself, but I am still not feeling confident. (Chen)

What is worth noting here is the perceived consequences of having insufficient proficiency in Chinese, which weakened Chen's professional identity as a native Chinese language teacher. On another informal occasion, Chen mentioned that China's higher education system has become more interested in hiring Western-trained scholars with excellent English literacy skills, who were able to make immediate contributions at the international level on behalf of the local university. However, as Chen revealed, most of her returnee fellows had taken a considerably long time to acquire sufficient Chinese academic literacy to compete with local educated peers in Chinese publications.

As distinct from Chen, Tan showed more confidence in her Chinese academic writing ability, though she also disclosed that she had had few training opportunities in Chinese academic writing. Tan used Chinese more for reading and writing but less for conference presentations. As she explained,

It is much easier for me to read and write in Chinese. I learned it simply through reading other people's articles. You just keep writing and writing. (Tan)

Language is not a problem. It is the way we conceptualise ideas. When I first came back, I had a long time translating my ideas from English to Chinese; it took me a long time to figure out the Chinese way of conceptualizing my paper. (Tan)

As can be seen from Tan's response, she thought that native Chinese speakers' academic writing skills could be acquired through modelling sample papers without explicit instruction. For example, she revealed in the interview that she always needed to translate her ideas from English into Chinese because she was trained to conceptualize a research paper in English. This was also echoed in Shi's (2001) study with returned scholars from Western institutions, whose research paradigms and academic thinking were initially developed in English (p. 627). Tan also believed that Chinese teachers must become 'experts in reading and writing Chinese', and be able to produce high quality pieces of work to 'strengthen the Chinese academic community'. Her career mission was also shared by Zhang, in terms of promoting the sense of responsibility for constructing knowledge in Chinese:

> I wouldn't advise young scholars to spend too much time on English writing. Instead, I would encourage them to use English as a tool to express Chinese ideas. Let Chinese voices be heard through English. There are many important works to do in Chinese, but our students are all too busy with passing English exams.

After four years of PhD study in the UK, Zhang argued very strongly for the importance of developing balanced bilingual academic literacy for Chinese teachers to construct knowledge in English as well as Chinese. He recalled from his days in the UK that language education research was largely Eurocentric. He pointed out that the invisibility of Chinese voices in the international foreign language education research community could further marginalise local knowledge. Regarding academic literacy practices, Zhang read in both English and Chinese, but wrote mostly in Chinese after he returned to China. For keeping an international research profile, he used English for developing networks with friends and research collaborators in overseas. Zhang was very fluent in English, but he believed that he would prefer, if possible, to give presentations in Chinese instead of English because he regarded it as a responsibility for scholars from China to promote the use of Chinese as much as possible.

Notably, Tan and Chen both expressed an increasing anxiety about losing their English academic literacy. They saw English as highly valued 'cultural capital' to distinguish international scholars from local ones in China's higher education. They also argued that the key to gaining access to the international research community was English academic literacy. For example,

> The longer I teach here and do my daily admin job, the more fear I have of losing my English literacy. I subscribed to two English radio podcasts, and I read English news every day to keep my English skills. I want to get a PhD from Canada or US. (Chen)

> There is not as much English exposure as I had when I was abroad, so I must keep reading and writing in English whenever I have time. [...] My next career plan is to find an opportunity to work as a director in a Confucius Institute in the UK. (Tan)

Clearly, their long-term career aspirations were related to increasing their professional recognition at the international level. Being able to read and write in English for research purposes was regarded as one of the most desirable language skills for Chinese language teachers to secure higher faculty positions, opportunities to teach abroad or run a Confucius Institute as a director and so forth. In this study, the three participants all stated clearly that English was the most important linguistic capital for their career development. Zhang also shared this view:

> English is definitely an edge, an asset for all of us. Without English, we wouldn't be able to have opportunities to study abroad, let alone having a good job in a good university. (Zhang)

It is very clear that participants all understood very well that English literacy is critical to their career development. Chinese teachers have perceived an undisputed trend for English to be one of the fundamental language tools to internationalise knowledge in the discipline of Chinese language teaching. However, participants also mentioned that 'English capital' was not always readily available for many Chinese scholars, due to limited internet freedom, the high price of English academic books and the lack of full subscriptions to academic journal databases such as ProQuest, JSTOR, Elsevier and the like. I observed quite a number of photocopied versions of English books in the three participants' offices. Their choices of language for research related activities were very different from each other. The following section will discuss the factors influencing their language choices.

Factors Influencing Bilingual Academic Literacies Development

Three major common categories emerged illustrating the factors that influenced participants' language choice for academic purposes: sociolinguistic context, professional community and personal experience. Under each category, there were sub-categories that further explained the factors that exert influence in bilingual scholars' academic literacies practices and development (see Figure 9.1).

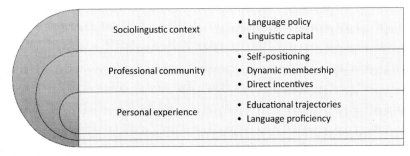

Figure 9.1 Factors that influenced teachers' bilingual academic literacy development

Sociolinguistic context

The sociolinguistic environment of the three participants' workplaces was almost exclusively monolingual in Chinese. Their faculty libraries have a wealth of Chinese collections, and their offices have a lot more Chinese reading materials and documents than English ones. Interestingly, however, the public Information Boards in the faculty's buildings had as many English posters and notes as Chinese ones. English notes were mostly for the benefit of beginning Chinese learners whose Chinese proficiency remained limited in reading important notifications in Chinese. Other English posts were posters for academic conferences to be held outside China. Overseas return-ees might have been prompted by the monolingual environment to alter their language choices to fit into the home academic culture from the day they started working in their faculties.

In view of the increasing nationalism and language pride in Chinese, the study confirmed the influence of social language attitudes on CFL teachers' language choices in teaching and research (Wang, 2014). The ability to use Chinese without mixing any foreign codes was considered a basic require-ment for CFL teachers to demonstrate their professional legitimacy as good Chinese language teachers. Codemixing, codemeshing or translanguaging was strongly discouraged (Canagarajah, 2011):

> I noticed that Taiwan scholars like to give English translations to Chinese terms, which is good for us to see the English origin of the term. When I published my first article in China, I was asked to minimise the number of English references and remove all English terms. What also bothered me was the English font in Chinese publications. For a long time, the English letters were always squeezed together like alien codes. (Zhang)

In the interview, Zhang shared an unpleasant experience of publishing a Chinese article with English annotations and references ten years ago. As he recalled, Chinese authors were often asked by journal editors to take out the English terms from their papers owing to 'typesetting difficulties'. A deep-rooted linguistic purism and lack of typographic technology have contributed to keeping English and Chinese codes partitioned in one paper. In recent years, despite the fact that an increasing number of English references were cited in Chinese journals, the English font problem continues to challenge readers.

Professional community

The study observed participants' personal efforts in developing Chinese literacy and English literacy at the same time for professional development. For some, it seemed common sense that for Chinese language teachers in China, Chinese academic literacy should enjoy primacy at the local level; however, others disagreed. First of all, teachers' different self-positioning in their careers may lead to different language choices for academic writing and publishing:

> I have published a few Chinese papers already, so my current writing plan is to publish one or two good English papers on Chinese linguistics in international journals. (Zhang)

> I have no CSSCI paper published in Chinese so far. I must first get known in China. (Chen)

Their professional positioning decided their choice of language. Zhang positioned himself as an international scholar, with a professional obligation to introduce Chinese knowledge to the global readership. In contrast, Chen, as a young scholar, found it urgent to establish her professional expertise as a scholar in CFL research at the local level after she returned from Canada as a student. She also realised the importance of 'getting known' in Chinese academic communities to help her secure promotion opportunities.

Efforts to maintain a dual professional membership in two academic communities were also found to be vital to long-term career development for participants. Being able to obtain and eventually maintain such membership was subject to the number of publications that a scholar has authored in a particular language. In the interviews, participants constantly made comparisons between the size and culture of the Chinese-medium academic community and the English one.

> The Chinese academic community is pretty small. I will strengthen my participation in the English academic world after I am settled in the Chinese community. (Chen)

> There is a long way for Chinese scholars to go if we want to publish in the top English journals. I hope I can publish one or two next year. But at the same time, I need to continue writing as many Chinese articles as possible. (Zhang)

> It takes more effort to publish a Chinese paper because there is only a handful of good Chinese journals. Although I want to publish more in Chinese, I do not always have the luxury of time. The opportunity cost is too high. (Tan)

The three participants, though at different career stages, were all managing to maintain and develop a dual professional membership. Lastly, direct incentives were identified in the study as another factor which motivated participants to use English for academic writing. Speaking about his own experience, Zhang gave an example of how Chinese and English publications were valued in China's universities:

> Now the situation is interesting – to publish in English, you get a handsome cash reward; to publish in Chinese, you have to pay page charges to the journal. Then how can we encourage our own young graduates and Chinese scholars to write in Chinese for publication? (Zhang)

These cash rewards, as explained by Zhang, consisted of money given by faculties to authors who published research papers, preferably in English SSCI journals with high impact factors. In contrast, some local Chinese journals required page charges even before the papers were taken for review by the journal editor. In a sense, Zhang's comments pointed to the fact that the overall publication culture in China's academic communities might be unfavourable to encouraging scholars to be devoted to Chinese writing and publishing (Shi *et al.*, 2005). Moreover, the insufficient number of academic Chinese journals had to some extent failed to accommodate the boom in CFL education research. The recent rise of China's economy has greatly increased the country's soft power in culture and language (Wang & Adamson, 2014; Zhao & Huang, 2010). Zhang also commented that this was 'the best time' for China to seize the opportunity to encourage quality participation in the international research community.

Personal experience

Teachers' educational backgrounds, particularly their knowledge of research methodology and ethics, were found to be affecting their participation in academic writing. In this study, the three participants reported first studying research methodologies during the time they were abroad, which enabled them to collect and analyse data following standard procedures. Speaking of their research colleagues in China, they were all aware of various degrees of knowledge of research methods and ethics.

> One time, a reviewer asked me to remove the part about data collection from my paper. He thought it was not important for a linguistic study. (Tan)

> At a conference last month, I can't believe I heard a Chinese scholar say that research methodology was nothing but a 'Western concept'. (Chen)

Tan's and Chen's story showed that the lack of proper knowledge and attitudes towards research methodology in the local community might have left Chinese-medium only publications in a marginalised corner. Tan found it very important to present data with proper acknowledgement of the sources. Clearly, different personal educational trajectories and research training may introduce different research paradigms and different levels of familiarity with research design. However, apart from those who were trained overseas, based on the three participants' observation, a good number of current CFL scholars have never had proper training in research skills and ethics in their PhD programmes in China.

In the meantime, the three teachers frankly expressed concerns that their English proficiency was not adequate for them to write effortlessly. English was the L2 of the three participants, who were born and educated in China during their formative years. Even though they learned research skills through English while they were abroad for a few years, reading and writing in English remained less developed than in their native language. For example, Chen argued it was necessary to learn how to write research proposals in English for collaborations with friends from overseas. Zhang was looking for new strategies to improve his reading comprehension of academic English articles because he was exploring new theories in linguistic studies. 'Now I understand what life-long learning is', said Chen in the interview to describe her determination to develop balanced bilingual academic literacies.

Perceived Differences in English and Chinese Writing Conventions

In order to understand how the participants in this study perceive writing conventions in Chinese and English, this study elicited their ideas by inviting them to comment on their own writings. Firstly, they were asked to describe the differences they perceived in academic writing in Chinese and English. Following this, they were invited to select one example of their publications in a Chinese-medium journal and one in an English-medium journal to demonstrate the perceived differences. Differences at discourse level mentioned by the participants are shown in Table 9.2. It is worth noting that the results were based on participants' perceptions in this study only, which do not necessarily reflect objective linguistic or broader social differences.

These perceived differences seem to have shaped the participants' views of publishable content. Participants perceived these as underlying publishing requirements, epistemological paradigms and communicative conventions, established by a broader research community that the authors felt they belonged to or were familiar with.

At the sentence level, participants' mentioned difficulties for them in knowledge construction and transfer when introducing and translating new concepts into each academic community. The study presented a few examples to briefly illustrate the difference in perceived conventions. In order to

Table 9.2 Perceived textual conventions of Chinese and English academic writing

Chinese	English
Subtle	Straightforward
Less structured	Structured (e.g. problem, method, results, implications)
Suggestive ideas	Explicit, clear ideas
Implicit logical structure	Use of logic markers (e.g. therefore, however)

protect participants' confidentiality, the following extracts were slightly modified.

> …提出教师职业发展应该注重 "三教" 问题。

> …proposed that the teacher's professional education should focus on 'Three Jiao' problems.

This Chinese sentence was extracted from an abstract of a research article. As the journal editor asked the participant to provide an English abstract at the end of the article, the participant translated the Chinese one into English. The participant found it particularly difficult to translate a well-established Chinese abstract to English because she felt she had to create new terms in English. However, the Chinese 三教 (Sān Jiào) was an abbreviated term representing Jiào Shī (Teacher), Jiào Cái (Textbook) and Jiào Fǎ (Teaching method). The participant further commented that

> English seems not to encourage this type of term construction. I translated 三教 (Sān Jiào) to 'Three Jiao' but I doubt its acceptability in English. I have thought about 'Three T', which seems even worse.

The participant hesitated and questioned the legitimacy of the new knowledge she had personally constructed in English. The three participants had all had experience of thinking or conceptualising in English while writing in Chinese. The two examples below were extracted from participants' manuscripts to illustrate how English has affected their Chinese writing.

> 学生可以学习更多, 了解更多, 收获更多。

> Students can learn more, know more and harvest more.

Clearly, to Chinese speakers, the participant was thinking in English when she was writing in Chinese. She used 更多 as an adverb to translate and replace 'more' in English. In the manuscript, I noticed that this sentence had been later changed to 学生可以学习和了解更多的相关知识, 有更多的收获 [Students can learn more related knowledge and reap more benefit], where "更多" was used as an adjective rather than an adverb, and objects were also complemented. The revised sentence, as commented on by the participant, made her feel 'more comfortable' when she read her paper in Chinese. In another example, the participant seemed to have translated the English sentence into Chinese without amending the word order:

> 一般的检测手段不能胜任排除无关变量 〈在这个复杂的大型的量化研究〉。

> [... general assessment methods are not able to eliminate unrelated variables in this complicated and large-scale quantitative research.]

In the Chinese writing convention, the preposition phrase (marked by < >) should not be left at the end of the sentence. Instead, it should be placed at the beginning of the sentence. However, the participant had only noticed this mistake when he read the paper to his students in class. Frequent translation between English and Chinese was an important part of their everyday scholarly work, but also the most challenging part.

Conclusion

This study has presented the case of three CFL teachers' involvement and aspirations in developing bilingual academic literacies. Three categories of factors were found to have influenced their choice of language for writing and publishing and intellectual engagement: at sociolinguistic, professional and personal level. In general, their educational background, knowledge in research, and most importantly, their English language proficiency have largely determined or limited their choices of language. Other factors that may exert an influence on participants were their different professional positions and expectations as well as their varied perceptions of the role and function of Chinese language education in Chinese society and the world. The study did not intend to generalise the research results because there could be more sub-categories identified in a larger population of CFL teachers.

In this study, the acquisition of bilingual academic literacy was more or less restricted to their personal efforts. Chinese language teachers found it essential to develop a balanced literacy in Chinese and English, yet training in both remained largely separate and insufficient. According to Hornberger's (2003) continua of bilingual academic literacy, the more contexts of learning and use allow people to draw from across the whole of each and every continuum, the greater are the chances for their full bi-literate development and expression. Even though the overall social conditions were less favourable for developing a bilingual academic literacy in China, Chinese teachers have demonstrated estimable personal efforts to study and write in both Chinese and English. Their professional aspirations to achieve international recognition have motivated them to work against all odds to obtain a membership in both the local and global academic community. Their stories exemplified the painstaking effort that CFL teachers have to make to develop and maintain their bilingual research proficiency in China. Unlike TESOL teaching professionals, CFL teachers need to find a good balance of academic community participation both in Chinese and in English. While TESOL scholars may not need to write extensively in their home languages after they have returned from English-speaking countries, CFL teachers in China, as well as foreign language teachers working in home contexts, must be able to demonstrate sound local knowledge and maintain visibility in the local academic community.

The study has implications at the levels of policy development, teacher education and second language writing research. On the theoretical level, it is important to focus research into bilingual research literacies through empirical studies with bilingual scholars. On the practical level, it is useful to offer courses and workshops on academic writing in both L1 and L2 for junior scholars. Academic communities may need to articulate and theorise how research articles are developed to a standard level in scholars' L1's; different academic writing conventions should be explicitly taught. It seems clear to all that having adequate knowledge and academic literacies in both English and local research communities would help a local scholar establish a successful academic profile.

References

Barkhuizen, G., Benson, P. and Chik, A. (2013) *Narrative Inquiry in Language Teaching and Learning Research.* London: Routledge.

Bates, R. (2008) Teacher education in a global context: Towards a defensible theory of teacher education. *Journal of Education for Teaching* 34 (4), 277–293.

Bell, J.S. (1995) The relationship between L1 and L2 literacy: Some complicating factors. *TESOL Quarterly* 29 (4), 687–704.

Canagarajah, S. (2002) *A Geopolitics of Academic Writing.* Pittsburgh, PA: University of Pittsburgh Press.

Canagarajah, S. (1996) 'Nondiscursive' requirements in academic publishing, material resources of periphery scholars, and the politics of knowledge production. *Written Communication* 13 (4), 435–472.

Canagarajah, S. (2011) Codemeshing in academic writing: Identifying teachable strategies of translanguaging. *The Modern Language Journal* 95 (3), 401–417.

China Daily. (2010) *Beware of English Invasion.* See http://www.chinadaily.com.cn/china/2010npc/2010-03/10/content_9564151.htm (accessed February 2015).

Cho, S. (2010) Academic biliteracy challenges: Korean scholars in the United States. *Journal of Second Language Writing* 19, 82–94.

Cummins, J. and Swain, M. (1986) *Bilingualism in Education.* New York: Longman.

Curry, M.J. and Lillis, T. (2004) Multilingual scholars and the imperative to publish in English: Negotiating interests, demands, and rewards. *TESOL Quarterly* 38, 663–688.

Gentil, G. (2005) Commitments to academic biliteracy: Case studies of Francophone university writers. *Written Communication* 22, 421–471.

Gentil, G. (2011) A biliteracy agenda for genre research. *Journal of Second Language Writing* 20, 6–23.

Hanban. (2016) *About Confucius Institutes and Confucius Classrooms.* See http://www.hanban.edu.cn/confuciousinstitutes/node_10961.htm (accessed July 2016).

Hornberger, N. (ed.) (2003) *Continua of Biliteracy.* Clevedon: Multilingual Matters.

Johnson, K. and Golombek, P. (2013) A tale of two mediations: Tracing the dialectics of cognition, emotion, and activity in novice teachers' practicum blogs. In G. Barkhuizen (ed.) *Narrative Research in Applied Linguistics* (pp. 85–104). Cambridge: Cambridge University Press.

Kachru, B. (1985) Standards, codification and sociolinguistic realism: The English language in the outer circle. In R. Quirk and H. Widdowson (eds) *English in the World: Teaching and Learning the Language and Literatures* (pp. 11–36). Cambridge: Cambridge University Press.

Kirkpatrick, A. (2011) English as a medium of instruction in Asian education: Implications for local languages and local scholarship. *Applied Linguistics Review* 2, 99–120.

Kramsch, C. (2014) Teaching foreign languages in an era of globalization: Introduction. *The Modern Language Journal* 98 (1), 296–311.

Li, Y.Y. (2006) Negotiating knowledge contribution to multiple discourse communities: A doctoral student of computer science writing for publication. *Journal of Second Language Writing* 15, 159–178.

Lillis, T. and Curry, M.J. (2006) Professional academic writing by multilingual scholars: Interactions with literacy brokers in the production of English-medium texts. *Written Communication* 23 (1), 3–35.

Lillis, T. and Curry, M.J. (2010) *Academic Writing in a Global Context.* London: Routledge.

Malinen, O., Väisänen, V. and Savolainen, H. (2012) Teacher education in Finland: A review of a national effort for preparing teachers for the future. *The Curriculum Journal* 23 (4), 567–584.

Orton, J. (2008) *The Current State of Chinese Language Education in Australian Schools.* Melbourne: University of Melbourne.

Orton, J. (2011) Educating Chinese language teachers – Some fundamentals. In L. Tsung and K. Cruickshank (eds) *Teaching and Learning Chinese in Global Contexts* (pp. 151–164). London: Continuum.

Ruan, Y. (2013) Can tasks be used to teach Chinese culture at the beginner level? In X. Du and M. J. Kirkebæk (eds) *Exploring Task-based PBL in Chinese Teaching and Learning* (pp. 78–98). Newcastle upon Tyne: Cambridge Scholars Publishing.

Scrimgeour, A. (2014) Dealing with 'Chinese fever': The challenge of Chinese teaching in the Australian classroom. In N. Murray and A. Scarino (eds) *Dynamic Ecologies: A Relational Perspective on Languages Education in the Asia-Pacific Region* (pp. 151–167). Netherlands: Springer.

Shi, L. (2002) How Western-trained Chinese TESOL professionals publish in their home environment. *TESOL Quarterly* 36 (4), 625–634.

Singh, M. (2013) Worldly critical theorizing in Euro-American centered teacher education? Preparing bilingual teacher-researcher theorists for the twenty-first century. In X. Zhu and K.M. Zeichner (eds) *Preparing Teachers for the 21st Century* (pp. 141–168). Berlin: Springer.

Singh, M. and Cui, G. (2011) Internationalising Western doctoral education through bilingual research literacy. *Pertanika Journal of Social Science and Humanities* 19 (2), 535–545.

Singh, M. and Han, J. (2009) Engaging Chinese ideas through Australian educational research. *Discourse* 30 (4), 397–411.

Street, B.V. (1984) Literacy in theory and practice. Cambridge: Cambridge University Press.

The Economist (2010) *Chinese Purism: saving Chinese from English.* See http://ww3.economist.com/blogs/johnson/2010/12/chinese_purism (accessed February 2015).

The Wall Street Journal (2015) *Chinese Education Minister warns against 'infiltration' of Western Ideas.* See http://blogs.wsj.com/chinarealtime/2015/01/30/education-minister-warns-against-infiltration-of-western-ideas/ (accessed February 2015).

Wang, D. (2014) *English in the Chinese Foreign Language Classroom.* Frankfurt am Main: Peter Lang.

Wang, D. and Adamson, B. (2014) War and peace: Perceptions of Confucius Institute in China and USA. *The Asia-Pacific Education Researcher* 24 (1), 225–234.

Wang, D. and Kirkpatrick, A. (2012) English as a lingua franca in teaching Chinese as a foreign language in Beijing: An investigation into teachers' language beliefs. *The Journal of Multilingual Education* 2 (3), 1–18.

Wang, D., Moloney, R. and Li, Z. (2013) Towards internationalizing the curriculum: a case study of Chinese language teacher education programs in China and Australia. *Australian Journal of Teacher Education* 38 (9), 116–135.

Wang, S. C. (2007) Building societal capital: Chinese in the U.S. *Language Policy* 6 (1), 27–52.

Yan, Y. and Deng, T. (2009) On Chinese loan words from English language. *English Language Teaching* 2 (4), 22–37.

Zhang, G.X. and Li, L.M. (2010). Chinese language teaching in the UK: Present and future. *The Language Learning Journal* 38 (1), 87–97.

Zhao, H. and Huang, J. (2010) China's policy of Chinese as a foreign language and the use of overseas Confucius Institutes. *Educational Research for Policy and Practice* 9 (2), 127–142.

10 Biliteracy as Policy in Academic Institutions

Beverly Baker, David M. Palfreyman, Gwenn Hiller, Wilson Poha and Zina Manu

This chapter presents issues of policy around biliteracy in four higher education institutions:

- a multilingual university in a border area in Europe: European University Viadrina in Germany;
- a bilingual university in a minority language context: Te Wānanga o Aotearoa in New Zealand;
- a bilingual university in a highly globalized emerging state: Zayed University in the United Arab Emirates;
- a bilingual university in a bilingual country context: The University of Ottawa in Canada.

In this chapter we aim to explore how macro (societal) level aspects of language policy are formed and implemented in interaction with meso and micro level processes and strategies (Baldauf, 2006). Focusing primarily on literacy policies and practices, for each institution we present first a macro view, i.e. the historical and political contexts underlying the multilingual character of each institution. We then take a meso view, discussing aspects of institutional programs and courses that enact each institution's multilingual literacy policies. Finally, for each institution we present examples at a micro level of literacy and translanguaging practices among students, teachers, and other stakeholders in the classroom and in other university spaces. While all four contexts are quite different, all underscore the challenges in reconciling the aspirational nature of multilingual policy at the national/institutional level with the everyday challenges of enacting such policies on the ground. Such challenges include negotiating the unequal statuses of the languages involved, and locating and deploying linguistic support when needed.

Case 1: European University Viadrina

European University Viadrina (EUV) is located in Eastern Germany near the border with Poland. Although EUV is not officially multilingual, it is a highly international university which de facto fosters the use of more than one language for academic purposes, and offers insight into relevant issues and best-practice examples of multilingual literacy.

EUV: Macro level

In recent decades in Germany, it has been rare for new state universities to be founded. Thus the foundation of EUV in 1992, following the reunification of Germany, had a highly political and symbolic meaning: the new university gave itself the mission on the one hand of being a bridge to Poland and Eastern Europe, and on the other hand of strengthening the European idea through research, study programs and a mixed composition of students and staff. Language education, especially with regard to Polish and German students learning the language of their respective neighbouring country, was one basic goal of the new institution: the relationship with Poland has always been especially difficult, due to several German invasions of Poland and border shifts in history.

While the basic language of the university is German, it has several international degree programs offering double degrees fully or partially taught in different languages; some programs require multilingual skills when applying. Language instruction also plays an important role at EUV in general, with most of the programs requiring the acquisition of additional languages. Another key feature of EUV is the internationally oriented range of courses offered (in terms of course content) with integrated language courses and obligatory periods spent abroad. Its proportion of international students (25.4% in 2015) is one of the highest within Germany.

Students come from more than 70 countries, but a majority comes from EU countries and/or Eastern Europe (e.g. Russia, Turkey, Ukraine and Belarus – EUV, n.d.). Many of them have a migration background and are bilingual, though not necessarily biliterate; academic proficiency in L1 may be limited.

With its international focus, EUV attracts specific groups of students, and it is not surprising that a considerable number of students are bi- or multilingual in an impressive way. For example, one of our student assistants has the following language competence profile: Ukrainian and Russian (native); German and English (fluent); French, Polish, Italian, Spanish and Swedish (advanced); Finnish (basic). A large part of these language competences were acquired during her studies at EUV.

In Germany, so far as we know, the idea of offering multilingual academic programs is still in its infancy; in this regard, EUV wanted to seize the opportunity to be a pioneer. There is no official policy of multilingualism codified in the university's statutes, but an analysis of its website and programs shows that the university is trying to anchor the concept of multilingualism at the macro level by presenting it explicitly as an inherent part of its profile. The university's website defines the specific profile within a *General Rationale for Internationalization*:

> In addition to its concentration on Poland, East Central Europe and the EU, Viadrina has placed emphasis on multiple language competencies in addition to English. Graduates [...] are expected to have a high level of proficiency in multiple languages including field-specific language skills. Aside from the geographic focus of Viadrina, the motivation to impart its students with multilingual communication skills shall be furthered to expand the university's unique profile. (EUV, 2015)

It can be noted that the language skills are not specified in particular competences like reading, writing or speaking. However, this statement, which was formulated in 2002, shows the uniqueness of such a linguistic education in the German university landscape. Actually, more than twelve years later, not much has changed. Multilingualism has a strong significance in the university, but it can be stated that EUV is still an institution 'in flux', with its aspiration to be a multilingual university implemented in varied ways by different departments and faculty.

Although more and more lectures at Germany's universities are being held in English, EUV is still one of few places where foreign languages other than English are in the focus of attention in written as well as oral skills. However, needless to say, besides German, English is the most dominant language used. Promoting students' literacy skills in English, which serves as a lingua franca in business and in the academic world, is pragmatic and outshines the other – more idealistic – endeavours at EUV. But still the university holds on to the political/idealistic dimension of multilingual education in Europe, as seen in statements such as the one above.

Hence EUV, although not officially a multilingual university, is in practice multilingual, and many actors strive to 'live' multilingualism in the form of various small-scale initiatives involving biliteracy. These will be presented in the next section, showing how they are embedded in aspects of the university curriculum (the meso level).

EUV: Meso level

All three departments (Law, Business and Social & Cultural Sciences) offer programs where students can develop biliteracy. For instance, some programs require BA students to gain proficiency (including writing, reading and speaking skills, according to the Common European Framework of Reference for Languages) in two languages other than their primary language, and they can choose among several languages offered by the language center. Several MA programs require for admission proficiency in two or even three foreign languages; for example the MA in Intercultural Communication Studies requires proficiency in two additional languages and supplementary acquisition of Polish during the two years of study (with Polish students learning another additional language).

A look at the course catalogue shows that EUV actually offers courses and lectures through the medium of several languages (English, Polish, French, Spanish) in all departments. In these courses, students speak, read and write in the given language. Concerning the language of the exams, faculty are rather flexible: according to faculty interviewed at EUV, as far as the lecturer is able to evaluate exams in a given language, often s/he would accept it.

A best-practice example of an international, multilingual program is the MA in European Studies (MES), which offers the opportunity to graduate in a double Masters with Istanbul Bilgi University, Turkey (where students have all classes in English) or with Adam Mickiewicz University in Poznań, Poland (which requires English and Polish literacy). In general, the program requires proficiency in one foreign language of the student's own choice at a high level of literacy (assessment is in the form of either an examination or a written assignment). A unique feature of the program is that MES students can gain an additional Multilingual Certificate by fulfilling the following criteria:

- At least 24 ECTS [European Credit Transfer System] Points in at least 4 modules taught in foreign languages [i.e. other than German] must be obtained.
- At least two foreign languages must be studied and at least 6 ECTS Points obtained for each Module
- If only two foreign languages are taken [...], 12 ECTS Points must be gained in each language.
- If a student studies in more than three foreign languages then only 6 ECTS Points must be obtained in each language. (EUV, 2016)

These requirements clearly promote a fairly balanced academic literacy in a range of languages, for those students who wish to gain this qualification.

An innovative type of teaching format which supports biliteracy comprises a seminar accompanied by a course focusing on academic language, a combination which is very appreciated among the students. This seminar type is well-established in the MES, where native French-speaking Political Sciences professors regularly teach in French, while a French language lecturer supplements the course with an academic literacy course. In this course, the professor teaches in French, using mostly French sources; in the accompanying French course, the lecturer supports the students to understand the texts and be able to discuss them (Bahr, forthcoming).

The university also offers several support structures to help students develop academic biliteracy; for instance a peer tutoring program in academic writing for non-native writers, which is widely known and adapted in other institutions in Germany (Voigt & Girgensohn, 2015). Here students are supported in all academic writing tasks they meet during their studies, with the focus mainly on writing in German and English.

Challenges appear, especially when university policy and student needs are not congruent. To take just one example, one of the university's most popular MA programs (Intercultural Communication Studies) was from its very inception based on a German-Polish cooperation concept (for political reasons). Students were only admitted when having a good command of two additional languages of their choice. During the MA all non-Polish speakers had to learn Polish; the intention was that the students should be proficient in Polish when they finish their MA. However, reality has shown that it was very difficult to motivate them to continue with Polish after the required basic classes. German native speakers consider Polish a very difficult language, and it is true that expecting students to reach a level which enables them to study in Polish within these two years is very ambitious. As a consequence of this, the seminars in Polish struggled with a lack of potential participants; the programme was reformed, and most of the Polish professors now offer classes in German or English.

EUV: Micro level

As part of a study concerning academic practices in internationalized contexts (Hiller, 2014), EUV students and professors were asked about their daily experience and about the challenges they face. The findings suggest that there are plenty of linguistic challenges for both students and professors; I will briefly discuss two of these which involve literacy practices.

Email interaction between students and professors can lead to culture-based misunderstandings, as both groups often vary in their linguistic conventions for e-mail communication. To take an example given by one professor, a request from an Asian student might include a detailed description of his sickness; at best, the professor is amused, while at worst s/he is irritated by the physiological details and ignores the message. As Rost-Roth (2003) has shown, a long story in combination with a request is not well received in the German-speaking context. Irritation may also occur when a student fails to use an appropriate form of address for their professor's academic status (e.g. 'Hallo', 'Hi', 'Hello' or absence of any salutation formula whatsoever). One professor I interviewed reported receiving an e-mail from an Australian student beginning 'Hi Barbara' (the professor's first name): she never answered the mail and deleted it, feeling the student was being cheeky. Research shows that differences in conceptions of linguistic politeness in professor-student interaction can often lead to failure in communication, leading to a restriction of learning opportunities (Hiller, 2014; House & Lévy, 2008).

Academic text genres also clearly differ between languages; for example an 'essay' in English, an *'essai'* in French or an *'Essai'* in German, despite being similarly named, have different purposes and conventions (Hufeisen, 2002; Durand *et al.*, 2006). As Hiller (forthcoming) shows, there are different expectations concerning the genre, which can lead to low marks. An American professor teaching in Germany mentions:

> The way they have to write their essays [in my course] is a little bit different, I was told, from the usual essays they are used to [...]. I think, based on what I have heard from other professors [...], students might not have known [what to do]. What I require my students to do, is writing essays which are very much like writing academic papers, where they have to cite correctly. (Interview)

In Germany and France an *Essay/essai* is not considered an academic text *sensu stricto*: in France it requires rather a dialectical discourse, and in Germany too it is considered more a philosophical genre than academic.

In conclusion, EUV is one of the first universities in Germany to gather considerable experience with multilingual literacy in higher education. Directed not by an official language plan, but rather by an institutional commitment enacted by enthusiasts of the European ideal, biliteracy develops through an unsteered striving of actors within the institution, in the form of various small initiatives. It is clear, however, that students very much appreciate the literacy and other language competences they acquire. In an alumni survey, former students in the Faculty of Cultural and Social Studies stated that the language skills they acquired were extremely valuable for their careers: 85% of alumni rated this very positive/positive (Hennings & Rössler, 2011). Support programs and course formats such as co-teaching between disciplinary professor and language instructor show innovative ways to support students in developing academic biliteracy.

Case 2: *Te Wānanga o Aotearoa* (TWoA)

Te Wānanga o Aotearoa is a large, multi-site institution in New Zealand which aims to foster the culture and language of the indigenous Māori people. While English is extensively used in teaching and learning, a number of students take up an option to write coursework in the Māori language, *Te Reo Māori*.

TWoA: Macro level

Māori are regarded as the indigenous people of New Zealand and *Te Reo Māori* (TRM) was the first language of New Zealand. The first Māori arrived more than 1000 years ago from Polynesian islands, while the first Europeans arrived in the late 1700s. In 1840 the Treaty of Waitangi was signed by representatives of Queen Victoria and over 500 Maori leaders. The signing of the Treaty of Waitangi disadvantaged Māori, and British colonists believed they were now in charge of – rather than in a partnership with – the Māori. There followed over 130 years of colonization, exploitation and oppression of Māori; Māori knowledge, language, culture and practices were eroded, negated and discouraged (Walker *et al.*, 2006).

Between the 1930s and the 1960s, the number of Māori who could speak TRM as their first language had dropped from 96.6% to only 26%, and a new generation grew up not knowing how to speak Māori. This led to fears that Māori would become a 'dead' language unless serious efforts were made to revive the language and encourage people to speak Māori again (May *et al.*, 2006).

In 1987, Māori were able to lay a claim against the Crown through the Waitangi Tribunal for failing to protect the Māori language. It was argued that the language is the core of our Maori culture and *mana* (prestige) (Durie, 1998). It is unique, spoken nowhere else in the world, and is part of a rich heritage and culture that is also unique. There is a great body of Māori history, poetry and songs that depend upon the language. If the language dies, all of that will die and the culture of hundreds of years will ultimately fade into oblivion (Waitangi Tribunal – Department of Justice, 1986).

As a result of this claim, the Māori Language Act came into force in 1987, and Māori language policy objectives were created. One of these objectives is to increase opportunities to use TRM by increasing the number of situations where Māori can be used. This resulted in a significant development in TRM education. Since the later 20th century there has been an explosive growth in Māori-driven initiatives, such as Kāhanga reo (preschool language 'nests'), Kura Kaupapa Māori (Māori-language immersion primary schools), Wharekura (Māori-language immersion high schools) and Wānanga (Māori tertiary institutions). A framework has emerged which acknowledges that

> language revitalisation is not about going back to a past linguistic state, but about recapturing a lost language and culture in the context of the present and in imagining the future[, …] going back and forth between discourse modes and the bilingual continua of the community. (García, 2009: 118)

Te Wānanga o Aotearoa (TWoA) is an indigenous Māori tertiary institution, founded in 1983 in Te Awamutu, as a training provider in response to a recognized need for an organization to provide education to those who had not fared well in the mainstream education system – specifically targeting Māori. From these humble beginnings, it is now a tertiary provider with over 50 locations throughout New Zealand serving over 31,000 *tauira* (students), of whom over 50% are Māori (Te Wānanga o Aotearoa, 2014). This tertiary institution has distinctive points of difference that set it apart from all other tertiary providers in New Zealand (Hoani, 2012). TWoA has a culture, a language, a way, a cultural soul that moves to a unique heartbeat and rhythm (Pohatu, 2008). Our exploration of this topic will be from the perspective of kaiako (teachers) of TWoA who work closely with tauira.

TWoA: Meso level

In June 2015, TWoA released its 'Reo Strategy' for all employees. The aim of this strategy is that by 2030, TRM will be in common use throughout TWoA and will be the language of choice when we conduct our business. As kaiako, we will converse, laugh, debate and joke in TRM. TWoA will also celebrate *Te Reo Māori*, uphold it and revere it as a *taonga tuku iho* (a gift handed down).

This initiative was instigated as a result of a survey completed by employees of TWoA, which highlighted that only 19% of kaiako (total staff 1700) have an advanced level of TRM. Although this proportion is quite low, the encouraging finding is that 94% of kaiako have said they want to improve their ability to converse and write in TRM (TWoA, 2015a). Paralleling policy at the University of Ottawa (see below), official email communication from our CEO and senior management are written in TRM first, followed by English. Also all department names and job titles have been or are in the process of being renamed. The organization aims to reclaim TRM amongst staff; when this becomes a reality, TWoA can then expand to becoming a multilingual institution.

Earlier we mentioned that TWoA has distinctive points of difference that set it apart from all other tertiary providers in New Zealand. One of these points of difference is the stated values of the organization, which are

> embedded in and woven through the actions we take to achieve successful outcomes for our tauira, as by achieving success for tauira we achieve success as an organisation. (TWoA, 2015b)

These values comprise:

> Te Aroha: Having regard for one another and those for whom we are responsible and to whom we are accountable.

> Te Whakapono: The basis of our beliefs and the confidence that what we are doing is right.

Ngā Ture: The knowledge that our actions are morally and ethically right and that we are acting in an honourable manner.

Kotahitanga: Unity amongst iwi [Māori tribe] and other ethnicities; standing as one. (TWoA, 2015b)

Within the context of these values and the historical context described earlier, TWoA (in contrast with Zayed University and the University of Ottawa – see below) shows a degree of institutionalized translanguaging. As in the list of values above, the policies in TWoA (2015c), for example, are presented with Māori main headings, while subheadings and text are mainly in English but with consistent use of a range of Māori terminology. TWoA offers considerable support for Māori(-oriented) literacy, notably in *Te Pātaka Māramatanga*, the 'largest indigenous academic library in the world' (Lal & Walker, 2014), which

proactively collects materials in Te Reo Māori [and] materials published by Māori, for Māori and about Māori. (p. 6)

Programmes of study at the university vary in the balance of Māori and English used. *Te Reo Rangatira* (Māori language programmes) have the majority of their class delivery and assessments in TRM. In the first year of study in these programmes there is a majority of English used, then as a tauira progresses through the levels, TRM becomes the only language used and assessed (unless the assessment requires TRM to be translated back into English). Programmes that make moderate use of TRM are *Toi* (Māori and Indigenous Art), *Whakairo* (Carving), *Raranga* (Weaving) and *Angitu* (Maori And Indigenous Peoples' Development). Programmes delivered and assessed mainly in English are *Hauora* (Health and fitness), *Te Arawhānui* (Business, Computing and Innovation), *Te Hiringa* (Education) and Social Services; however, TRM is woven into these programmes as all classes start and end with *karakia* (prayer) and *waiata* (song), while Māori case studies, frameworks and ways of learning are used throughout tauria course material. As part of the Reo Strategy, all staff who need to develop their ability to communicate in TRM will have personalised strategies implemented in their professional development plans to ensure that they are actively taking steps to increase their reo. One step in this process (introduced in 2015) is to encourage staff to enrol on TWoA Te Reo Māori programmes, initially with a focus on conversation. It is still to be determined whether these classes will be held during work hours or after hours.

One way that TWoA implements the value of Te Aroha is through a policy that allows all tauira (students) to complete their assessments in TRM. The policy states the following:

All assessments are accepted in Te Reo Māori and/or English (unless it is a Te Reo Māori assessment). Tauira need to advise the Kaiako/Kaitiaki [teacher] of their preferred language before the due date of the assessment. The kaiako/kaitiaki will provide an appropriate assessor/s. (TWoA, 2015c: 12)

Most assessments for all programmes consist of essays, reports and other written course assignments. Every tauira enrolled on a TWoA programme throughout New Zealand is advised of this language opportunity during their interview or during their first class as part of their induction.

TWoA: Micro level

A survey was conducted to identify whether any tauira had taken up the opportunity to complete their assessments in TRM. Information about the total number of tauira in New Zealand who have completed their assessments in TRM was unavailable to us, but we sent a survey to students at Te Awamutu campus and received responses from 15 tauira. Tauira were asked what motivated them to complete their assessments in TRM; how they felt about being able to be assessed in TRM; and whether they received feedback on their assessments in a timely manner.

When tauira were asked what motivated them to complete their assessments in Te Reo Māori, they shared views exemplified by the following:

I felt that the true essence of what I wanted to put across was better articulated in Te Reo Māori.

Māori is my first language. I believe it is my right to speak and be assessed in Te Reo Māori, no matter what institute I attend.

I am of this land. My language has been gifted to me by my ancestors. I am indigenous to this Land and I have a responsibility to future generations. i.e. the survival of our language.

Another tauira who chose to complete our survey is from England, and had been learning TRM since living in New Zealand. He was studying a programme that did not require him to complete his assessments in TRM, so he was able to choose his preferred language to complete his assessments. He shared what motivated him to complete his assessments in TRM:

I have been learning Te Reo Māori for the past 15 years as well as customs and traditions. Māori is the official language of New Zealand. I also believe we (non-Māori) have an obligation to support the use of Te Reo wherever we can, after all Te Reo was denied to the Māori people for over 100 years.

This tauira who has embraced TRM brings to mind the Māori proverb *Ko te manu e kai ana i te miro, nōna te ngahere; ko te manu e kai ana i te mātauranga, nōna te ao,* which means 'the bird that partakes of the miro berry reigns in the forest; the bird that partakes of the power of knowledge has access to the world'. This tauira has chosen to access the world through Māori lenses, as TRM has its roots embedded in its culture. These comments by tauira demonstrate a 'heteroglossic vision' (García, 2009: 118), which engages with the bilingual continuum students bring to the classroom. These students see their bilingualism as a right, and work towards the acceptance of all their linguistic and cultural differences.

Tauira were asked how they felt about being able to complete their assessments in TRM. Responses included the following:

> It is something to treasure for future generations. I always ask to do my assessments in Te Reo only to support the language both spoken and written. It is an honour to be assessed in Te Reo Māori.

> To me, this is one of the great things about TWoA. I think it is excellent that I can choose how I want to be assessed without feeling embarrassed. This is also what separates TWoA from mainstream. i.e. TWoA actually encourages student be assessed in Te Reo if it makes them more comfortable. It is not the 'what' but the 'how' they go about doing this.

As kaiako, we have observed that the way tauira live, learn and experience deeply influences and shapes their knowledge and worldview, which means the ability for people to possess knowledge is deeply dependent on their worldview. By allowing tauira to have the choice to be assessed in TRM, they are able to

> explore (k)new approaches to learning so they are free of the high levels of dis-ease and dis-comfort that can be experienced when unable to express oneself in their first language. (Edwards, 2011: 3)

Edwards further explains that to express oneself in one's first language

> allows a person to re-invent and re-connect with our ways of knowing, doing and being. It also supports the idea that we are capable and should take responsibility to develop our own frameworks of being. (ibid)

These tauira have a strong ethnic identification with a language that survives in rituals and ceremonies, and among some of their community (García, 2009); for example, at the start of each academic year at TWoA, each campus will hold a *powhiri* (traditional Māori welcome) to welcome all tauira to the start of their education journey for the year. Also, many programmes also hold their classes in *marae* (traditional Māori meeting houses) instead of in classrooms on campus. This gives tauira an experience to learn Māori customs and protocols while learning TRM.

Tauira were also asked if they knew whether their kaiako or someone else fluent in TRM marked their assessments. This was asked because many staff do not speak TRM. Most tauira had their assessments marked by their kaiako, or assumed it was their kaiako who did their marking; no respondent had experienced delays in getting their assessments back.

As part of our research we also conducted a focus group with kaiako to identify how they dealt with marking assessments in TRM. The kaiako we selected were in the *whare toi* (arts programmes). We found that the majority of kaiako in this focus group were able to mark their tauira's work, as most of them are fluent in TRM. Those who were unable to mark such work passed the assessments to colleagues to translate: they did not find it difficult to find a colleague who would be able to translate from TRM to English, and the kaiako is able to mark the assessment once it is translated into English. The *kaiako* who participated in our focus group were able to get assessments back to tauira in a timely manner because they have colleagues who are proficient readers of TRM.

In conclusion, the revival of Te Reo Māori has been supported by *Te Wānanga o Aotearoa* in many ways, one of which is a policy that allows tauira to complete their course assessments in Māori. Our research shows that tauira who chose to complete their assessments in Te Reo Māori have identified this opportunity as a treasure, an honor, a responsibility to future generations, and an obligation; and that staff find the policy workable in practice. These comments embody the essence of the revival of the Māori language.

Case 3: Zayed University, United Arab Emirates

Zayed University (ZU) is a university of about 8000 students in the United Arab Emirates (UAE), a relatively small, oil-rich country located on the Persian/Arabian Gulf coast between Saudi Arabia and Oman. Its stated and implemented policies illustrate issues of biliteracy, identity and modernity in the learning, teaching and assessment of content and language.

ZU: Macro level

The UAE was established in 1971 as a federation of seven small emirates, which had recently, with the discovery of large oil reserves, begun to move from a largely subsistence economy under British protection into a phase of highly accelerated economic, demographic and cultural change. The 1970s and following decades have seen extremely rapid development in the UAE's economy, infrastructure and services, staffed largely by foreign guest workers from the Indian subcontinent, other Arab countries, South-East Asia and Western countries (in decreasing proportion). As a result, indigenous Emirati citizens now find themselves a minority (about 15% of the population) in a state which is orally highly multilingual (in Urdu/Hindi, Arabic, English, Tagalog, Farsi, etc.), and for most public purposes (road signs, utility bills, media and education) biliterate in Arabic and English.

Most students at ZU and other state education institutions are Emirati; for most of these students Arabic is their 'first language' and English is their 'second'. However, the permeability and variations in this apparent dichotomy show how biliteracy is truly a complex combination of continua (Hornberger, 2002). The Gulf dialect of Arabic which our students use in their community is very different (often to the point of incomprehensibility) from the Modern Standard Arabic (MSA) promoted by the university, itself a recently and incompletely codified compromise between the archaic, literary Classical Arabic of the Qur'an and the various regional dialects. Diglossia exists between MSA and Arabic dialects, so MSA is no-one's first language, but must be gradually learned throughout schooling: first in writing, then for formal speaking contexts. English, on the other hand, surrounds most of these young people almost from birth, with outsourced childcare, shopping, films, songs and even family members (Palfreyman, 2011) using this language, often hybridized with Arabic, Hindi or other languages. English has connotations of modernity, and although students' academic written proficiency in English may not be what is expected by their Western(ized) teachers, English is very familiar to them; orally they are surprisingly fluent and compared with the Levant and North Africa there is a great deal more mixing of English (as well as Hindi and Farsi) with Arabic. The fluidity of languages is reflected also in the everyday use of the very dissimilar Arabic and English scripts across language boundaries, with people regularly writing Arabic text messages with the English alphabet or English words such as 'bye' in Arabic script. Translingual phenomena such as these have led to public concern about the purity and future of Arabic in the UAE (Holes, 2011).

In higher education, Findlow (2006) highlights how the founding missions of state insitutions in the UAE have reflected changing aspirations for the country. The first, United Arab Emirates University (UAEU), was established in 1976 with the assistance of Egyptian scholars, aiming to establish the UAE as a centre of education in the Arab world, with most subjects taught at least partly in Arabic; the second, the Higher Colleges of Technology (HCT), was established in 1988 as a network of technical colleges adopting Canadian/British models and expertise and using almost exclusively English as a medium of instruction. Zayed University, in contrast, was founded in 1998 with the mission of 'advancing the UAE as a participant in a modern, global society' (Findlow, 2006, cited in Findlow, 2006), i.e. as 'not the modern centre of the Arab world but [...] the Arab centre of the modern world' (Nicolson, 2006). Although the majority of ZU faculty are from Western countries, from the beginning the university placed emphasis on using both

English and Arabic as media of instruction, and currently states one of its six global learning objectives for all graduates thus:

> ZU graduates will be able to communicate effectively in English and Modern Standard Arabic, using the academic and professional conventions of these languages appropriately. (Zayed University, 2014: 10)

Nevertheless, Findlow (2006) correctly noted that ZU's

> initial reported plans to teach in equal proportions of Arabic and English were soon shelved and only a minority of subjects are now taught in Arabic. (p. 26)

At the time Findlow was writing, pressure to include Arabic in the curriculum was based on its association with traditional indigenous values, and hence national identity/unity in the face of massive demographic and social change (thus paralleling to some extent the efforts described above to support/revitalize Te Reo Māori). In recent years, the latter has been given greater emphasis, as the country's rulers seek to establish (in the wake of the 'Arab Spring' revolutions) that their modern state has not abandoned the traditional identities of their people. Official emails and decisions from senior administration are now issued in Arabic followed by an English translation. In terms of employability, it has become apparent that although English literacy is a key medium for advanced knowledge in modern domains, graduates also need to be able to apply, explain and discuss this knowledge in Arabic with professionals or other stakeholders within their community and the Arab world more broadly. As a result of these conflicting pressures, all three state institutions have converged towards a predominance of English as medium of instruction together with an established place for Arabic, including some linkage of Arabic (more noticeable in UAEU, less so in HCT) with the content of their disciplines.

ZU: Meso level

Undergraduate programmes at ZU consist of three main phases:

(1) the Foundation programme (lasting from eight weeks to two years), focusing on basic English for Academic Purposes and aiming for IELTS level 5. Ten to 15% of students come to university having already gained this level, and so are exempt from this programme;
(2) the General Education (GE) programme (lasting about two years), which aims to give all students a grounding in academic literacy (English and Arabic), information literacy, mathematical and scientific thinking, information technology and the historical/global context of their country's development;

(3) Major programmes (lasting about two years, often overlapping with GE) leading to a degree in a specific discipline such as Journalism, Education, Graphic Design or Information Technology.

Institutional policy assigns Arabic as a medium of learning only to courses focusing on Arabic language and/or Islamic Studies; all other courses in the university are English-medium. The Foundation programme focuses entirely on English language and skills, and this is followed up in the GE programme with a sequence of three English Composition courses which focus on using sources to write discursive and argumentative texts of increasing length/complexity. In each Major programme, one or more courses include a focus on English language development for professional purposes. Arabic provision has a similar structure in the second and third phases shown above: it begins with a sequence of three GE courses, the first of which, *Arabic Concepts*, focuses on organization of academic paragraphs and essays as well as some oral presentation skills. The second and third courses in this sequence are designated as Islamic Studies, and explore the history of Arab/Islamic thought through analysis of texts and (written) discussion of contemporary issues; since the 'Arab Spring', an additional Arabic-designated GE course *Emirates Studies* has been instituted, involving students in discussion of economic, cultural and political developments and participation in the UAE. Finally, each Major programme includes two half-credit Arabic 'Lab' courses, each of which is linked to and supports an English-medium content course; several majors also offer optional whole-credit courses focusing on Arabic language – for example for journalism or education, as well as a course titled *Technical Writing (Arabic)* comparable to the above-mentioned *Technical Writing* (in English).

It seems from the above that academic literacy in Arabic and English at ZU as a whole reflects the modernizing mission of the university and the dualism described by Findlow (2006) between

> cultural authenticity, localism, tradition, emotions, religion [associated with Arabic, and] modernity, internationalism, business, material status, secularism [with English]. (p. 25)

Thus the default language of instruction and assessment in the University is English, while Arabic-designated courses tend to focus on Arabic language and/or Islamic discourses. Interestingly, one of the few Arabic-designated courses at HCT is a morally-oriented course titled *Internet Safety on Social Media*, which apparently aims to discipline one area of students' extracurricular literacy:

> help[ing] students identify and avoid harmful, on-line behaviours and situations regarding Social Media and Networks. (Higher Colleges of Technology, 2014: 134)

In contrast, the Islamic Studies courses at ZU, for example, are presented as

> plac[ing] the Islamic identity within a wider global perspective containing all different civilizations and cultures. (Zayed University, 2014: 113)

This latter goal suggests some attempt at diffusion across the Arabic-English dualism, while professionally-oriented Arabic labs/courses in the Majors show that Arabic literacy is treated as important in the modern (Arab) world.

ZU: Micro level

Language policy at ZU (as at the University of Ottawa – see below) is bilingual but not heteroglossic (García, 2009): the curriculum clearly distinguishes between Arabic and English courses. However, as in the other institutions discussed in this chapter, in practice there is plenty of translanguaging in ZU as course texts are discussed and prepared. Despite an explicit English-only policy in most GE courses, students in all courses often discuss ideas in Arabic; some faculty understand this discussion, and also aim to use culturally relevant examples for learning purposes, which sometimes involves use of Arabic terms or quotations, or Arabic-associated discourses. Although translanguaging is not officially sanctioned, the policy on Arabic literacy has been adapted (one might say 'relaxed') at an institutional level to deal with different entry competences among students. One major issue has been with a small but significant set of students who enter the university with low proficiency in Arabic. Some of these are the gradually increasing number of non-Arab international students (for example from Kenya or Korea) who wish to study at the university but cannot realistically fulfil the GE Arabic language requirement; this has led the university to run a parallel sequence of three GE courses titled *Arabic for International, Nonnative Students*.

More problematic for the established conception of Emirati identity are Emirati students (sometimes from families where one of the parents is from a non-Arab background such as India or the Philippines) who have studied in private, English-medium schools. When these students enter the university they typically have conversational proficiency in Emirati dialect and fair academic written proficiency in English, but minimal skills in MSA. After a period of trying to ignore or assimilate these students, ZU introduced further parallel courses: two in *Remedial Arabic* and two titled *Arabic for Heritage Students* (AHS); then, since these students still struggled with the later Arabic language Islamic Studies courses, two courses in *Islamic Civilization for Non-Native Speakers* were added, which involve for the first time official reading and discussion of Islamic content in English. There are also suspicions among Arabic teachers that some incoming students deliberately underdisplay their skills in the initial Arabic placement test in order to be placed in the AHS courses, which are perceived as easier than the main Arabic course sequence.

In the Major programmes, a translingual aspect is most visible in the form of translation skills, which are incorporated into Arabic 'lab' support courses and also form the main focus of professionally-oriented courses such as *Media Translation* and *Technical Translation*. These have been driven largely by feedback from graduate surveys and work internships that students need to be more able to mobilize their knowledge and expertise across languages. In the case of Media or IT graduates, translation could be seen as an integral professional skill; but also Education students, who take their developed literacy in English to teaching jobs in Arabic-medium state schools, have so often been called upon to translate in an informal capacity at work that a translation course has been instituted for the College of Education as well.

The English Composition and Arabic language programmes are coordinated at the institutional level (course objectives such as 'writing a well-organized essay' and 'critical reading' exist in both course sequences). However, there is little co-reference at the teaching level; and in the author's experience as a member of the English department and as a cross-disciplinary educational developer there has been relatively little contact between faculty in the two departments in terms of methodology or language. Occasional exceptions to this have been Arabic faculty members seeking ideas about writing skills from English faculty, rather than *vice versa*. On the other hand, there has at times been a degree of coordination across the GE programme in terms of content, with the topic of 'globalization', for example, studied in the first Global Studies course and supported (sometimes ad nauseam) in the concurrent courses in both Arabic and English; so there seems to be the potential for some transfer of knowledge and literacy skills between the courses.

In order to investigate whether students perceived any connections in learning across their two language course sequences, students in their first semester of GE were surveyed about this topic. My first question was *Does what you learn in your English Composition course help you in your Arabic writing?* Overall, the response to this was lukewarm: about 50% of students answered 'No, not much', while 38% selected 'Yes, some' and just 12% 'Yes, a lot'. Responses to the question *Does what you learn in your Arabic course help you in your English writing?* were even less positive, with 61% answering 'No, not much', 28% 'Yes, some' and 11% 'Yes, a lot'. However, it was interesting to see the responses of those who saw some connection, when I asked for examples. Students who saw the English course as helping their Arabic writing tended to mention common content knowledge:

> We have been taught about the Globalization in English in the first week and in the second week we had an Arabic essay to write and it was about Globalization, so we had some information that we used it in the Arabic essay.

or genre knowledge about the organization of academic writing:

> topic sentences and how to began a sentence with a strong word such as 'moreover'.

In terms of how Arabic instruction helps English writing, again some students cited content knowledge:

> For example I didn't know a lot about globalization and the Arabic course helped me a lot to understand.

A few, though, highlighted the interesting possibility of bringing a more expressive element into academic writing in their second language:

> Arabic helps me in developing creative ways in expressing feelings and ideas because usually Arabic is full of metaphorical quotations and imagery.

In conclusion, higher education policy in the UAE has been strongly influenced by the linguistic dualism analysed by Findlow (2006), and by changing political pressures towards one or the other side of this dualism. However, at ZU at least there has been some transition towards recognizing the 'glocal' (Robertson & White, 2007) use of Arabic for modern, professional purposes. Translanguaging remains for the most part excluded by institutional policy; but the nature of the Emirati context and more complex linguistic identities have forced some adaptation of policy. Informally, students constantly cross and combine between English and Arabic as they learn about both language and content; in their written work, actual writing in a mixture of languages does not as yet fit into the expectations of the university context; but there are signs of potential for 'covert' transfer of ideas and ways of writing between the languages.

Case 4: L'Université d'Ottawa/The University of Ottawa, Canada

Located in the English-dominant province of Ontario, the University of Ottawa (uOttawa) is North America's largest bilingual university, and the world's largest officially bilingual English-French university, with approximately 42,000 part time and full time students. Exploration of the bilingual nature of this institution raises many critical questions about overt and covert translanguaging practices. I am presenting this institution from my perspective as a faculty member and Director of Language Assessment at uOttawa's Official Languages and Bilingualism Institute, a university unit dedicated to supporting and studying bilingualism and multilingualism.

uOttawa: Macro level

Canada is officially bilingual in English and French – in fact, 'bilingualism' as a term in Canada is used almost exclusively in referring to *French-English* bilingualism. Within the province of Quebec, French is the dominant language and English is a protected minority language. However, within the larger Canadian and North American context the opposite is true. Bilingualism is a highly valued commodity in Canada; Canadians fluent in both English and French have even been shown to earn more than those who speak only one official language (Christofides & Swidinsky, 2010). These two languages have relatively higher prestige than other languages spoken by Canadians of immigrant backgrounds, as well as the dozens of aboriginal languages, which receive relatively little support.

uOttawa: Meso level

Institution-wide language policies affect all areas of university functioning and all stakeholders, with explicit, detailed and enforced requirements for programs and class offerings, for staff hiring, for faculty members as conditions of promotion and tenure, and even for electronic communication within the institutional community. The institution dedicates an enormous amount of resources to encouraging individual bilingualism.

The majority of these policies reveal a preoccupation with creating equality in the use of French and English in all contexts, because like the wider Canadian context there is a power imbalance favouring English over French. Enrolment at the university by language most used is currently about 31% French and 69% English (University of Ottawa, 2014). About one-third of uOttawa students are registered in French-only programs or bilingual English-French programs.

Bilingualism is a long-standing mandate: following the *Report of the Task Force on Bilingualism at the University of Ottawa* in 1971, the University's Senate and Board of Governors (1974) adopted the Regulation on Bilingualism, which is still in force. The university's Senate Standing Committee on Francophone Affairs and Official Languages enforces this Regulation on Bilingualism – which is more explicit for communication in writing than for speaking. The Senate Standing Committee (2006) lists the following among its functions:

> To monitor how faculties and services control the quality and level of bilingualism of written communication.

All official email communications with the university community, for example, must have exactly the same message in French and in English, with the French appearing first. A large part of the Senate Committee's mandate is the processing of complaints related to issues of 'linguistic balance' in writing, such as the 'unilingual' nature of internal communications on campus posters and signs.

At a more functional level, resources are dedicated to realizing the level of bilingualism set out in these official policies. For example, uOttawa offers extensive linguistic support for staff, students, and professors. Staff can benefit from free lunch-time and evening language courses; and French-dominant professors who teach in English (and *vice versa*) can have their teaching and lecture materials proofread for them. For students, as at the European University Viadrina (EUV), some courses are accompanied by academic language support courses (through uOttawa's French Immersion Regime).

Despite this support, French learning is particularly challenging for English-dominant professors and students, and not only because the city of Ottawa is more English dominant. Firstly, sometimes macro-level policies are too ambitious and underestimate the time and effort required to acquire the languages to an academic level. In addition, because English is the dominant language of international academia, most readings are in English and professors feel pressure to publish in English journals and present in English at conferences.

The institutional commitment to linguistic balance has resulted in the creation of dual monoglossic spaces rather than bilingual spaces – that is, the two languages are strictly compartmentalized (Lamoureux *et al.*, 2014). For example, there are two student newspapers – one in English and one in French. This is an example of García's observation (2009) that

> schools often demand the total control of two bounded autonomous systems instead of honoring and capitalising on [actors'] bilingual practices. (p. 141)

Nowhere is this compartmentalisation starker than in the university's assessment practices – both in the assessment of French and English as languages, and in the assessment of other subjects through either French or English. Many programs require entrance and/or exit tests in the language of the program, and these tests are all firmly monolingual. Recourse to the other official language is often an explicitly-stated basis for lowering a test-taker's grade. Shohamy (2011) has discussed this contradiction between pragmatic acceptance of translanguaging practices in pedagogical settings and their proscription in any accompanying assessment.

On the other hand, as at TWoA and in some cases also at the EUV, students are allowed to submit their assignments in their choice of language (either English or French) in almost all programs and courses. This policy presents possible challenges, such as assuring reliability in grading. Students are also not encouraged to submit translanguaged or bilingual assignments – they must choose one language for a given assignment. In French immersion courses, where English-dominant students take subject area courses in French, there are incentives in place to encourage submission of classwork in French, such as assurances that the students' grades will not be unduly affected. However, most students do not bother, missing out on a chance to improve their written French. In this case, the language of submission policy conceivably has the effect of discouraging bilingual literacy development. One might wonder if more English students might decide to attempt more French writing if they could mix it with English.

Beliefs about the compartmentalization of languages in assessment are very strongly entrenched. However, one possibility in this context may be found in a reimagining of the test currently administered to certain professors who as part of their contract negotiations are required to attain 'passive bilingualism'. Currently, this test is conceived as a target language proficiency test of reading and listening comprehension. The entire test, including instructions and multiple choice test items, is written in the target language. There is a possibility, however, to operationalize passive bilingualism as a truly bilingual practice. These professors are expected to be only 'passively bilingual' because in their work they will probably never need to speak or write in the second language. They might be expected, rather, to attend a meeting where both languages are being used and follow everything. Therefore, to assess this ability, a professor could be asked to listen or view a simulated department meeting or class seminar which takes place in both languages (a very authentic situation at uOttawa) and summarize the content or answer comprehension questions – either task could be written in the first language. Such an approach would expand the already problematic construct of 'passive bilingualism' with an authentic task that makes explicit the value of dynamic bilingual literacy practices.

uOttawa: Micro level

Despite regulations that institutionalise dual monolingualism, spoken interactions in multiple university domains – faculty meetings, student-teacher conferences, and service interactions, to name a few – are characterised by dynamic and organic translanguaging practices. Even a brief visit to the campus reveals students and other members of the university community actively marshalling the resources of their two languages (or in some cases, two of their multiple languages) in negotiating meaning in academic and social spaces. These practices are modeled for students, often unconsciously, by their instructors. For example, a history class ostensibly being held in French only might feature mixed French and English discussions of an English reading. This suggests a tacit understanding by instructors and students of the potential educational benefits of using both languages 'to construct understandings, to make sense of the world and of the academic material' (García, 2009: 148).

However, this flexibility and tacit acceptance of translanguaging are much less evident in written texts, which is not surprising: written products are explicitly discussed in the university regulations on bilingualism in a way that spoken interactions are not, and they can be more easily controlled and monitored. However, as Canagarajah (2011) reminds us, 'Translanguaging cannot be completely restrained by monolingual educational policies' (p. 402). Student-teacher emails and other electronic classroom communication (such as online discussions) constitute one such example. While officially evaluated submissions remain in one language, there is much anecdotal evidence that electronic as well as classroom written communication includes more dynamic use of both languages.

To conclude, the official bilingualism policies of the University of Ottawa have much to commend them: they celebrate and promote the cultural and educational benefits of bringing Canada's official languages into contact. In addition, concerns for the vitality of French are justified and their increased use in all areas of the university community must be promoted. Currently, accomplishing these goals has meant the enactment of a dual monolingual model; this is especially evident in policies related to written communication. A revision of these institutional language policies would be welcomed that embraces a dynamic bilingual model. These policies could embody a new definition of linguistic balance: the need to combine the protection of a minority language with the encouragement of facilitative translanguaging practices that actually represent highly proficient biliteracy.

Discussion

As this chapter has demonstrated, bilingual and multilingual literacy policies are enacted at universities for a variety of reasons: to enable a global perspective on education for pragmatic as well as idealistic reasons (EUV); to revitalize and give a voice to an indigenous language (TWoA) or to protect a minority language and reflect larger country-wide policies (ZU, uOttawa). These goals are rooted in the ways that nations and communities define themselves; and these self-definitions evolve with changing local and global circumstances. The association of literacy with prestige and durability of a language means that having a place for the written language in university contexts is often a goal in itself; further steps to formally support particular literacy skills or to set and reach appropriate proficiency objectives are less clearly articulated – although emergent, micro-level initiatives may sustain an institutional culture of biliteracy even without a specific institutional policy (EUV). Policies may focus on empowering languages (such as French at uOttowa or Arabic at ZU) and/or on empowering individuals to exercise rights or to make decisions (as at TWoA and perhaps at EUV). Research concerning daily teaching and studying practices in biliterate contexts shows that there are still plenty of challenges to be met in applying these policies on the ground, in particular on the level of individual written communication. Ways to address these challenges include the following:

- moving to become officially bilingual or multilingual as an institution, as a way of solidifying commitment to multilingual practice;
- acknowledging that multilingual practices are more than multiple monolingual practices – opening the door to language mixing within written communication; and
- providing the support necessary for an institution to achieve its high aspirations.

In addressing these challenges, intercultural didactics, which considers more perspectives than mere language acquisition – i.e. providing training in different communicative skills not only at a linguistic but also at a social level – will be a relevant field in the years to come.

Hornberger and Skilton-Sylvester's continuua of biliteracy model (2000) is a useful framework to apply here to the language policy issues that all four institutions face, as linguistically diverse as they are. The monolingual-bilingual and the oral-literate continua are an especially useful lens by which to view the explicit language policies of uOttawa, which appear to be in place less to encourage biliteracy development than to counteract unequal power relations between the two languages – a direct result of both the majority of English speakers on campus and in the city, and the dominance of English in academic publishing and research dissemination. Unfortunately, a dilemma occurs when the protection of a language leads to the creation of 'dual monoliteracy' practices which are at odds with the fluid translanguaging occurring in oral communication.

In some cases policy aims to increase the diversity of the media of biliteracy (for example Maori as an alternative to English in New Zealand, or the wide range of options at EUV); while in others it aims to focus literacy development on a small number of prestige languages (for example in the United Arab Emirates, where biliteracy exists in a multilingual, multidialectal context). Contexts (academic or related to institutional management or graduate employment) are a key element of implementing biliteracy policies: rituals and ceremonies, from Maori *powhiri* to university exams or decrees from senior administration, are associated (*de jure* or *de facto*) with particular media and types of literacy. Assessment is typically the context in which policy is implemented with most rigour, in terms of giving students rights and/or obligations to use a particular linguistic code, with less tolerance of translanguaging. Interactions in class, on the other hand, typically play out in more fluid patterns of language use around texts.

In terms of development of biliteracy, the cases described in this chapter illustrate how learners and teachers may differ widely in their literacy skills in different codes and contexts. These skills are also dynamic, developing or changing with time and the demands of different ideologies. The development of biliteracy is also social, as illustrated for example by the teachers at TWoA seeking help in marking students' work from colleagues who have a greater proficiency in Maori. Policy may in some cases stimulate coordination and transfer between courses in different languages, encouraging students and teachers to compare and contrast content, genres, skills and strategies across languages, drawing on various points of the continua of biliteracy as proposed by Hornberger and Skilton-Sylvester (2000).

Hornberger's continua for the content of biliteracy are particularly salient in the cases described in this chapter: from the use (or non-use) of German, French or Polish in different programmes at EUV to the use of the 'local' language for more 'locally' oriented courses in New Zealand or the United Arab Emirates, literacy practices in different languages are associated with certain content areas – uOttawa seems to approach most closely the offering of the same programmes in different languages. Again, however, the continuum nature of these oppositions is highlighted by the way languages are strategically mixed (as at TWoA) or distinctions are pragmatically negotiated (at ZU) to bring the domains of the two languages together in institutional policy. Universities inevitably respond to a range of drivers from symbolic traditions to material/human resources and employability demands; and literacy policy and practices are reshaped and rebalanced as these factors change with time.

References

Bahr, A. (forthcoming) Deutsch-französische Wissenschaftskommunikation – interkulturelles Lernen durch Integration von Fach- und Sprachlehre. In K. Dietrich-Chenel, F. Duchene-Lacroix, G. Hiller, H.-J. Luesebrink, A.-M. Pailhes and C. Vatter (eds) *Interkulturelle Kompetenz in deutsch-französischen Studiengängen: didaktische Konzepte, Methoden, Materialien/Les compétences interculturelles dans les cursus franco-allemands: modèles didactiques, méthodes et supports d'enseignement*. Wiesbaden: VS Verlag.

Baldauf, R.B. (2006) Rearticulating the case for micro language planning in a language ecology context. *Current Issues in Language Planning* 7 (2–3), 147–170.

Canagarajah, S. (2011) Codemeshing in academic writing: Identifying teachable strategies of translanguaging. *The Modern Language Journal* 95 (3), 401–417.

Christofides, L.N. and Swidinsky (2010) The economic returns to the knowledge and use of a second official language: English in Quebec and French in the Rest-of-Canada. *Canadian Public Policy* 36 (2), 137–158.

Durand, B., Neubert, S. and Viallon, V. (2006) *Studieren in Frankreich und Deutschland: Akademische Lehr- und Lernkulturen im Vergleich*. Berlin: Avinus-Verlag.

Durie, M. (1998) *Te Mana, Te Kawanangatanga. The Politics of Maori Self-determination*. Bookpac Production Services: Singapore.

Edwards, S. (2011) *Ako Wānanga: The Art, Science and Spiritual Endeavour of Teaching and Learning in a Wānanga: A Localised Approach*. Te Awamutu: Te Wananga o Aotearoa.

European University Viadrina (2015) Viadrina's specific profile. See https://www.europa-uni.de/en/internationales/Partnerships/profil.html

European University Viadrina (2016) Master of Arts in European Studies: Languages. See https://www.kuwi.europa-uni.de/en/studium/master/es/Studieninhalte/Sprachen/index.html

European University Viadrina (n.d.) Studierendenstatistik der Europa-Universität Viadrina Frankfurt (Oder) im Wintersemester 2014/2015 nach Herkunft der Studierenden. See https://www.europa-uni.de/de/struktur/zse/pressestelle/informationen/studierendenstatistik/Studistatistik-Herkunft2014-2015.pdf

Findlow, S. (2006) Higher education and linguistic dualism in the Arab Gulf. *British Journal of Sociology of Education* 27 (1), 19–36.

García, O. (2009) Education, multilingualism and translanguaging in the 21st century. In A. Mohanty, M. Panda, R. Phillipson and T. Skutnabb-Kangas (eds) *Multilingual Education for Social Justice: Globalising the Local* (pp. 140–158). New Delhi: Orient Blackswan.

Hennings, M. and Roessler, I. (2011) Verbleibstudie Europauniversität Viadrina: Erste umfassende Absolventinnen und Absolventenbefragung. See http://www.kuwi.europa-uni.de/de/profil/studienziel/CHE_AlleFakultaeten_Viadrina_Mai_2011.pdf

Higher Colleges of Technology (2014) Course descriptions. See http://www.hct.ac.ae/content/uploads/HCT-Catalogue-1415-Course-Descriptions.pdf

Hiller, G.G. (2014) Kulturelle und sprachliche Diversität in der Hochschule: Am Beispiel von E-Mail-Kommunikation. In A. Moosmüller and J. Möller-Kiero (eds) *Interkulturalität und kulturelle Diversität* (pp. 233–258). Waxmann, Münster.

Hiller, G.G. (forthcoming) Lehr- und Beratungskompetenzen in der internationalisierten Hochschullehre. Befunde und Empfehlungen auf Basis einer empirischen Studie zu E-Mail-Kommunikation. In M. Merkt, N. Schaper and C. Wetzel (eds) *Professionalisierung der Hochschuldidaktik*. Reihe: Blickpunkt Hochschuldidaktik; N° 127, W. Bertelsmann Verlag, Bielefeld. In Vorbereitung.

Hoani, S. (2012) Kaupapa Wānanga: A philosophy for life. In Te Wānanga o Aotearoa, WIPCE Conference Proceedings Peru, 2011 (p. 84). Te Awamutu: Te Wānanga o Aotearoa.

Holes, C.D. (2011) Language and Identity in the Arabian Gulf. *Journal of Arabian Studies* 1 (2), 129–145.

Hornberger, N.H. (2002) Multilingual language policies and the continua of biliteracy: An ecological approach. *Language Policy* 1 (1), 27–51.

Hornberger, N.H. and Skilton-Sylvester, E. (2000) Revisiting the continua of biliteracy: international and critical perspectives. *Language and Education* 14 (2), 96–122.

House, J. and Lévy, M. (2008) Universitäre Kontaktgespräche als interkulturelle Kommunikationssituationen. In A. Knapp and A. Schumann (eds) *Mehrsprachigkeit und Multikulturalität im Studium* (pp. 107–135). Frankfurt am Main: Lang.

Hufeisen, B. (2002) Ein deutsches Referat ist kein englischsprachiges Essay. Theoretische und praktische Überlegungen zu einem verbesserten textsortenbezogenen Schreibunterricht in der Fremdsprache Deutsch an der Universität. Innsbruck etc.: Studien-Verlag.

Lal, M. and Walker, J. (2014) What can mainstream libraries learn from Te Pātaka Māramatanga – an indigenous academic library: Lesson from Wānagogy. LIANZA Conference 2014 (pp. 12–15). Auckland, New Zealand: Library and Information Association of New Zealand. See http://www.lianza.org.nz/mohan-lal-and-jock-walker-what-can-main-stream-libraries-learn-te-p%C4%81taka-m%C4%81ramatanga-indigenous

Lamoureux, S., Daoust, J.-L. Bourdages, J., Vignola, M.-J. and Malette, A. (2014) *Developing University Literacy and Promoting Academic Success Across Disciplines: A Case Study of French-Language University Literacy*. Toronto: Higher Education Quality Council of Ontario.

May, S., Hill, R. and Tiakiwai, S. (2006) *Bilingual Education in Aotearoa/New Zealand: Key Findings from Bilingual/Immersion Education: Indicators of Good Practice*. Ministry of Education, New Zealand.

Nicolson, A. (2006) Boom town. *Guardian*. See http://www.theguardian.com/business/2006/feb/13/unitedarabemirates.travel

Palfreyman, D.M. (2011) Family, friends and learning beyond the classroom: Social networks and social capital in language learning. In P. Benson and H. Reinders (eds) *Beyond the Language Classroom* (pp. 1–26). Palgrave.

Pohatu, T. (2008) Takepu: Principled approaches to healthy relationships. In the *Traditional Knowledge Conference Proceedings, Te Tatau Pounamu: The Greenstone Door, Traditional Knowledge and Gateways to Balanced Relationships* (pp. 241–247). University of Auckland, New Zealand: Nga Pae o te Maramatanga.

Robertson, R. and White, K.E. (2007) What is globalization? In G. Ritzer (ed.) *The Blackwell Companion to Globalization* (pp. 54–66). Oxford: Blackwell.

Rost-Roth, M. (2003) Anliegensformulierungen: Aufgabenkomplexe und sprachliche Mittel. Analysen zu Anliegensformulierungen von Muttersprachlern und Nichtmuttersprachlern am Beispiel von Beratungsgesprächen und Antragsbearbeitungs-Gesprächen im Hochschulkontext. In N. Baumgarten, C. Böttger, M. Motz and J. Probst (eds) *Übersetzen, Interkulturelle Kommunikation, Spracherwerb und Sprachvermittlung: das Leben mit mehreren Sprachen*. Festschrift für Juliane House zum 60. Geburtstag. Zeitschrift für Interkulturellen Fremdsprachenunterricht 8 (2–3), 1–23.

Senate Standing Committee on Francophone Affairs and Official Languages: Task Force on Programs and Services in French (2006) French at the University of Ottawa, Volume II: State of Affairs for Programs and Services in French.

Shohamy, E. (2011) Assessing multilingual competencies: Adopting construct valid assessment policies. *The Modern Language Journal* 95 (3), 418–429.

Te Wananga o Aotearoa (2014) Te Puronga. Annual Report 2013. See http://www.twoa.ac.nz/getmedia/2c587bb6-dd34-4445-a3e0-357d586a3049/17446-TWOA-Annual-Report-scr.pdf.aspx

Te Wananga o Aotearoa (2015a) Reo Ora. See https://tekete.twoa.ac.nz/communications/TWoA%20Panui/ReoOraHeRautakiReo.pdf

Te Wānanga o Aotearoa (2015b) Ngā uara: Our values. See http://www.twoa.ac.nz/Te-Whare/Nga-Uara

Te Wananga o Aotearoa (2015c) Tikanga Ako. See https://tekete.twoa.ac.nz/DocumentCentre/Educational%20Regulations/Tikanga%20Ako%202015.pdf

University of Ottawa (1974) The regulation on bilingualism at the University of Ottawa. See http://www.uottawa.ca/about/policies-and-regulations/bilingualism

University of Ottawa (2014) Quick facts, 2014. See http://www.uottawa.ca/institutional-research-planning/resources/facts-figures/quick-facts

Voigt, A. and Girgensohn, K. (2015) Peer tutoring in academic writing with non-native writers in a German writing center: Results of an empirical study. *Journal of Academic Writing* 5 (1), 65–73.

Waitangi Tribunal, Department of Justice (1986) Report of The Waitangi Tribunal on The Te Reo Māori Claim. See https://forms.justice.govt.nz/search/Documents/WT/wt_DOC_68482156/Report%20on%20the%20Te%20Reo%20Māori%20Claim%20W.pdf

Walker, S., Eketone, A. and Gibbs, A. (2006) An exploration of kaupapa Maori research, its principles, processes and applications. *International Journal Social Research Methodology* 9 (4), 331–332

Zayed University (2014) Course catalog. See http://www.zu.ac.ae/main/files/contents/docs/New_Catalog_2014-2015_Oct26.pdf

11 Afterword: Moving Forward with Academic Biliteracy Research

Guillaume Gentil

This book expands our understanding of strategies and challenges for developing academic literacies in more than one language in and for higher education contexts. Researching and fostering multilingual literacies in higher education is timely in today's postsecondary landscape, given the convergence of at least three factors: the appeal of academic literacies in English as a global language, continuing investments in national languages as mediums of instruction and scholarship, and new demands and opportunities for education in marginalized languages. Yet much research on multilingual academic literacy development to date has focused on elementary school settings, typically in the context of bilingual programs or officially monolingual programs dealing with multilingual student populations (Baker, 2011), or on multilingual scholars' publishing practices (e.g. Lillis & Curry, 2010). While there is considerable research on second language writing among undergraduate and graduate students (cf. Belcher, 2012; Leki *et al.*, 2008), much of it has been concerned primarily with the acquisition of literacy in English (or less commonly another language) as a second or foreign language rather than multilingual writing development per se (but see Gentil, 2005; Kobayashi & Rinnert, 2013).

In contrast, most chapters in this volume illuminate ways to foster multilingual academic literacies among undergraduate students. Indeed, one of its strengths is that several contributors are educators who are directly involved in, and dedicated to, designing and implementing pedagogical strategies for their students. I trust that they will inspire like-minded readers to adopt and adapt some of these strategies for their own contexts. Of particular interest to me are the authors' attempts to offer and document ways to help multilingual writers draw on their entire linguistic repertoires as they 'write to learn' and 'learn to write' (Manchón, 2011) in and across languages. Even when educational contexts officially aim to develop bilingual or multilingual literacies, as in what Baker (2011) calls the 'strong forms of bilingual education' (p. 210), bilingual education programs such as French immersion in Canada or two-way education in the United States have been premised on what Cummins (2007) labels the 'two solitudes assumption' – the rigid separation of the languages of instruction so that only one language is used at a time, for a given subject matter, and in a dedicated classroom. Calls for rethinking such monolingual instructional strategies (Cummins, 2007) or 'monoglossic' bilingual education arrangements (García, 2009) have been made; however, research into these alternative strategies and their effectiveness is still relatively underdeveloped compared to the wealth of research on second and bilingual education in the monoglossic paradigm.

Given the wealth of the contributions in this volume, this afterword will not review them individually. Rather, I attempt to capture the main themes or take-home messages that I see emerging from these accounts. I then venture some reflections on the ways these findings might be best theorized and yet also contribute to theory building. Indeed, because one strength of the book is to describe practices of and strategies for multilingual academic literacies in specific instructional settings, one question that loomed increasingly larger as I was reading it relates to the theorizing of these practices and strategies. One concern I have with the current state of research in this area is the proliferation of constructs vying for attention (e.g. *translingual, translanguaging, biliteracy, pluriliteracies, multilingual literacies*). While I appreciate the nuances and affordances that each of these constructs might bring, as well as the efforts that have been made to show their interrelationship and complementarity, I remain concerned that such new-fangled terminology might distract from core concepts (including literacy, writing, and language) and be a source of confusion as well as new insight. This can be seen in the tensions between the ways in which the constructs are defined in theoretical frameworks and the ways in which they appear to be used in the description of student and instructor texts and practices. In light of this state of affairs and taking stock of the research space that this book has opened and begun to explore, I conclude with some suggestions for further inquiry.

Take-Home Messages

It is much to the credit of this volume to offer descriptions of students' and teachers' engagement with multilingual academic literacy in a wide range of world regions (Hong Kong and Mainland China, continental US and Puerto Rico, South Africa, Wales). It further compares and contrasts the language policies and practices of four higher institutions in Germany, New Zealand, the United Arab Emirates and Canada (chapter by Baker, Hiller, Manu, Palfreyman & Poha). Of particular interest are comparisons of different institutional contexts within the same national context, especially when these institutions differ in their official language policies. For example, two chapters focus on South African contexts. However, while Antia and Dyers document a pedagogy of multilingual literacies in the University of Western Cape – a university that officially embraces (to various degrees) English, Afrikaans and Xhosa for internal communication and instruction – Hurst, Madiba and Morreira report on educational strategies for multilingual support within an officially English-medium institution. Similarly, the contrasts among an English-only university in the US Midwest grappling with a linguistically diverse student body (Kiernan), an English-only university on the US-Mexico border (Esquinca, Mein, Villa & Monárrez), and a bilingual Spanish-English program in Puerto Rico (Mazak, Rivera & Mangonéz) are quite revealing about the prevailing influence of institutional and demographic contexts on educational opportunities and demands for multilingual academic literacy development.

Despite or through the diverse peculiarities of these situations, a number of common trends emerge. First, it is clear that most situations of language contact entail a certain degree of asymmetry among the languages and their users. Generally, the linguistic resources in circulation are not used interchangeably but for different functions and in different contexts and to index certain identities. These distinct uses reproduce and reinforce the differentiation of linguistic resources into distinct sets that are socially recognized under different labels (e.g. English or Spanish), with these labelling practices further delineating boundaries between languages and language speakers. A telling example of this is given by the Hong Kong students in Costley's chapter who report mixing English with Cantonese in informal conversations but avoiding a mixture of Cantonese and Mandarin in an effort to distance themselves from mainland China. They further refrain from mixing English with Cantonese in formal written academic assignments to conform to the university's monolingual policy. Even in a context like Puerto Rico, with high levels of bilingualism and biliteracy in Spanish and English and within a institutional context that officially allow professors the choice of Spanish and English in their classrooms, subtle rules regulate the use – and mixing – of the languages. For instance, Mazak *et al.* report that professors are 'quite aware of the preference of students for professors to speak Spanish', but the use of English readings is taken for granted.

At the root of these differentiated language uses lie power imbalances between language users at individual and collective levels. For example, the lack of reading materials in Spanish in Puerto Rican academic contexts most likely reflects the dependency of Puerto Ricans on an English-dominated academic publishing industry based in the continental US. But the preferred use of Spanish in spoken interactions is an affordable way of indexing difference from continentals. Similar dynamics (oral negotiations in Spanish or Welsh of written academic content in English, given the paucity of reading resources in the minority language) seem to be at play in the Texan and Welsh contexts as well (Esquinca *et al.*; Ifan & Hodges). The contributions to this volume consistently and tellingly demonstrate that multilingual users are aware of these power imbalances and of the rules regulating the use of linguistic resources in given contexts. They further show that educational spaces generally reflect these imbalances but can also be used as opportunities to help redress them, for example in helping students take pride in the identities associated with their home languages. Encouraging illustrations of this can be seen in post-apartheid South Africa. Hurst *et al.* report how even in an official monolingual English institutional context, two educational strategies – language histories and multilingual glossaries – allow students from historically disadvantaged groups to validate and leverage their rich linguistic repertoires in order to deepen their understanding of core course concepts. Similarly, Antia and Dyers show how the provision of multilingual lecture materials fostered critical re-evaluations of isiXhosa and Afrikaans vis-à-vis English while facilitating comprehension of course content. In Puerto Rico, Mazak *et al.* illustrate further the enabling effect of bilingual lecture slides not only in the development of subject-matter knowledge but also to model and authorize the use of more than one language for cognitive, metalinguistic, and attitudinal benefits.

Perhaps one of the most important and recurring messages of this book is that allowing multilingual students to draw on their entire linguistic repertoires is a desirable educational strategy for a number of reasons: it facilitates language and literacy development, content understanding, metalinguistic awareness, cognitive development, and identity affirmation as well as helping to redress social, economic and historical inequities. These findings – the prevailing influence of contextual demands and affordances on language and literacy development, linguistic asymmetries reflecting and reproducing social and economic imbalances of power, the role of educational spaces and strategies to redress them, and the importance of validating and capitalizing on multilingual students' entire linguistic repertoire – are not in themselves new. The contribution of this volume, however, is to confirm that what we have learned from several decades of research on bilingual education mostly in K-12 contexts (see, e.g. Baker, 2011; Cummins, 2000; García, 2009) also applies to higher education contexts – a timely contribution in today's globalized era. This book further proposes a number of useful pedagogical strategies and policy recommendations for multilingual academic literacy development and associated cognitive benefits and learner empowerment, which I hope will inspire literacy educators, curriculum developers and policy makers worldwide.

Theorizing Practices and Practising Theories

Thus far, in my attempt to capture what I see as the main take-home messages of this volume, I have tried, as much as possible, to limit the use of educational jargon to a few key concepts – *language, literacy, bilingualism, biliteracy* – which are also used by non-specialists, arguably with less precision and sophistication than in bilingual education circles. This was quite deliberate, firstly for the sake of simplicity and secondly because I wanted to postpone a question which has been simmering in my mind while I was reading the book and to which I now turn: What might be the most productive ways of theorizing the book's main findings – productive in the sense of generating most insight in the clearest and most parsimonious way; in other words, in having most explanatory power?

To identify the constructs used throughout the book and investigate their use in a somewhat systematic way, I loaded all the chapters (including the introduction but excluding this concluding chapter) into AntConc corpus analysis software (Anthony, 2014). This provided some insight into the core concepts by the authors in their studies of multilingual academic writing development. Unsurprisingly, these included, in declining order of frequency *language, languages, literacy* (and *literacies*, although five times less frequent), *multilingual, bilingual, writing, learning* (and *development*, quite frequent as well). Each of these words occurs at least 200 times in this volume. Of greater interest, perhaps, are frequent recourses to two neologisms, *biliteracy* (frequency = 186) and *translanguaging* (f = 179), along with related, though much less frequent, coinages such as *pluriliteracies, multiliteracies, languaging, translingual* and *translingualism*. Words like *knowledge, ability* and *skills*, are also worth mentioning, with approximately 100 occurrences each. Other concepts such as *code*, typically in hyphenated phrases such as *code-meshing* or *code-switching*), and *genre* appear at lower frequencies (about 40 occurrences each).

Views and uses of *language(s)*

Concordance searches led to further insight into how these concepts were defined and used. Among the core concepts, I could not locate a definition of *writing* (or *reading*). Arguably, this construct might be considered too basic to deserve a definition. The word *language*, however, receives greater attention. With remarkable consistency, most authors distance themselves from commonly held views of languages as 'bounded autonomous systems' (Baker *et al.*, citing García) or as 'separate, distinguishable, countable entities' (Esquinca *et al.*, citing Pennycook), underscoring instead the 'tenuous and porous dividing lines between languages' as well as 'bilinguals' fluid movement across languages' (Esquinca *et al.*). *Language* is further defined as 'action and practice, and not a simple system of structures and discrete sets of skills' (Hurst *et al.*, citing García) and 'an action – a dynamic, never-ending process of using language to make meaning' (Esquinca, citing Swain) and thus better used as a verb than as a noun. Such a reconceptualizing of *language(s)* was articulated with reference to Canagarajah's (2013) critique of the 'monolingual orientation' arising from the European nation-state model of 'one nation, one language' and assuming, inter alia, that 'for communication to be successful we should employ a common language with shared norms' and that 'languages have their own unique systems and should be kept free of mixing with other languages' (p. 1). Alternatively or additionally, this conceptual shift was part of a critique of a 'deficit orientation' toward multilingual writers deemed to be at odds with a multilingualism-as-a-resource orientation. It is interesting that the word form *resources* ($f = 166$, also occurring in the singular, $f = 14$) is among the top 25 content words in this volume. Indeed, arguably the most prevailing metaphor to describe *language(s)* is that of a resource or set of resources (*linguistic resources*, $f = 28$).

I embrace attempts to combat deficit orientations to multilingual writers and appreciate that this effort may involve reconsidering common assumptions about the ways in which we think about language(s). However, we should be wary of an apparent disconnect in current research on multilingual literacy between the ways in which the word *language* gets defined in a rather celebratory manner – as action, as fluid, as unbounded, as process, as dynamic – but still used in more established senses. In this book, for example, participants' language repertoires are described and constructed as belonging to separate languages with distinct labels ('Cantonese', 'Mandarin', 'Zulu mixed with Sotho and a little bit of English'). Indeed, references to specific languages, notably English, Chinese, and Spanish, are very frequent. Clear distinctions are also made between *a/the/their first/home language* ($f = 84$) and (*a/their/the) second/foreign language* ($f = 79$) as well as between the *most dominant* and *the weaker language*. Furthermore, countable and plural uses of *language* are plentiful, and nowhere is *language* used as a verb. Somehow, future research on multilingual writing development needs to find ways of reconciling how the word *language* is defined and how it is actually used. It is interesting that Esquinca *et al.*'s chapter, which attempts a more elaborate definition of the term, draws on the work of M.A.K. Halliday in systemic functional linguistics (SFL) to define 'language as primarily a resource for making meaning'. Central to SFL, however, is the idea that languages such as English or Spanish are linguistic systems, each with their own meaning potential. Indeed, much of SFL work in language typology aims to compare the constitutive systems of particular languages so as to identify what they may share and in what ways they may differ (Caffarel *et al.*, 2004). This is arguably a worthwhile enterprise for language educators interested in understanding and explaining to their students how particular languages may compare in how they realize similar meanings. Cummins (2007) enlists the systematic comparison of cognates as one useful bilingual instructional strategy to expand vocabulary among speakers of English and romance languages. Vocabulary, however, is only one candidate for systematic crosslinguistic exploration of language structures. Grammar (which SFL views as closely related to lexicon), phraseology, discourse organization as well as genre and register might be worthy of cross-linguistic exploration as well. As the exploration of this field progresses, researchers should not overlook the resources that work in intercultural rhetoric, comparative stylistics, and language typology might offer for multilingual writing development on the grounds that they are based on separatist views of language; my sense is that this would be like throwing the baby out with the bathwater.

Unclear as well, from the participants' testimonials, is how 'fluid' their movement is across languages. Several chapters do describe how students find it useful to shift back and forth between, and mix, languages in informal conversations and in talk around written texts – either surreptitiously or with the sanction of their instructors, depending on the institutional context. But in most of the contexts described, the participants must conform to the prevailing monolingual orientation, and at times painfully so. Amelia's testimonial, reported by Esquinca *et al.*, is a sad reminder of the lack of fluid, dynamic movement across languages upon first exposure to a new language: freshly arrived in Texas from Mexico, having to take mathematics for the first time in English was so hard that it made her cry. One might argue that educational institutions should permit L1 use and fluid language practices not only in informal small group interactions but also in whole class lectures and for examination. Some chapters, particularly Mazak *et al.*'s in a Puerto Rican context, illustrate the benefits of this. But this would require that the instructors themselves have the linguistic repertoires that allow for this. Even with good will, adding a new language to one's repertoire takes time – often several years. In Amelia's South Texan setting, as in countless of other language contact situations, while some multilinguals can act as language brokers effortlessly mixing or switching languages depending on the interlocutor, monolinguals cannot.

That languages are social constructs is well established, but as Berger and Luckmann's (1966) seminal work demonstrated, social constructs create realities that cannot be wished away. Gender and race too are social constructs, but changing or transgressing one's gender in a gendered society is a long and arduous process in a person's life, and being non-racist in a racist society is next to impossible. Similarly, the bounded nature of language systems is hard to ignore lest ontogenetic and historical time scales be collapsed. In the successive moments of meaning making, the use of linguistic resources may aptly be described as a flux of meaning in which language systems are both constantly drawn upon and reshaped in minute ways. However, languages evolve on a different time scale. English and French as we know them today, for example, are the products of several centuries of a codification process that has instituted them into distinct systems despite a long history of contact and reciprocal influence. It is not surprising, then, that in the time scale of a person's life, it may take years for a speaker raised in one linguistic tradition to learn another. Physicists have proposed a dual view of matter as wave and particle. This perspective might offer a useful lens for linguists to think of language in a dual way: as system and action, as state and flux, as langue and parole. And much as wave properties may be hard to detect for macroscopic objects, flux properties may be elusive at the more macroscopic levels of language.

Two closely interrelated assumptions of the monolingual orientation that have come under criticism are firstly that successful communication needs to rely on maintaining shared linguistic norms, and secondly that this can be achieved by keeping languages free from mixing so as to preserve the integrity of each language as a distinct system (Canagarajah, 2013). Isn't there some value, however, in these assumptions? To return to French and English, whose numerous cognates rarely fully overlap in meaning, the use of 'sensible' to mean 'sensitive', as it commonly does to French users, is likely to be a source of misunderstanding to the unsuspecting English speaker. These ambiguities are avoided in multilinguals' fluent inter- and intrasentential code mixing because phonological, orthographic, and other language markers cue interlocutors to the linguistic systems that are intended as frames of reference at specific junctures. When incipient bilinguals are learning a new language system, their attempts at meaning making may not be construed as intended. While in the context of an English composition class, such ambiguities may be celebrated as transformative or heuristic, in the context of an engineering course lexicogrammatical precision can be paramount. Language codification may be reviled for its exclusionary and disempowering consequences; it nonetheless enables precise academic communication.

This volume offers numerous examples of the value of allowing students to draw on their entire linguistic repertoire to make sense of course content and facilitate their literacy development. It also illustrates how, especially under the constraints of a timed exam, it may be most expedient to use the first language that comes to mind to display knowledge (Mazak *et al.*'s chapter). Perhaps the value of having to use one normatively standardized linguistic system may be more openly acknowledged as well. Wang, for example, relates the difficulty of Chinese scholars in finding English equivalents of Chinese concepts when translating abstracts. In my own research work on academic biliteracy, I reported the formidable challenge of a francophone doctoral student struggling to write a review of gender studies in French given the lack of a simple translation equivalent for *gender* (Gentil, 2005). Basically she was trying to write about gender using the word for 'sex', as French only has one word for both concepts. If one embraces the free mixing of linguistic resources, it is tempting to simply borrow a missing term from another language. Often, however, such loans do not have the same resonance in the host language, having restricted usage as fairly shallow signifiers. An alternative strategy is to draw on the meaning potential of the home language; the advantage of this strategy is that it creates an opportunity to explicate the concept with novel linguistic and metaphorical means, resulting in a deeper understanding, as vividly illustrated by the productive use of multilingual glossaries in Hurst *et al.*'s chapter. The celebration of fluid multilingualism and free language mixing should not lead us to forget that one original rationale for language separation in bilingual education programs was to avoid the natural tendency for dominant languages to displace minority languages in asymmetrical contact situations. If the goal is the cultivation of linguistic diversity, then preserving some language separation and having rules over which language may be used in a given context may indeed be desirable.

Views and uses of *literacy* and *biliteracy*

Another pair of core concepts running through this volume is *literacy* and *biliteracy*, which are both commonly conceptualized as a set of skills and as a set of social practices (or uses):

> Bilingual research literacy is briefly defined as the *ability* to use two languages for research purposes. Singh and Cui (2011) argued that the term 'bilingual research literacy refers to the *use* of two languages for the purposes of generating, interpreting and/or analysing evidence' (p. 539) (Wang's chapter, emphasis added)

> ... biliteracy in academic contexts: that is (adapting a definition from Hornberger, 1990) the *use* in a higher education context of two or more languages in or around writing for the purpose of broadening or deepening knowledge .... we regard academic biliteracy as an individual's *ability* to read and write more than one language in an academic setting .... (Introduction to this volume, emphasis added)

Table 11.1 shows that although *literacy* is more commonly construed as a form of practice, with reference to Brian Street and work in New Literacies Studies, its construal as a set of skills is quite frequent as well. It is common for words to have more than one meaning. However, polysemy raises two sets of questions: How do the meanings interrelate and is there any ambiguity in how the word is used in a given context? Perhaps clarifying the relationship between literacy as practice and literacy as skill may deepen our

Table 11.1 Frequencies of literacy as skills vs. as practices

literacy skills	8	*literacy practices*	33
biliteracy skills	4	*biliteracy practices*	18
		literacy event(s)	24
writing ability	2	*literacy activities*	3
biliteracy capacity	1		
Total	15	*Total*	78

understanding of what we may mean by *learning* (f = 200) and *(bi)literacy development* (f = 15).

With regard to *biliteracy,* unsurprisingly, all but one chapter made at least a passing reference to Hornberger (the most cited theorist in this volume) and several authors used Hornberger's continua of biliteracy as part of their analytical framework. A central tenet of this framework is that

> the more students' contexts of language and literacy allow them to draw from across the whole of each and every continuum, the greater are the chances for their full language and literacy development and expression (Hornberger & Link, 2012: 243).

The chapters in this volume provide ample illustration of this principle, namely that helping multilingual students to draw on their entire linguistic repertoires, including linguistic resources at the traditionally less powerful ends of the continua, facilitates biliteracy development. It also further provides much evidence for the claim that 'individuals' biliteracy develops along the continua in direct response to contextual demands placed on them' (Hornberger & Link, 2012: 244).

Views and uses of *translanguaging* and *translingual*

The concept of *translanguaging* has been the focus of several publications in recent years and is emerging as a staple metaphor in bilingual education scholarship; Hornberger and Link (2012) have endeavoured to demonstrate the mutually beneficial relationships between *translanguaging* and *biliteracy* as two key constructs for understanding and promoting multilingual literacy development. Both occur with great, and almost equal frequency in this volume, with 186 occurrences for *biliteracy* and 179 for *translanguaging* (*Translingual* (f = 45) might be regarded as a close cousin, popularized by Canagarajah (2013) in US-based composition studies. The notion of *translanguaging* is worth attending to, given that one of the main goals of the book identified in the introduction is to address Lewis *et al.*'s (2012) concern that 'the effectiveness of translanguaging strategies [has] yet to be researched, evaluated, and critiqued' (p. 650).

In their illuminating review of the origin and development of the term, Lewis *et al.* (2012) remark that

> there can be no exact or essentialist definition as the meaning of translanguaging will become more refined and increasingly clarified, conceptually and through further research. (p. 642)

An interesting question, then, is in what ways this volume might contribute to the conceptual clarification and refining of *translanguaging* while shedding light on its effectiveness as an educational strategy for academic biliteracy development in higher education. One ambitious aim of this volume, again candidly stated in its introduction, is to 'showcase divergent views of translanguaging in an attempt to build on current conceptions'. These divergent views are reflected in the array of definitions and uses in evidence throughout these pages. Through my corpus-informed lexicographic analysis of the word, I was able to identify the following depictions of translanguaging as:

- *practices*, specifically 'the multiple discursive practices in which bilinguals engage in order to make sense of their bilingual worlds' (García, 2009: 45);
- *skills* that include 'reading, understanding and summarizing' and are related to but different (in what ways?) from translation and codeswitching;
- a *pedagogy* or a set of pedagogies or pedagogical strategies for language and literacy development that centres on the idea that 'drawing on multilingual students' full communicative repertoires [can] foster meaningful educational experiences' and 'empower multilingual students to develop creativity and criticality';
- a 'lens', *'perspective'* or an 'approach' to multilingualism and bilingual education that is premised on a number of key assumptions, such as the lack of 'clear-cut boundaries between the languages of individuals' and the 'dynamic and mobile' nature of the linguistic 'resources that multilingual users bring to every communicative act';
- an *'ideology'* or 'attitude' that language teachers can display in their practices;
- a 'feature' of biliteracy.

Occasionally (six times), *translanguage* is employed as a verb (as in 'some students chose to translanguage in their written assignments'), but *translanguaging* is also something (a strategy?) that can be 'used' (as in '[the bilingual participants] used translanguaging with ease to accomplish writing tasks'). Adding to the terminological complexity, five chapters also use the term 'translingual,' mostly in reference to Canagarajah's (2013) *Translingual Practice*, which justifies the use of 'translingual' as distinct from 'translanguaging' in that the latter has 'hitherto been defined largely in cognitive terms' (p. 10). While this may have been true of the earlier conception of the term in the Welsh context (see Lewis *et al.*, 2012), this does not seem to be the case in its more recent development, as García and Li (2014: 40) pointed out in their response to Canagarajah. Indeed, how distinct the two terms are is not always clear from the five chapters in this volume that use both. There may well be a bit of a trademarking battle going on here – it is a sad reflection on education scholarship that new coinages are often a means of accruing symbolic capital. This is not to say, however, that these new concepts have no potential value. In a recently published book devoted solely to *translanguaging*, García and Li (2014) provide a useful definition of it as

> ... an approach to the use of language, bilingualism and the education of bilinguals that considers the language practices of bilinguals not as two autonomous language systems as have been traditionally the case, but as one linguistic repertoire with features that have been societally constructed as belonging to separate languages. (p. 2)

What this definition captures is the tension, palpable in this volume, between the desire to consider the linguistic resources of multilinguals as forming one linguistic repertoire and a prevailing backdrop of assumptions, practices, and discourses that create them as separate languages. Overcoming this tension is a formidable challenge, as evidenced in the tensions noted earlier in the ways the word 'language' is defined and used in this volume. As philosophical hermeneutics reminds us, being aware of the socioculturally and historically situated nature of one's conceptual horizon does not mean that one can escape it (Dreyfus & Rabinow, 1982). Be that as it may, one lesson I draw from this volume is that the concept of *translanguaging* can prove difficult to handle. To be pedagogically useful in biliteracy education, its different meanings – as a theoretical orientation to biliteracy, a type of biliteracy practice, and an educational strategy for biliteracy – await further delineations and interrelations.

Parting Thoughts

Thus far I have focused mostly on issues related to theory building because these were most salient as I read this volume. The time seems to be ripe for scholars interested in academic biliteracy or multilingual academic literacies to engage in the type of meta-disciplinary thinking that characterizes the coming of age of a field of academic study (Matsuda, 2003). As suggested above, one direction these meta-disciplinary reflections might take is to ponder on the definitions and uses of core concepts – literacy, language(s), writing/reading, development/learning. In closing, I wish to briefly point to three other possible directions for reflection and future research on academic biliteracy in higher education: (1) cross-disciplinary pollinations, (2) untapped research methodologies and (3) research contexts awaiting exploration.

When addressing second language writing scholars, I have sought to demonstrate how looking into literacy and bilingual education studies might be a useful source of insight (Gentil, 2011). In reverse, I would like to encourage specialists of biliteracy and bilingual education – particularly those interested in higher education settings – to turn to the field of second language writing (Belcher, 2012; Leki *et al.*, 2008). Over the last five decades or so, second language writing scholars have generated a considerable body of work illuminating, *inter alia*, the role and use of the L1 and codeswitching while composing in a second language, the bidirectional transfer of first and second language writing skills, and the interrelationships between learning to write in a language and writing to learn (a language or a subject matter) as well as between language proficiency and writing expertise. It is noteworthy that several contributions to this volume have focused on issues related to the multilingual management of vocabulary and terminology, such as finding translation equivalents for key concepts. These undeniably constitute an important aspect of biliterate work and development, especially in higher education contexts. However, second language writing scholarship has also paid much attention to text organization beyond the sentence level, as well as the relationships among sentence-level lexicogrammatical choice, text-level structuring, and the purpose and context of writing, particularly from the perspective of genre theory. Surely, these are important dimensions of academic biliteracy development; much as genre research might benefit from a biliteracy agenda (Gentil, 2011), biliteracy research might benefit from genre research.

Another source of potentially fruitful crosspollination is with translation studies. Most chapters in this volume in one way or another make reference to translation as an integral aspect of biliterate work. Yet none draws on translation studies to raise attention to strategies that professional translators might use. Kiernan, for example, reports on a translation narrative assignment, which appears to be most pertinent in the particular educational context she describes. As part of this assignment, students must reflect on their attempts to translate a short academic text of their choosing. One participant shared her belief that 'it was important for [her] to keep the order of the words the same as well as using the closest translation of the word', even though she also noted that this was not always easy and that one of her classmates did not translate 'word-by-word'. While this activity appears to have been a useful consciousness-raising exercise, we cannot tell from Kiernan's chapter whether the course later offered an opportunity to discuss well-known translation principles, one of which is to focus on idea units and avoid word-by-word renditions (Delisle, 2013). Baker *et al.* report that translation skills were added to the curriculum in Zayed University in response to student demand in light of their anticipated usefulness for the workplace. I would be interested in research on the impact of the teaching of translation strategies on biliteracy development. Translation studies have contributed much insight into multilingual terminology management, comparative stylistics, and computer-assisted translation; it would be a pity for biliteracy educators to reinvent what translation specialists have already established.

In terms of research methodologies, it is noteworthy that most authors in this volume used a combination of qualitative research methods, mostly interview, survey or written narrative data about participants' perceptions

and experiences, writing samples, course materials, and observations of naturally occurring learning and teaching practices. Such research methods are
common and appropriate for providing insight into academic biliteracy development in specific contexts from the participants' perspective at a given
point of time. Future research, however, might benefit from looking further
into multilinguals' composing processes and biliteracy strategies, for example
as they write in one language from sources in another. Screen capture technology in particular affords a relatively unobtrusive and ecologically valid
way of recording writing processes in home or school environments (Seror,
2013). More longitudinal research would also provide additional insight into
multilingual literacy development over time (see, e.g. Gentil, 2005; Kobayashi
& Rinnert, 2013). More mixed-methods and quantitative research studies
would be welcome as well. Biliteracy development has been well researched
in K-6 bilingual education programs that are based on the two-solitudes
assumption because these programs are well established; Lambert and
Tucker, for example, documented English-French biliteracy development in
the context of a French immersion program over seven years and using a
variety of indicators (Baker, 2011). In contrast, translanguaging approaches
to biliteracy development are much more recent and the research base for
their effectiveness has yet to be built, particularly in higher education contexts. This research base is necessary to convince stakeholders of the sound-
ness of such approaches and to flesh out the details of the most promising
educational strategies.

This volume, understandably, has focused on multilingual literacy practices in contexts known for their language diversity or history of language
contacts, including Wales, South Africa, Canada and the US Southwest. It is
not difficult to think of other types of context in which research on similar
initiatives would be of interest, for example South Asia, East Asia or Latin
America. To take one context I am more familiar with, there has been much
debate in France over the introduction of English as a medium of higher
education. It would be interesting to research how the type of pedagogical
strategies described in this book might help domestic and international students in French universities develop academic literacies in both English and
French. Indeed, I would hope this book will inspire future research and educational initiatives in one-state-one-language countries where global English
and linguistic diversity challenge well-established traditions of higher education in the national language.

References

Anthony, L. (2014) AntConc (Version 3.4.3). See http://www.laurenceanthony.net/
Baker, C. (2011) *Foundations of Bilingual Education and Bilingualism* (5th edn). Bristol:
    Multilingual Matters.
Belcher, D. (2012) Considering what we know and need to know about second language
    writing. *Applied Linguistics Review* 3 (1), 131–150.

Berger, P.L. and Luckmann, T. (1966) *The Social Construction of Reality: A Treatise in the Sociology of Knowledge*. Garden City, N.Y: Doubleday.

Caffarel, A., Martin, J.R. and Matthiessen, C.M. (2004) *Language Typology: A Functional Perspective*. Amsterdam: John Benjamins.

Canagarajah, A.S. (2013) *Translingual Practice: Global Englishes and Cosmopolitan Relations*. New York: Routledge.

Cummins, J. (2000) *Language, Power, and Pedagogy: Bilingual Children in the Crossfire* (Vol. 23). Clevedon: Multilingual Matters.

Cummins, J. (2007) Rethinking monolingual instructional strategies in multilingual classrooms. *Canadian Journal of Applied Linguistics* 10 (2), 221–240.

Delisle, J. (2013) *La traduction raisonnée: manuel d'initiation à la traduction professionnelle de l'anglais vers le français* (3 edn) Ottawa, ON: Les Presses de l'Université d'Ottawa.

Dreyfus, H.L. and Rabinow, P. (1982) *Michel Foucault: Beyond Structuralism and Hermeneutics*. Chicago, IL: University of Chicago Press.

García, O. (2009) *Bilingual Education in the 21st Century: A Global Perspective*. Malden, MA: Wiley-Blackwell.

García, O. and Li, W. (2014) *Translanguaging: Language, Bilingualism and Education*. Basingstoke: Palgrave Macmillan.

Gentil, G. (2005) Commitments to academic biliteracy: Case studies of Francophone university writers. *Written Communication* 22 (4), 421–471.

Gentil, G. (2011) A biliteracy agenda for genre research. *Journal of Second Language Writing* 20 (1), 6–23.

Hornberger, N.H. (1990) Creating successful learning contexts for bilingual literacy. *Teachers College Record* 92, 212–229.

Hornberger, N.H. and Link, H. (2012) Translanguaging in today's classrooms: A biliteracy lens. *Theory Into Practice* 51 (4), 239–247.

Kobayashi, H. and Rinnert, C. (2013) L1/L2/L3 writing development: Longitudinal case study of a Japanese multicompetent writer. *Journal of Second Language Writing* 22 (1), 4–33.

Leki, I., Cumming, A.H. and Silva, T.J. (2008) *A Synthesis of Research on Second Language writing in English*. New York, NY: Routledge.

Lewis, G., Jones, B. and Baker, C. (2012) Translanguaging: Origins and development from school to street and beyond. *Educational Research and Evaluation* 18 (7), 641–654.

Lillis, T.M. and Curry, M.J. (2010) *Academic Writing in a Global Context*. New York: Routledge.

Manchón, R. (2011) *Learning-to-Write and Writing-to-Learn in an Additional Language*. Amsterdam: John Benjamins.

Matsuda, P.K. (2003) Second language writing in the twentieth century: A situated historical perspective. In B. Kroll (ed.) *Exploring the Dynamics of Second Language Writing*. (pp. 15–34). New York: Cambridge University Press.

Seror, J. (2013) Screen capture technology: A digital window into students' writing processes. *Canadian Journal of Learning and Technology* 39 (3), 1.

Singh, M. and Cui, G. (2011) Internationalising Western doctoral education through bilingual research literacy. *Pertanika Journal of Social Science and Humanities* 19 (2), 535–545.

Index